ADVERTIS

Fourth Edition

ADVERTISING

Fourth Edition

Roderick White

McGraw-Hill Publishing Company

London . Burr Ridge, IL . New York . St Louis . San Francisco . Auckland . Bogotá .
Caracas . Lisbon . Madrid . Mexico . Milan . Montreal . New Delhi . Panama .
Paris . San Juan . São Paulo . Singapore . Sydney . Tokyo . Toronto

Published by
McGraw-Hill Publishing Company
Shoppenhangers Road
Maidenhead
Berkshire SL6 2QL
England
Telephone + 44 (0) 1628 502500
Facsimile + 44 (0) 1628 770224
Website   http://www.mcgraw-hill.co.uk

British Library Cataloguing in Publication Data
A catalogue record for this book is available from the British Library

ISBN 0 07 709458 1

Publisher: Dominic Recaldin
Desk Editor: Alastair Lindsay
Editorial Assistant: Caroline Howell
Cover by Simon Levy Associates

Created for McGraw-Hill by the independent production company
Steven Gardiner Ltd TEL +44 (0) 1223 364868 FAX +44 (0) 1223 364875

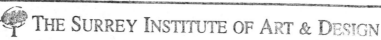
McGraw-Hill

A Division of The McGraw-Hill Companies

Printed in Great Britain by Bell and Bain Ltd, Glasgow

Contents

Foreword

Good books about advertising are amazingly rare. There are just a handful of well-written autobiographical books by practitioners. There are many books criticising the advertising process, but they are mainly academic—in every sense—in nature, and only a fraction are interesting. There are thousands of academic 'how-it-works' books on the subject of advertising, but precious few give any indication that the author has ever had any contact whatsoever with the real world of brands, media buyers and sellers, and ad agencies.

This book is different. It is obviously written by a practitioner. By someone who has lived and breathed for many years in the hot-house world of advertising, and who consequently knows his subject very well indeed. It is a very good, immensely practical guide for anyone about to get involved in the world of advertising. Roderick White explains, in simple, jargon-free, clear language, the basic concepts and techniques which the beginner needs to know about, to avoid confusion in what is a fairly complex business. The author strikes a splendid balance between over-simplification and unnecessary detail.

It is consequently an ideal book for anyone about to get involved in advertising for the first time, for people in a first job in advertising or marketing, and for teachers or students requiring a straightforward but reasonably detailed introduction to the subject.

In addition, the book describes the advertising business in sufficient depth to be of use to specialists actually working in advertising who would like a broader knowledge of the business in which they work.

Best of all, this book has been carefully updated (perhaps one should say upgraded) and rewritten over the years by the still practising author. As a consequence, most of the less well-covered elements of the original work have been gently improved, leaving an informative, well-thought-out and highly readable whole.

This really is a very good book about advertising.

MJ Waterson,
Research Adviser
The Advertising Association

Preface and acknowledgements

This book owes its origins to Mike Waterson, and its contents to many people, both colleagues and clients, with whom I have worked over the years at JWT and what is now Conquest London, together, increasingly, to a wide range of contacts, correspondents and authors who contribute their thinking to *Admap*.

This fourth edition owes its existence particularly to Dominic Recaldin, and its production to my editor, Alastair Lindsay. My thanks to them and their various aiders and abettors at McGraw-Hill.

Thanks are due too to those organisations who have allowed me to use advertisements or other illustrative material reproduced in this book: Aldi Stores Ltd, Alfa Romeo GB Ltd, Appletise Ltd, Bank of Scotland plc, Brintons Ltd, BUPA, Cable & Wireless Communications Ltd, De Beers Consolidated Mines Ltd, Dell Computer Corporation Ltd, Electrolux Ltd, Elida Faberge Ltd and Ogilvy & Mather, Help the Aged, KP Foods Ltd, Luxis Ltd, Master Foods Ltd, Mazda Cars UK Ltd, Mercedes-Benz GB Ltd, Mines Advisory Group and Conquest, Nikon UK Ltd, Prestige & Collections Ltd, Roche Products Ltd, Sacla Ltd and Mitchell, Patterson, Grime, Mitchell, Seagram UK Ltd, UDV Ltd., Vauxhall Motors Ltd, Virgin Atlantic Airways Ltd, ESOMAR, *Admap, International Journal of Advertising*.

Most thanks, however, are due to Stephanie, for putting up with my monopolising the computer and devoting too much windsurfing time to finalising the book.

1 Introduction

> There is a myth that people in advertising and communications ... are on
> the cutting edge of progress and that they are quick to change. This is not
> necessarily so.
>
> Martin Sorrell, CEO, WPP Group, Admap, January 1997

The first edition of this book was written in 1980. Since then, the world has
changed, and advertising with it. There is still a substantial role for conventional
media advertising in the marketing communications of most businesses, but it is no
longer the case (if it ever was) that the automatic response to the question 'How can
we sell more, profitably?' is 'By advertising'; and the answer to the next question
'On TV, of course'.

So, any book that aims to provide a practical introduction to advertising needs to
change, and alter its focus. It must take into account: changes in people's use of
media, and in the media available, for relaxation, information and entertainment;
developments in our understanding of how people respond to, or use, commercial
communications of all kinds; fashions in film and TV; changing technologies; shifts
in the balance of power between various forms of retail distribution; even changes
in the Spirit of the Age, if that means anything, much, outside the more pretentious
newspaper headlines.

It should, too, recognize that advertising is increasingly unconfined by national
boundaries. 'Global advertising' was effectively invented, as a concept, by Saatchi
& Saatchi in the 1970s, and it would be unrealistic to write about advertising as if it
only happened in one country. Even if this was ever true, you now only have to log
on to the Internet to be faced by ads from sources all over the world, in a completely
international medium.

In all this, you must recognize that the advertising business has little sense of
history. This means that the wheel gets reinvented with startling frequency, though
it may sometimes be hard to be sure that it really *is* a wheel beneath the camouflage.

Anyone who writes about advertising has to retain a healthy scepticism when faced
by the latest magic novelty that will solve all the problems of every advertiser in the
world. While Martin Sorrell, quoted above, is probably right about the slowness
with which ad agencies embrace change, I suspect this is partly because agency
people become almost preternaturally sensitive to the possibility that what is new is

likely to be only superficially different. After all, the word 'new' is one of the half-dozen most frequently occurring words in ad headlines, and most of the so-called 'new' products that we meet in our daily lives have little or no significant novelty about them.

That means, then, that although this is a thorough rewrite of the original book, much of the content reflects long-established thinking. In other words, it is only a bit more than a typical 'New, Improved!' product: a relaunch, in fact.

Advertisements – not just advertising

This book is mostly about how to make and use advertisements—not about 'advertising', an abstract whipping boy for media pundits and politicians to cite as the cause of the ills of society. When I talk about advertising, I will usually be using the word either to describe the process of using advertisements to sell things, or to refer to the industry that produces the ads.

I will be talking, too, mainly about advertising in the media ('above-the-line'), as opposed, for example, to point-of-sale messages (which, with other marketing communications, are 'below-the-line': this is an obsolete but still-used distinction, originally based on the way marketing budgets were laid out). In reality, anything that calls attention to a product or service can be advertising: it *adverts*. It could be a crudely written postcard in a newsagent's window, offering a second hand pram, or babysitting; or a 60-second commercial on peak-time TV. It makes saying 'advertising does this' or 'advertising causes that' look pretty daft, when you recognize this. The fact is that advertisements are not limited to a page in the *Sun* or a TV commercial. In a sense, almost anything a company does to call attention to its wares is an advertisement—but people rarely go into paroxysms of fury, or into deep sociological analysis, about brochures, branded book matches or beer mats.

While this book aims to be a 'how to' book, please do not expect to find all the answers. Devising advertisements is an imaginative and chancy business, and no one has ever produced a foolproof technique for having imaginative ideas—let alone the right ones. The business of advertising is, too, a changing one, and some of the most successful people in it have, in effect, rewritten the rule book. So this will be a fairly comprehensive toolkit, but I can't promise to turn anyone into a proficient cabinet-maker. That requires years of practice and hard work.

Advertising in context

Advertising is a small part of the day-to-day life of business, governments and of the publics with which each seeks to engage. It is, on the other hand, a business that offers the people who work in and with it endless excitement, fascination, frustration and, sometimes, satisfaction—together with the opportunity, from time to time, for a great deal of fun and even for making a massive contribution to the success of a brand.

As a small and fragmented industry (in the UK, the 200-odd member agencies of the Institute of Practitioners in Advertising, the agency trade association that covers virtually all the agencies of any size, employ in total only some 13 000 people), this is a business that attracts interest and comment well above its apparent status. There are, I believe, good reasons for this. Advertising revenues pay for a large part of the media—television, newspapers, magazines, radio—that we rely on for information and entertainment; and the journalists who work for these media are interested in the strange world that pays much of their salaries. Advertising is, too, the most visible and immediate point of communication between most businesses and their customers—the public—and there is plenty of evidence that many people find advertisements, from time to time, a subject for lively discussion.

From the business person's point of view, advertising and the processes that lead to the development of advertisements and advertising campaigns represent a change from the day-to-day tasks of managing. Agencies are 'different' from the run of customers or suppliers with whom they deal; and the subject matter is usually more enlivening than the quality of the latest batch of widgets or the contents of the customer complaint file. It is possible to believe, for a moment or two, that you are involved in a creative process that is somehow out of the ordinary.

The advertising business, of course, goes out of its way to reinforce the view of its activities as highly original and—even—daring or outrageous: this is good for the self-esteem of the people who staff the agencies, and helps create a mystique about the business that other forms of marketing communications have not acquired. Public relations and sales promotion may seem, in comparison, relatively obscure and dowdy, while the dynamically growing specialism of direct marketing is firmly—and unfairly—linked to the dismissive put-down 'junk mail'.

What these comparisons point up, however, is that advertising is just part of a much wider world of business communications. True, it tends to take the largest part of the funds spent by companies in talking about their wares to their various publics, and it has managed to attract a glamorous aura: but, in the last analysis, media advertising (which is what most people usually talk about) is merely one of a number of possibly alternative tools that a company can use to help communicate with its customers.

What's more, the available evidence suggests that media advertising is becoming less, rather than more, important in the overall scheme of marketing communications. As we shall see (Chapter 13), this is not necessarily for especially good reasons, but the facts are there. A key factor is that fast-moving consumer goods (fmcg) manufacturers have discovered, from supermarket checkout scanning data that provide weekly, detailed consumer sales feedback, that it is easier to shift sales in the very short term through a variety of forms of sales promotion than through advertising. As a result, in the USA and increasingly in the UK too, marketing budgets have been shifted 'below the line' into various types of price cutting.

The accumulating evidence of detailed analysis and mathematical modelling of what happens as a result of sales promotions, and of advertising expenditure, is leading to this practice being questioned. It seems that constant price promotion has the effect of increasing the price elasticity of brands, of encouraging a quite substantial minority of consumers to follow the price offers, and of turning price promotion into a self-defeating exercise. There is very little, if any, evidence to suggest that price promotion brings any long-term benefit to a brand, in terms of market share, sales or profit. Conversely, there is reasonable evidence, though this can be hard to unravel, that consistent media advertising can and does build the long-term strengths of brands—in the modern jargon, it increases or builds brand equity (a concept I will return to in Chapter 4).

The brand and the marketing mix

Advertising is just part of the marketing activity of a company, and part of the range of communications that can support a brand. Marketing, as a business discipline, can be thought of as the essential interface between a business and its customers or consumers. It is marketing's job to ensure that the business is, as far as possible, providing customers with what they want, rather than simply trying to unload on them what the business happens to have available to sell. In other words, it acts as a conduit, with the aid of market research, for consumer demand to reach the business. It then has to turn this demand into profitable sales, and, in most businesses, be sure that the customers are satisfied sufficiently to buy again—or, at least, not bad-mouth the company to all their friends.

To do this, the business deploys a range of tools and techniques, collectively known as the *marketing mix*: product formulation and variation; packaging; sales literature; the sales force, selling either direct to consumers or to retail distributors; pricing; sales promotion; direct mail; advertising; market research (see Figure 1.1). In particular, it usually aims to do this through the use of *branding*. The distinction between a product and a brand is important, because it explains much of what marketing tries to do, and much of the use of advertisements.

A *product* is simply something that may be offered to potential buyers: it may be good of its kind, but will not be systematically presented in a way that distinguishes it from its competitors. A *brand*, on the other hand, is a product whose producer

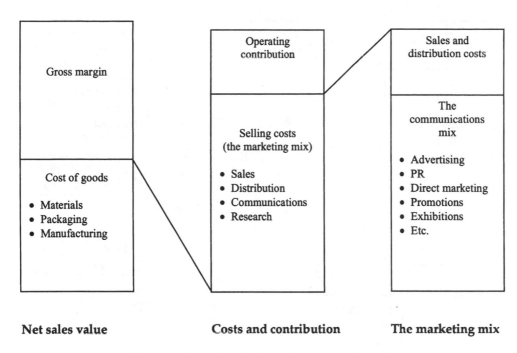

Figure 1.1. Advertiser's costs: a schematic view

has made every effort to make it uniquely desirable to potential buyers, consistently using every element in its presentation to do so. If this is done well, it makes the brand difficult to compete against—not necessarily because it is technically superior (though it may be), but because it has acquired an aura (a 'brand image') which makes it appear better than its competition. A classic UK example is Heinz Baked Beans.

A brand is created by all the elements of the marketing mix working together, consistently, to create a positive prejudice in people's minds: it has a place in their minds, where a mere product is simply a means of fulfilling a physical need. Indeed, it has been said that brands only exist in the minds of consumers. Certainly, a successful brand is seen by its market as having both rational and emotional characteristics that combine into a coherent and distinctive picture. The way a brand acquires this status can be illustrated simply by a diagram—which is, of course, a representation of the marketing mix (see Figure 1.2).

The role of advertising

Clearly advertising is just one of the constituents of the mix that goes to build the brand. Advertising exists to help to sell things. In the case of off-the-page direct

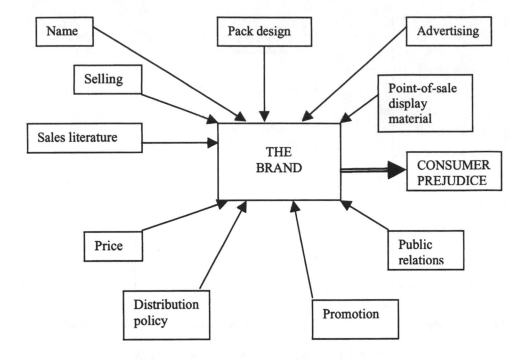

Figure 1.2. How a brand fits together

response ads, they actually *do* sell things, but mostly the process is less direct than this (see Chapter 4).

Advertising is mainly about brands. It is designed, consciously or unconsciously, to create and strengthen consumer impressions of the brand advertised, so that they will be more likely to buy it, or to buy it more often. (An apparent exception to this is public service advertising, where governments use ads, for a variety of purposes that are essentially non-commercial in character.)

However, a brand does not *have* to be advertised through media advertising. It is perfectly possible to devote the marketing budget to having salespeople knocking on consumer's doors or telephoning them to make a sales pitch, or to concentrate entirely on persuading (or bribing) suitable retailers to put the brand on their shelves so that the packaging and presentation will sell it to visitors to the store. The task of the marketing manager is to weigh up the costs and the likely benefits of alternative uses for the budget, and act accordingly. If advertising can be avoided, this can save a lot of money for other purposes.

What is reasonably certain, though, is that to do this will limit the brand's reach. Advertising is an ideal tool for reaching large numbers of people economically. As

Procter & Gamble pointed out in evidence to a Monopolies Commission inquiry on detergents in the mid-1960s, their multi-million-pound expenditure enabled them to talk to virtually every home in the country on TV, for 30 seconds or more, several times a year—for a sum that would allow them to send every home just one postcard. The scale of this arithmetic still applies.

As we shall see (Chapter 13), there is a growing view that mass advertising and mass marketing are no longer the way forward for most consumer businesses, but it is equally true that the alternatives have their limitations. People still like to buy brands of which they have heard, and which they believe to be popular, in some sense. Media advertising is still the cheapest way of making sure that a brand is broadly known and recognized.

Integrated communications

One aspect of thinking about advertising and the marketing mix that is gaining currency is the idea that advertising must go hand in hand with other parts of the marketing mix—for instance, there is evidence that promotions are more effective, and brand building, when they are combined with advertising. This is an element in a change that has been developing for some years in how we approach advertising within the overall marketing and marketing communications mix. *Integrated communications* is now a well-established piece of jargon in the advertising and marketing world, although there is still a considerable debate about precisely what it means in practice, how to achieve it and who should be managing the process.

The principle is clear. If you accept that a brand is a combination of a product (which can be a service, like life assurance or a meal in McDonald's) and of the communications about the product, it should go without saying that all the various communications designed to help present and sell the brand to its target consumers ought to work together to build a coherent, compelling picture of the brand.

They don't need all to be saying *exactly* the same thing, because they all work rather differently: what is needed is synergy between them, to make the sum of the communications more powerful than they would otherwise have been. Each of the activities—PR, advertising, direct mail, trade promotions, consumer promotions, packaging design, point-of-sale signage, brochures and other literature, spin-off merchandise, sponsorship, the web site . . . —will have its own individual role in helping to achieve the marketing objectives for the brand. But each of them will also have a role in contributing to the brand's reputation among its customers. Some will communicate facts, or usage instructions and hints; some will be focused on convincing the potential buyer that the brand is excellent value for money; some will be providing it with positive and motivating associations; some will be calling

	Spending priority	Expect to Increase in Budget	Return on Investment
1.	Brochures	Internet	PR
2.	Trade press	Database marketing	Database marketing
3.	PR	Direct mail	Direct mail
4.	Direct mail	PR	Brochures
5.	Exhibitions	CD-ROM	Seminars
6.	Database marketing	Distributor support	Telemarketing
7.	Seminars	House journals	Trade press
8.	Distributor support	Trade press	Distributor support
9.	House journals	Brochures	Sales promotion
10.	National press	Sales promotion	Exhibitions

Figure 1.3. Business advertisers' top rankings of communication activities—1997 top ten, for each heading (Source: CHJS Survey, reported in Jeans *et al.*, *Admap*, October 1997)

attention to the brand's presence in the store, on the street, in a catalogue, on the Internet.

Advertising, then, should be regarded simply as *part* of a total continuum of communications about the brand. It may have a leading role, and carry the greatest budget: but it can be merely cast in a supporting role for a campaign of activity centred around—for example—a programme of sponsored pop concerts.

Thinking of advertising like this is second nature to many of the (mostly smaller) agencies that specialize in business-to-business advertising. A recent analysis of the business-to-business market showed that media advertising comes some way down the business marketer's list of priorities and is rated below a number of other forms of communication in terms of cost-effectiveness (see Figure 1.3). This reflects the smaller and more tightly defined target groups that these advertisers and their agencies are trying to reach; but as the marketers of consumer goods and services try to define their prime target markets more precisely and tightly (see Chapter 5), a similar way of thinking becomes realistic here, too.

Advertising agencies dealing mainly with consumers have found it quite hard to come to terms with integrated communication thinking, though it has been part of their vocabulary for at least 20 years. There are a number of reasons for this. The primary benefit of media advertising is that it enables a business to talk directly to a very large number of potential (or actual) customers, very economically. This was possible in newspapers, or on posters, before the invention of television; but it was TV that really opened up the mass market. Not only did peak-time TV reach very large chunks of the population: the qualities of moving pictures enabled TV commercials to be extremely powerful selling messages, or so it seemed. Media advertising, and especially TV, advertising rapidly came to dominate advertisers' marketing budgets, and this was emphasized as modern retailing and distribution enabled the manufacturers of fmcg products, who led the process, to reduce their salesforces and direct-selling costs, and transfer the money into advertising.

Specializing in the creation and placing of TV ads became a dynamic and highly profitable business, and the best agencies grew bigger and richer on the back of TV. Other media took a back seat, and although many agencies set up subsidiary units or companies to provide a range of other marketing services, the action, the prestige and the interest became firmly centred in TV advertising. Few agency managers bothered to acquire a detailed knowledge of non-media communications, and most agencies do not, routinely, think in an integrated way.

At the same time, from the point of view of the advertisers ('clients', to ad agencies), media advertising became the focus of the marketing budget, and managing the agency relationship an important part of the marketing job—certainly in comparison with other forms of communication. It is only quite recently that large marketing communications budgets have appeared in a far wider range of markets than the fmcg and automobile categories that dominated expenditures in the 1950s and 1960s. At the same time, TV audiences that were once apparently monolithic have become fragmented (though the four networks in the USA still take 60 per cent of the audience, for example), and marketers have begun to recognize that the core target audiences that they need to influence are often tiny minorities in the population at large (see Chapter 6). Encouraged by the learning from direct marketing, there have been significant shifts in thinking about how best to influence customers, and—in many cases—retain their loyalty, rather than to acquire new customers.

The effect of all this, together with the move by fmcg manufacturers into sales promotion, has been to weaken the hold of mass-media advertising on the consciousness of advertising clients. These managers have had to discover for themselves the need to integrate a range of communications in order to build and protect their brands. In trying to do this, they have mostly had precious little help from their ad agencies, because these agencies, as we have seen, have had no interest in integration, and have either hived off or lost the craft abilities, let alone the thinking, that would make it possible.

At the same time, it seems reasonably clear that advertisers do not greatly wish to hand the task of managing the integration of their communications over to a third party. Quite apart from the loss of control this involves, there are real doubts about the ability of any agency, whatever its claimed expertise, to deliver objective advice about budget allocation between activities; let alone to provide top-quality service for every one of the rather different skills and disciplines involved in—say—TV advertising, direct mail, sponsorship and related promotions and public relations.

Marketing directors and managers are used to buying the different elements of the mix from different specialists, and as advertising has tended to become a higher level decision, the other mix elements have provided the manager with freedom to take decisions and organize his or her own activity.

For anyone becoming involved in advertising, then, the problems of achieving success, which were already quite complex, have been amplified. It is no longer enough to try to understand as much as possible about making and using advertisements as a subject in its own right: you have to become knowledgeable and sensitive to the other means available to support a brand. It has to be possible, and realistic, to say 'We don't need to advertise this brand', or 'Wouldn't it be better to organize a public relations programme around a series of sponsored events?' or 'Shouldn't we devote our budget to direct mail?

The rest of the book

After this very broad introduction, which introduces a number of the themes that will appear later, the rest of the book will cover the main areas that someone more or less new to advertising will need to know about:

- Advertising agencies: how they work, how they are organized, and how to choose and use one.
- Advertising strategy: how to think about what the ads are trying to do, and understanding the people they are aimed at.
- How good advertisements can be created.
- Media: what is available, and how it is bought, sold and planned.
- Putting a campaign plan together.
- Judging advertisements and evaluating campaigns.
- The law, regulation and self-regulation.
- The relationship between advertising and the economy and society.
- Advertising internationally and globally.

Summary

- Advertising is a core part of many companies' marketing mix: the activities that link a brand to its market and its consumers or customers.
- Traditionally, media advertising has taken the lion's share of marketing communications budgets, at least for most consumer goods companies, since it is a cost-effective means of reaching large numbers of people.
- As media and markets have fragmented, however, other forms of communication are gaining importance, and advertising is increasingly seen as just part of an integrated communications programme.

□   As such, advertising works together, and integrates with, a variety of other forms of communication.

Questions to consider

□   Is advertising becoming more or less important to companies? Why should this be so?

□   How might the marketing mix differ for a brand of frozen food, a charity and a bank?

2 The agency world

'Curiouser and curiouser' cried Alice

Alice in Wonderland, Lewis Carroll

No business absolutely needs an advertising agency. It is perfectly possible to handle all marketing communications in-house, or buy the services and processes involved from a series of separate specialists. However, most businesses find it easier to use an agency (or several). That way, they also gain the benefits of simple lines of communication, expertise, creativity and, often, a great deal of experienced advice that they might pay much more for from a firm of consultants.

Advertising agencies come in a variety of shapes and sizes, with, increasingly, a range of specialist firms carrying out parts of what used to be done by a single firm—the so-called 'full-service' agency, which was able and willing to carry out the entire range of advertising processes, and often a number of other related activities in addition. While full-service agencies are still common, it is increasingly rare for their clients to demand the full range of services. This chapter starts from the full-service advertising agency, but also looks at how an advertiser may choose to use a creative agency in conjunction with other specialists.

The traditional agency

An advertising agency has four key functions (see Figure 2.1): planning the strategy for the advertising, creating and producing the ads, planning and buying the media in which to run them, and managing this process together with the client. It will also have its own business support functions—finance, personnel, progress/production, information/library, office management, IT—and may be able to offer other forms of marketing communications. These range from public relations to sales promotion, and larger agencies have usually hived these off into separate profit centres. Of course, this gets in the way of effective integrated communications.

Agencies have for years organized themselves in departments, corresponding to the key functions, and in large agencies these are usually found on separate floors. The main departments you will meet are:

- *Account management* The 'suits', whose job is to manage the agency's business with one or more clients. It is their responsibility to be in regular—

12

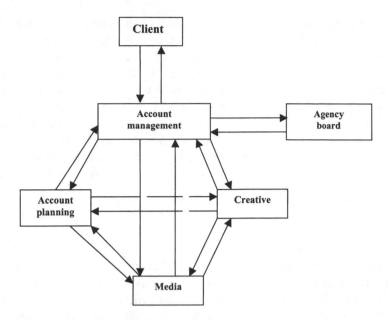

Figure 2.1. Traditional agency structure—the key departments

even intimate—contact with the client's key people; agree with the client the strategy, objectives and brief for each campaign or activity; ensure that the brief is understood within the agency; and organize the agency's resources to achieve the client's demands. This means that they have to understand the client's business in detail and be, in effect, business associates for the client. What's more, they are responsible to the agency's management for delivering a satisfied client and a continuing profitable business.

☐ *Creatives* These are the ones with jeans and trainers and unpredictable habits, who have the task of turning the brief into ideas that will sell. While they can be extremely professional business people, with a real grasp of the realities of the market, they are sometimes frustrated poets and artists manqués, and less disciplined than may seem ideal. Usually, creatives come in pairs ('teams'): an artist or visual thinker, and a writer; though the artist ('art director') may not be very good at drawing and the writer ('copywriter') can often be highly visual as well as reasonably literate.

☐ *Account planning* Planners were a British invention that is now widely followed, especially in the US. Their role is to use detailed understanding of the customer or consumer, based on market research, experience and any other information, to develop the brief for the advertising. This involves defining the target audience as precisely and evocatively as possible and creating a strategy that can inspire the creatives to do great work. Planners have to combine a good knowledge of research techniques and interpretation with a more or less magpie mind and the ability to empathize, and argue, with the creatives. In some agencies, it is the planner's job to carry out personally a large part of the qualitative research that supports the creative development process.

☐   *Media*   The department's job is to plan and buy media. They work with the rest of the team to identify the most effective and cost-efficient ways to reach the target audience, and then negotiate with the media to buy the specific spots or spaces to do the best job for the brand. With a growing range of media research available on-line, they have to be computer-literate and capable of extracting value from a mass of figures. Sharp negotiating skills are needed, too, to get the best value from the media owners—media planners and buyers are usually different people, though they have to work closely together.

Normally, as a client, you rarely meet anyone from an agency outside these functions, except for some of those involved in actually producing the ads, especially the agency TV production team.

Recently, the traditional agency structure has become a target for rethinking. This has taken two main forms: the hiving off of specialist functions into separate agencies and the development of more or less radical new ways of organizing agencies. While the first of these is longer established and more obviously successful, it is logical to start with the second.

New agency structures

Three key factors influence the ways in which new agency formats have emerged: technological changes, the growing importance of internationally held accounts for large agencies, and the recognition that different clients' demands on the agency vary widely. Allied to these is the belief that the old structures were not especially good at fostering teamwork and team thinking within the agency.

These factors have moved some agency managements to reorganize their businesses in one of several directions. The most common is to structure the agency around its clients, so that there is an office, or area of the office, for each account, with—often—the furniture, furnishings and decoration designed to reflect the client's business. This is—broadly—the practice at St Luke's, the UK spin-off from Chiat/Day, which is also organized as a cooperative*. It is easy to see how an area for Nike or Reebok might differ from one for Midland Bank or Chanel or a government anti-drug campaign. The idea is to create a focus for the account team, with an appropriate atmosphere to ensure that they keep close to the brand and what it stands for. It also gives the client the feeling that his or her interests are being closely cared for by a committed team—whereas, in every agency, almost everyone works on several accounts, and the team for each account will be

---

* See Andy Law, *Open Minds*, Orion Business Publications, London 1998.

different. Agencies build account teams on a mix-and-match, horses-for-courses basis (or, sometimes, simply because these are the only people available).

Closely related to the 'account room' approach, aided by modern technology, is the 'virtual account group' or 'virtual agency'. There is no real need to have everyone working on the account in the same room, the same building or even the same country. All you need is some carefully linked computers, an intranet, video-conferencing and ISDN or equivalent connections. There are virtual agencies and virtual departments in existence—in the UK, the Scottish Leith agency established a virtual planning department some years ago, which evolved into specialist planning agency Red Spider—and big international groups like WPP increasingly assemble electronically-linked teams from several countries to service international clients. The beauty of the virtual agency is that it can include, or leave out, anyone or any function: if the client needs specialized advice, a specialist consultant can join the team, for just as long as they are needed. If all that is required is an occasional ad, there is no need to keep a permanent operation in place.

Somewhere between these formats comes the use of 'hot desking'. Lots of agency people spend much of their time out of the office, at meetings, producing commercials or at photographic shoots, and space is expensive. So, in some areas of the office, desks are available on a first-come, first-served basis. (When everyone turns up at once, there's an unholy scramble.)

All this is trying, with varying degrees of success and conviction, to get away from the things agencies have always criticized in their clients: a focus on products and production and too little attention to the needs of customers. The traditional agency format was speciality-driven, with the built-in assumption that creativity was the sole property of the creative department. In practice, although it is the job of the creatives to come up with the actual ads, anyone on the team should be able to contribute to the creative process.

The growing range of specialists

There have always been specialist companies fulfilling some of the tasks that a full-service agency performs. Ad agencies themselves started in the early 19th century as brokers, selling advertising space for newspapers and news-sheets. It was only later that they realized that they could make more money, and give a better service, by providing the advertisers with copy to fill the space they had sold.

Media buying agencies

The big break-out from full-service dates back to the late 1960s, when a few pioneers set up specialist agencies to handle media buying. They recognized that this

Group	Parent	Indep/dependent	1998 billings £ m	% share of total adspend
1. Zenith Media	Saatchi	D	563	7.8
2. Carat Group	Aegis Group	I	494	6.8
3. MindShare Media	WPP Group	D	348	4.8
4. Mediacom/TMB	Grey	D	333	4.6
5. MediaVest	McManus Gp.	D	322	4.4
6. CIA Medianetwork	Tempus Gp.	I	318	4.4
7. Initiative Media	IPG	D	307	4.2
8. BMP OMD	Omnicom	D	306	4.2
9. Universal McCann	IPG	D	305	4.2
10. New PHD	Omnicom	D	264	3.6
TOTAL – Top 10			3560	49.0

Figure 2.2.   Top ten media buying agency groups: 1998 (*Source: Campaign*, based on MMS data)

activity was different in character from other agency tasks, and argued that by concentrating purely on buying they could offer better value to advertisers than the traditional agencies. Practices varied between countries: in France, where Carat rapidly came to dominate the media business, media shops could buy blocks of space or time from media owners at a discount, and then sell on to their clients at whatever prices they judged appropriate—they became, in effect, media wholesalers. In the UK this was never the practice, and was probably actually illegal, and the French situation became so non-transparent, and possibly corrupt, that legislation—the Loi Sapin—had to be introduced to prevent abuses.

One advantage media shops have is that they can usually sell their services to competing—'conflicting'—clients in the same field (in France, Carat handle 10 car accounts). Ad agencies have always found this difficult, both because of their own scruples about confidentiality and, more importantly, because few clients were prepared to put their business into an agency working for a competitor. (There *are* specialist agencies that handle competing clients within selected markets, but these are mostly small, such as London's Dewynters, who specialize in entertainment and leisure. World wide, the one big exception is Dentsu, the leading agency in Japan, and, indeed, the world.)

Media specialists have prospered and grown, and dominate the media markets in Europe: in the UK, where the market is still relatively fragmented, the top 50 media buyers account for 99 per cent of advertising expenditure, according to *Media Week,* and the top 10 alone account for 49 per cent (Figure 2.2), while further concentration is expected. As they have grown, media specialists have become more involved in media planning, though the creative agencies still expect to have a considerable input in this area. It is, as we shall see (Chapter 9), important to decide where exactly a particular ad should appear, to give the creative material its best chance to have an effect; and this is clearly a matter for discussion between creatives and media thinkers. There are now several UK media planning consultancies, such as Michaelides and Bednash, and concentration on planning is recognized as the next major trend in media, because fragmentation of traditional mass media has heightened the importance of precise, imaginative targeting, while buying has become almost a commodity, low-cost, low-margin business.

Media shops have become an important source of advertising research, with much original work being done, especially in the UK, by Carat, who have recruited researchers from agency planning departments as well as traditional media researchers.

The full-service agencies have not abdicated from their involvement in media. Several have established arm's-length subsidiaries, to carry out buying for their own clients and for other advertisers for whom they do not provide a creative service. The first of these, Zenith, was set up by Saatchi & Saatchi in 1988, to handle buying for the group's agencies in the UK, and then worldwide. Other agencies have followed suit, and the market now divides between 'media independents' such as, CIA, and 'media dependents' such as Zenith, and WPP Group's relatively new MindShare (see Figure 2.2). Some independents have moved into the creative field, either by acquisition or merger, or by establishing small in-house facilities, especially for direct mail.

Creative boutiques

Around the end of the 1960s, in the UK at least, several leading creative people from agencies set up 'creative hot-shops', an idea that had originated a little earlier in the US. These agencies originally did nothing but create ads to meet a brief from the client. In time, they often found themselves acting as an extra creative resource for agencies that found themselves under pressure, while the more successful ones, such as The Creative Business, branched out to include account planners on their staff. Nowadays, it is more common to find creative teams working as freelances, rather than whole agencies. These freelances may work directly for a client, or supplement the resources of an agency that finds itself short of time or talent.

Direct marketing

Direct marketing—direct mail, off-the-page selling and now direct response TV (DRTV), radio and the Internet—has always been part of the advertising business. Some of the industry's founding fathers and pre-eminent figures, such as Claude Hopkins in the 1920s and David Ogilvy more recently, have been direct marketing specialists. For many years direct marketing has been regarded as a distinct branch of advertising, and specialist agencies have developed to handle it. Some of these, such as Ogilvy One, are offshoots and subsidiaries of large full-service agencies, and often work very closely with the parent; others, like WWAV Rapp Collins, started as independents, but WWAV is now part of global advertising giant Omnicom. As in all areas of marketing services, large independent companies are becoming hard to find.

As direct marketing becomes more and more a key element in many companies' marketing, full-service agencies will expand their capabilities in this field: it certainly makes sense, in terms of integrated marketing, to have media advertising and direct marketing under common creative direction. Full-service agencies are acquiring or merging with direct specialists, or actively developing their own skills in the area, as well as moving into so-called 'new media' (the Internet and the World Wide Web). This last area is teeming with small specialist agencies and consultancies, though a shake-out seems inevitable.

Account planning

A relatively new phenomenon is the proliferation of specialist planning agencies. There have been one or two of these in the UK for years—The Planning Shop and The Planning Partnership, for example. The last few years have seen many more, such as Red Spider and Forrest Associates, spurred by a combination of the recession of the early 1990s and the realization that modern technology makes it perfectly possible for planners to operate outside the walls of an agency. There is a developing grey area between planning shops, marketing strategy consultants and market research companies with a planning focus.

The rationale for planning specialists lies in the way in which planning has developed: downsizing by agencies has led to planners being thinly spread across accounts, and downsizing by advertisers has meant that marketing departments need more help. Agency planners' ability to work in depth has been reduced. This provides the opportunity for specialist organizations either to take over the planning role for an agency, or to act as a supplementary source of ideas for agency or advertiser.

Management consultants

Recently, some senior agency managers, notably Martin Sorrell of WPP, have suggested that corporate managements have turned to the big general consultancy firms for advice on brand strategy, thus excluding ad agencies from a key traditional role and cutting off an important part of the agency's influence with its clients.

It has been argued—probably rightly—by some agency thinkers that this fails to recognize that agencies, uniquely among consultancy organizations, not merely analyse and recommend strategies but create solutions to marketing problems, but the threat remains.

There is some evidence of a trend for major advertisers to set their own strategies and then run creative contests to see who can come up with the best ideas to fulfil them. One logical conclusion of all this has been suggested by Coca-Cola's use of an American creative talent shop, CAA, to produce creative ideas in response to briefs developed by Coca-Cola's own marketers.

Selecting an agency

Every year, in the UK, some 300–400 advertising accounts move agencies. The larger moves create massive speculation in *Campaign*, the London agency 'village's' weekly magazine. Agencies vie to pitch for the business. A short-listed few get invited to compete. Midnight oil is burnt. Members of agency teams explore the client's business, go out into the streets to interview and—often—film consumers talking about the brand. Speculative campaigns are created, argued about, torn up, redeveloped, researched, fought over. For large accounts, billing millions of pounds, a complete commercial may be produced. Over a brief period, the client's executives see formal presentations of strategy, creative material, media plans and unique 'deals', and a whole lot else. Eventually, a decision is reached: the account is assigned to a new agency (or perhaps the old one); there are headlines in *Campaign*, champagne in the winning agency, and then everyone goes back to normal.

This pattern is universal, all round the world, though increasingly pitches for large accounts are becoming international, regional or even global (see Figure 2.3).

The process is not wildly efficient: you do not easily choose a bride at a beauty contest, and this is effectively what happens. There have been numerous attempts to find a better way, and in the UK the ISBA (the advertisers' trade body) and the IPA (the agencies), together with the DMA (direct marketing), have published the *ISBA/ IPA/DMA Pitch Guide* to try to prevent abuse of the system as it stands. Some large agencies, such as Bartle Bogle and Hegarty (BBH), refuse to produce creative work for pitches, and insist on being judged on the quality of their strategic thinking, together with work they have done for existing clients.

This is realistic: an agency needs to get to know and work with a client and the client's market to produce creative work that is really right for the brand: very few pitch-winning campaigns ever see the real world, or not without modification. The essential dialogue between client and agency is omitted from the pitch process, however hard the agency—and client—may try to avoid this.

Advertiser	New agency	Old agency	Billings ($ m)
Compaq Computers	DDB Needham	Ammirati Puris Lintas	300
Ditto—media	Optimum	Ammirati Puris Lintas	
Danone Group	Y&R*	Saatchi, BDDP, Y&R	250
Frito-Lay Corp	BBDO*	BBDO, Y&R, DDB Needham	200+
Alcatel Alsthom-media	Zenith*	Optimum & others	160
Dell Computer	BBDO	JWT	100+
Ernst & Young	DMN&B	Grace & Rothschild Grey (media)	100
Motorola—media	Universal McCann	Initiative Media	100
Siemens	JWT*	Various agencies	100
Merrill Lynch & Co	JWT	Bozell	90
Chase Manhattan	FCB*	Wells BDDP, McCann Erickson	75

* Consolidation

Figure 2.3. Top 10 global account moves: 1998 (Source: *Advertising Age*, 11 January 1999)

The problem is human nature. Clients expect agencies to produce ads, and agencies like doing so. Indeed, agencies relish the freedom a pitch gives them to create ads without the detailed constraints that inevitably appear in a real-life relationship with any client's brands and management. So, even when the client has stipulated that creative work is not required for the pitch, it is a safe bet that one or more of the agencies will produce ads. Experience suggests that, if one agency does so and the others do not, that agency tends to win: so, of course, they all do it.

But how does a client decide who should pitch? There are over 200 agencies in the IPA in the UK, and at least as many more (mostly very small) outside. In the US, *Advertising Age* has quoted a figure of over 9 000, of which the majority are small and local. How do you find the right one?

You can start with directories: in the UK *Advertisers' Annual* ('The Blue Book') or the *ALF/BRAD Agency List* can provide details of agencies, covering key personnel, approximate size, lists of clients, etc. The *Standard Directory of Advertising Agencies* ('Redbook') provides similar listings in the US. The trade press regularly publishes lists of the larger agencies—*Campaign* has its 'UK 300', and *Advertising Age* in the US has both US and international agency listings in terms of size of billings and income.

It is useful to keep an eye on the marketing and advertising trade press, because it provides a good, if gossipy, overview of what is happening in the advertising business, and provides clues as to which agencies are 'hot' at any time. It is not

difficult, too, to take note of ads that you regard as being especially goo
out who is responsible for them. If an agency seems to be producing goo
its current clients, it may be able to do so for you. The only problem
probably working for one of your competitors, which would bar it fr
for you: but if your account is enticing enough—translation: if your
enough—it could be possible to seduce the agency to drop their existing
your favour.

Another thing you *could* do, is simply mention to the trade press that you are
looking for an agency: your phones, fax machines, email, receptionists will be
deluged with solicitations. This will happen, too, if it leaks out that you have set up
a pitch, even if you make it quite clear that you have a final shortlist, and there will
be no additions. Some good agencies (and one or two not-so-good) regard this as a
challenge, and every now and then one of these Johnny-come-latelies not only gets
into the pitch but walks off with the spoils.

In the UK, and in several other countries, there is a commercial organization called
the Advertising Agency Register (AAR) that keeps on file details of over 100
agencies, and will help an advertiser screen these down to a shortlist. This is not
entirely satisfactory, because it tends to be limited to larger agencies (who are
prepared to pay AAR's fees), but can provide a useful guide. Beyond this, there are
consultants, such as Agency Assessments, who specialize in finding and selecting
agencies for clients. They will, if required, take your brief, draw up and approach a
shortlist of suitable agencies, and even conduct the whole pitch procedure.

If this looks decidedly like dating, courting and marriage, it is. Normally, a client
hopes to establish a working relationship that can last for some years: changes of
agency are disruptive and expensive, and it takes time for a new relationship to bed
down. This means that the choice of an agency is not just a business decision of
some importance: it is also a matter of chemistry—of a mutual attraction between
the individual people involved and between the two companies' corporate instincts
and attitudes. For the client, it is a little like recruiting a key senior manager, but
with one critical difference: a new manager has to fit into the corporate culture and
blend with the organization, while an agency should, arguably, be picked precisely
because it can bring something different to the party, in addition. An agency can
become a true business partner and also a source of creative energy for the client to
exploit. The client and the agency management have to be able to carry on a
business relationship, while still allowing the agency's creative side to stimulate and
provoke in ways that may well threaten 'orthodox business practice'.

Choosing an agency, then, demands management time. It is not simply a matter of
deciding who has devised the best ad campaign, though that is obviously important:
you go to an agency for its creativity, because that is the main thing it has to sell,
and which you may find yourself lacking. It is more a matter of being able to work

with the agency in future: so you need to have positive answers to a series of screening questions (see Box 2.1). These or similar questions can form the basis for a scoring system used by all the members of the team choosing the agency: it may be wise to apply them not once, but two or even three times during the selection process.

Box 2.1   Screening questions—checklist for agency selection

- Have they fully understood the brief?
- Do they know how to use market research? Can they contribute to our thinking here?
- Is their strategic thinking sound?
- Is it imaginative? Have I learned anything useful from it?
- Are they professional and businesslike?
- Can I work with their senior people? And will they be actually working on my business?
- Are their capabilities high in all key areas—management, strategy, creative, media?
- Do they work well as a team—both among themselves and with our people?
- Is their creative work of a high quality?
- Is this confined to TV, or does it go across all media?
- Does this include below-the-line? New media? Can they offer an integrated service?
- Do they have real expertise in the specialist areas which we are looking at, e.g. direct marketing, new media?
- Can they work with us internationally (now or in the future)?
- How do they propose to evaluate the effectiveness of the campaign?
- What is their attitude to costs? Will they save us money?
- How will they relate to our media buying agency/ other specialists?
- Will they fit with our ways of working? Are they willing and able to be business partners, or will they simply be suppliers? (This depends—of course—on how we see our own style of dealing with agencies).
- How important to them will our account be? Will we be one of their larger accounts, or simply a small fish in a very large pool?

The importance attached by different companies to these factors varies quite widely. As a general rule, agencies are chosen primarily on the basis of creative solutions, together with 'chemistry' (Can we work with these people?). It is probably a more sophisticated approach to judge more on strategy and the agency's approach to solving problems.

Each client needs to determine in advance what the basis for its judgement will be: this process is, in itself, a distinctly useful one, and may teach the company more than it expects about how it handles the advertising process and its relationships with agencies. Drawing up a score sheet, and deciding how it should be weighted, is an essential basis for a rational decision in this area.

Paying the agency

Traditionally, agencies earned commissions on the space or time they bought in the media—a practice going back to their origins as space brokers. The media, in fact, paid agencies 15 per cent—sometimes only 10 per cent, occasionally 20 per cent—of the gross cost of the space (which translates in agencies' billing systems into 17.65 per cent of the *net* media cost). In addition, agencies charged the same mark-up (or more) on production of ads and other materials, and most agency groups would negotiate an extra commission for handling advertising in foreign countries, typically another 5 per cent.

This system survived intact until the 1960s, when the first stirrings of 'unbundling' of agency functions began. If the agency no longer does the media buying, how much is that worth on its own, and how much should you pay the agency for what's left? A sort of tariff for media buying rapidly emerged, ranging from as little as $1\frac{1}{2}$ per cent to as much as 5 per cent in some cases. This would leave the main agency, say, $12\frac{1}{2}$ per cent.

Then, some large clients, especially clients from areas that had not traditionally been heavy advertisers, started to question whether the standard commission was too high. Pressure began to be applied to agency managements to accept lower rates, and very quickly 15 per cent became 12 per cent and then 10 per cent, and some large retailers, in particular, negotiated rates of commission, for full-service business (including media) down to as low as 8 per cent. The fixed 15 per cent commission has been largely dead, in Britain at least, since the 1980s.

This has led to an extensive search for alternatives. Once you accept that 'commission' is outmoded, it becomes reasonable to ask how an agency ought to be remunerated. This has led to two broad approaches. The most widely used is modelled on the practices of many professions: the client is charged fees, either for time worked on the account (based on time-sheets); or, as an adaptation, the agency draws up a 'menu' of services, and these are charged at an agreed rate. Fees have the obvious disadvantage that they take no meaningful account of whether the service provided is any good (Did it work?) and that creativity is hard to pin down. A creative idea may be found extremely quickly, and the high hourly cost that the creator may be charged out at cannot compensate the agency for the lack of hours involved.

There is no doubt that fee systems are rapidly replacing commission, though the residual value of the commission system is that it is conceptually and administratively very simple to operate. The same is true of straightforward fee systems, which are, in fact, usually proposed by agencies on the basis of calculations about what the commission would have been. It is much more difficult to arrive at an effective payment by results (PBR) system that both motivates and rewards the agency and satisfies the client's desire for transparent value for money. A key factor promoting PBR is the growing pressure on marketing management to make their advertising budgets accountable: PBR provides a clear route to—at least—a specific, measurable result from the advertising. Of course, it still leaves open the trickier question of whether the advertising budget might have been better spent on other activities. We will return to this in Chapter 14, while remuneration systems are discussed in more detail in Chapter 3.

For the client negotiating with a new agency, the type of remuneration deal, and its level, is clearly important. It will not merely affect the bottom line (15 per cent of the ad budget is significant in relation to profits), but it will influence the entire relationship with the agency. Some clients take a very macho stance on these negotiations. This implies a relationship that is very much buyer–supplier. While this may be appropriate for some corporate styles, it is not, I believe, the best way to use an agency: if you have the right agency it can act very much as a business partner—though it has to earn the right to do so.

Summary

- Ad agencies grew up to perform the whole range of advertising services for clients: account management, strategy development, creative, production, media planning and buying. An agency that does all of these is a 'full-service' agency. These days, few of any large agency's clients will be on a full-service arrangement.
- Since the 1960s, agency functions have been at least partly 'unbundled', with specialist firms able to take on many of the agency's tasks. This process has gone furthest, worldwide, in media planning and, especially, buying.
- Agencies—even the large full-service companies—have responded, to an extent only, by rethinking their structures and working practices. Radically different formats, however, are only found among smaller, newer agencies.
- Selecting an ad agency usually involves a pitch process—even though this is not entirely satisfactory. Would you choose a bride at a beauty contest?
- Agencies used to be paid through commissions from the media. This system is breaking down, and fee systems are becoming more general.

Questions to consider

☐ Does it make sense for a modern agency to offer a full service? What are the arguments for and against?

☐ What are the pros and cons of using specialist agencies? How can their efforts best be coordinated?

☐ What are the possible alternatives to the traditional pitch, as a way of choosing an agency? What would be most likely to produce a satisfactory solution for the client?

3 Managing the client–agency relationship

Embrace the new agency into a long-term relationship

ISBA/IPA/DMA Pitch Guide

Once the pitch has been completed, and the client has selected the agency that is going to help the business to hitherto undreamed-of heights, the two parties to the deal have to do two things. One is relatively trivial in the greater scheme of things, though it may well carry the seeds of future divorce: agreeing the commercial and financial terms of the relationship. More important is the need to establish exactly how the relationship is going to work, on a day-to-day basis. The quote above is not the only way to run the relationship, though it is likely to be the most fruitful.

Exactly how this works will depend on the client company's attitude to its ad agency or agencies. Most agencies are hoping to arrive at a relationship with their clients where they become, in effect, business partners. Some clients, however, prefer to see their agency as simply a supplier: just another business from whom they buy, with the transactions concerned being tightly defined, and a subject for often aggressive price negotiation.

Setting the terms

In the last chapter, we saw that the ways in which clients pay their agencies have been changing. Indeed, the current situation can best be described as one of flux. There is a need first to define, in detail, precisely what the client expects of the agency; and then to define the methods of payment for this. The IPA and ISBA have combined to produce a guide to client-agency contracts,[1] which is a valuable starting point, though it needs to be adapted to the specific circumstances. The headings for the 'standard' agreement cover 41 items, together with schedules giving details of specific items covered.

Both agency and client need to have a clear understanding on a whole range of issues (see Box 3.1) as the basis for a formal contract. Within this, the key areas are likely to be remuneration, the handling of intellectual property, and—unfortunately—severance arrangements. The contract should be an essential element

---

[1] Suggested Terms and Provisions for Use in Client/Agency Agreements, Lewis Silkin, London, on behalf of ISBA, CIPS (Chartered Institute of Purchasing & Supply) and IPA, London 1998.

Box 3.1   Key headings from Standard Agreement format

- Services covered
- Agency status
- Conflict
- Authority and approvals
- Remuneration:
  - Media charges, refunds, commissions
  - Materials, services, expenses
  - Market research
  - International and currency fluctuations
  - VAT
  - Payment terms
- Audit
- Intellectual property
- Insurance
- Data protection
- Termination
- Severance

- Date and term
- Co-operation
- Confidentiality
- Contact reporting

- Selection/terms for suppliers
- Ownership/custody of materials
- Warranties and indemnities
- Advertising standards
- Notice period
- Dispute resolution

Source: Adapted from ISBA/CIPS/IPA.

---

confirming the relationship, though in my experience clients tend to be astonishingly reluctant to sign, and the ISBA's research shows that 40 per cent or more of client–agency relationships are not covered by formal contracts. The contract is not usually of day-to-day importance in a successful ongoing client–agency relationship—only when things start to go wrong (which, as Murphy's law states, they inevitably will).

From the agency's point of view, the vital issue is to be sure that they get paid, adequately, for everything they do for the client. The client, naturally, wishes to get as much as he can from the agency, while paying as little as possible. A good client will realize that the best way to achieve this is not, in practice, to screw the agency down and exploit every opportunity to get extra work beyond what is in the contract. This means that the scope of the agency's responsibilities should be clearly spelled out and agreed, and it should be recognized that the agency is entitled to ask for extra money if it is asked to go significantly beyond the agreed tasks. (This should not preclude the agency from taking a speculative initiative from time to time, but it should not expect to get paid for that: it is a standard ploy in the continuing game of seducing the client to give the agency more business.) In the last resort, both sides need to recognize that the agency is in business to make a profit. If it cannot do that on an account, it has to renegotiate the terms, or resign the account.

Methods of payment

In the last chapter, payment methods were discussed briefly. Essentially, there are four main methods, with a variety of variations and combinations (see Box 3.2). The issues that emerge when the agency contract is being drawn up are specific to the format used, and most of these provide opportunities for negotiation.

Box 3.2   Agency payment systems

  ☐ Commission: Fixed (up to 15 per cent, usually lower).
                                  Variable, usually on a sliding scale, related to the billings involved: e.g. up to £xk, 13 per cent, £xk-yk, $12\frac{1}{2}$ per cent, over £yk, 12 per cent)

  ☐ Fee: Fixed, usually calculated in relation to the commission likely on the account, as a benchmark
                                  Time/labour-based
                                  Creative/idea fee

  ☐ Payment by results: Normally linked to either fees or commission. An extra payment for achieving either specific quantified objectives or for meeting qualitative criteria relating to the agency's performance and the relationship with the client

  ☐ Work-unit pricing: A relatively small agency, ARM, has a sophisticated pricing system based on detailed analysis of the costs and time required for various activities, that allows them to quote precise prices, in advance, for all the work a client may require. This is ideally suited to fit with modern accounting practices, but has taken 15 years to develop. (See J. Orsmond, Fixed-cost working, *Admap*, October 1998)

Quite frequently, these different types of payment may be mixed or combined. For example, an agency undertaking a development project may be paid on a fee basis, until the brand receives enough advertising for a switch to commission; or the agency may be guaranteed a minimum income (in effect, a fee in lieu of commission unearned).

Commission

The main issue here is the rate of commission:

☐ Its absolute level.
☐ Whether it should vary with, for instance, different media, different levels of total spend.

□ How—if at all—it should apply to non-media items (mostly production costs).

The alert client will be aware, too, that while media discounts are built into media rate cards (Chapter 9), studios and production houses often pay discounts to agencies, which can make the production side of the business far more profitable to the agency than appears on the surface.

The key problem with commission, though, is that it distorts—or can distort—an agency's advice to its clients. There are clear benefits from persuading the client to use media and creative material that entail limited work by the agency for large expenditure, which is why large agencies have become rich on the back of TV campaigns. You produce one expensive commercial (or group of commercials in a campaign), on which you earn substantial production commissions, and then run the campaign for some time on national TV, the most expensive medium, without any need to do more creative work. By contrast, a good press campaign requires far more individual pieces of creative work for the same level of expenditure and is therefore significantly less profitable to the agency.

Fees

Time-based fee systems look like the answer to the problem just described. In essence, the agency is paid for the work it does on the client's behalf, and this should mean that every option is given equal weight in the agency's recommendations.

Again, however, there are problems. First, the agency has to have in place an effective and efficient time-sheet system as the basis for charging. Most agencies have such systems, as part of their internal financial controls, but they are not always the most religiously observed part of agency life. Then, the agency and the client have to be prepared to agree on the rate for the time of each member of the team. This may be easy enough, but it focuses the client's attention either on how costly it is to have the services of the top people, or on the fact that he or she gets a nice cheap deal, but never sees the top people who were promised, at the pitch, to be working on the business. Finally, from the agency's point of view, the most costly people are the creative talent, and the most valuable thing the agency can do for the client is to produce a great creative idea. Great creative ideas *may* take many hours' hard work, but are equally likely to emerge from 10 minutes' thought in the bath. This does not give the agency much reward for the idea.

Menu systems—work-unit pricing

These operate on a cost-per-task basis. The agency draws up a schedule of the types of activity it is likely to have to do for the client, and puts a price on each. Developing the idea for a national TV campaign will, on these systems, be considerably more costly than designing a sales brochure, even though the latter may involve more physical work, in time terms.

The main virtue of this approach is that it provides a transparent price structure, lends itself to tight cost control by the client and meshes well with standard cost-accounting processes. It also can be a valuable tool for the agency's management, since devising the scheme requires detailed understanding of how the agency's operating costs are structured, something many agencies are surprisingly vague about.

The obvious problem is that it treats the job of devising and producing a client's communication campaign as a series of discrete elements, and fails to allow for the possible existence, and value, of synergy between them. From the agency's point of view, too, it lays them open to the client looking for competitive quotes, purely on a price basis, which can quickly erode the scale of the business and the trust in the relationship between agency and client. Finally, it needs some way of dealing with quality: a cheap bad idea is no use to anyone, but how do you devise the necessary system for rewarding great ideas? Unless you can do this, the agency has little motivation to go the extra mile on your behalf.

Payment by results

Payment by results (PBR) systems are usually combined with one of the other approaches, so that the agency can earn a bonus for exceeding agreed targets, however these are set. Thus, Unilever's international agencies operate on commission, but can earn up to an extra 3–4% for above-target performance.

The obvious problem for both client and agency is to develop attainable targets and measure progress towards them. The obvious way of setting targets is in relation to sales, but there are considerable pitfalls in this (see Chapter 8), even for direct response operations. As a result, many clients adopt a 'softer' approach, agreeing ratings for each aspect of the agency's service, and rewarding attainment over a certain level. From the agency's point of view, it is probably better to have a system that focuses more closely on the attainment of agreed advertising objectives, expressed in the form of some type of communication measure. This will require the regular use of consumer research to monitor progress against the benchmarks. The crucial issue is that both client and agency have to be able to agree, fairly precisely, how they expect the advertising to work and what to measure to see that it has done so. This can be difficult to achieve.

The creative fee

One UK agency, Rainey Kelly Campbell Roalfe , take the view that what clients are buying is their creativity, so that that is what they will charge for. Their practice is to use a two-part charging system: they charge a monthly fee based on the proportion of the work of each individual assigned to the account that the client can be expected to require; this fee includes an allowance for overheads, and is designed to enable the agency to break even on its service to the client. Then, they determine a value for the creative idea that can meet the client's needs: this is agreed in advance, but payable only once the client is satisfied that the right idea has been delivered. The basis for deciding this fee varies, but may relate to the scale of the intended effect on the client's business, or be fixed in relation to the total marketing budget. For ideas used beyond the first year, there is a pre-agreed basis for charging, in effect, a royalty for continuing use of the idea. Similar arrangements can be agreed for use in international markets. Clearly, the major issues here are, first, to agree the basis for the fee and, second, to agree whether the creative solution is worth what is being charged for it.

Whatever system is used, there will need to be detailed arrangements to ensure that non-standard items are adequately covered. Mostly these will occur in the area of production and special events, such as sales conferences, in which the agency may become involved. A particular issue that the clients need to be aware of is that TV contractors expect to be paid in advance of the break of a campaign, and the agency will expect to be paid accordingly; no agency can afford to be a banker for its clients.

Running the relationship

Once the details are agreed—or, often, in advance of this—client and agency will actually start working together. Very often, the change of agency takes place with a view to developing a major new campaign with a considerable leadtime, but equally often there is on-going activity to be attended to, quickly.

This means that both teams have to get up and running very fast. They have to get to know each other, and to establish day-to-day systems for contact and contact reporting. These days, they will probably want to set up electronic links to exchange information and data, and to enable both sides to look at rough ads and other material without incurring massive courier charges. A video-conferencing link, too, may be needed.

At the same time, the agency team will want to learn everything they can about the client's business and the brands being advertised. This should involve visits to offices and factories, conversations with distributors or retailers selling the brand, a complete review of all available market research and, of course, getting to know each other's teams of people.

The most important immediate element to get into place, though, is the structure and basis of day-to-day contacts. Who will talk to whom, and how often? What arrangements should be made for reviews and evaluation? How should this all fit into the client's business planning cycle?

Structuring contact

The primary contact between the agency and the client is the account manager (account director, account executive or whatever). This manager is responsible for the smooth running of the account and the effective use of the agency's resources on the client's behalf. On a large account, or in a large agency, there will usually be two or even three levels of account management: an account director (who is often on the agency's board); a senior account executive or account manager (titles vary); and an account executive, who is usually quite a junior assistant, who may be learning the business.

On the client side, there will usually be a marketing director who is ultimately responsible for the advertising, along with the rest of the marketing mix. Increasingly, though, the chief executive takes an active interest in the advertising, and will want to be involved in major discussions. Under the marketing director, structures vary widely, and not simply with the size of the company. Some very large companies have specialist advertising or communications directors or managers, and perhaps also—again among the very largest—a specialist media manager. Most companies have some sort of brand or market manager system, where one or more layers of management take the responsibility for the marketing of specific brands or product categories within the business. They will always be involved in the preliminary stages of advertising development, but increasingly they are not in any position to give the final sign-off to a campaign. This decision will be taken at a higher level, and this means that brand managers can typically say 'no', but not 'yes', to an idea. Increasingly, too, the purchasing department has a role in the client's advertising management, particularly in the area of controlling production operations and costs.

Most agencies aim for a structure where, for a particular client, the agency has one contact person for each level of the client's business. Thus, the chairman or CEO talks to the managing director; the account director to the marketing director; and so on down the line. Obviously, this is purely formal and there is no reason, in principle, why the links should not cross each other: in practice they do, frequently, in most cases.

This is not least because most agencies these days like to have in-depth contacts with their clients. The appropriate people at the client company are able to talk with—say—the media planner, or the account planner, or the TV production department, without always having to go through the account management team.

The one possible exception to this, which is very much a matter of agency style, is that access to the creative department of the agency tends to be carefully protected.

There are two reasons for this. One is the practical one, that the creatives are supposed to be busy creating, and do not want their train of thought broken by an importunate client. The other is that creative people are widely—and sometimes rightly—seen as 'loose cannon' within the agency, and liable to tell the client a few unwelcome home truths that might do fatal damage to the relationship.

Formalizing contacts

Day-to-day contact

It makes sense for the key managers on either side to meet regularly: depending on the scale and nature of the business, this may be weekly, fortnightly or monthly; though at times of major activity meetings may be daily. These meetings are effectively progress chasing, as well as providing the opportunity to discuss new work, exchange a new brief, look at media plans, and the like. Obviously, between meetings there are always the telephone, fax and, increasingly, email (even if security dictates that this should be via a joint intranet) and even video conferencing.

Where the exchanges at these meetings are not in writing, each meeting or contact will be routinely (and briefly) reported, through what the business calls 'call reports', or 'contact reports'. These are usually simply a note of decisions made and areas discussed, not essays on the state of the world, and are circulated to everyone involved with the account, on both sides. They provide a record of decisions and, in some cases, a call to action by named individuals (see Figure 3.1).

Major meetings

Day-to-day meetings between the key managers are not an adequate forum for discussing major issues. These come in two main varieties: new briefs for major campaigns, the presentation of new campaign proposals, research debriefs and so on—what may be called 'operational' meetings—and 'review' meetings designed to look at progress and results and to develop ideas for the future.

Both categories demand a significant level of preparation from the agency, and sometimes (especially for new briefs) from the client as well.

'Operational' meetings most frequently consist of the agency presenting material or information in response to an earlier brief from the client. Typically, the agency will present a reprise of the relevant briefing material, perhaps with interpretation from new research or new thinking about the problem, and then, if creative work or media plans are involved, go through their proposals. This sort of meeting is likely

LANSDOWN CONQUEST | 4 FLITCROFT STREET LONDON WC2H 8DJ

TEL **0171 240 4949** FAX **0171 240 9094** ISDN **0171 397 3033**

Contact Report

CLIENT	PRODUCT	MEETING DATE	PLACE
XXXXXXXXXX	XXXXXXXXXX	30 March 1999	Flitcroft Street

PRESENT FOR CLIENT	PRESENT FOR AGENCY	CIRCULATION - CLIENT:	AGENCY:
J Smith	P Quinn	J Reid	Julian Saunders
R Robinson	R White	J Smith	Simon Frank
		PJ Proby	John Wringe
		L Martin	John Trainor
		R Robinson	Peter Cannon
			Paul Quinn
			Roderick White
			James Chinnock

ACTION BY:

1. Summer Campaign

Agency presented roughs for the proposed press
campaign, and recommended the "Theatrical" approach.
Client said he would like to discuss the
recommendation internally.

Client

2. Invoices

Agency reported that invoices N1475 and N1476,
dating from last October, had still not been paid.
Client asked for them to be re-submitted.

Agency

3. Media

Client asked whether the agency had considered using
Adshels in support of the Magazine schedule
currently proposed. Agency to comment.

Agency

Paul Quinn
30 March 1999.

IF THIS CONTACT REPORT IS IN ANY WAY INACCURATE PLEASE CONTACT US WITHIN 48 HOURS

Figure 3.1. Typical Contact report

to take place at intervals, and these will depend very much on the volume of activity involved. For some clients, it may be no more than an annual or six-monthly event; for others, it may be necessary to have one monthly or even more frequently.

What I have called 'review' meetings are more varied. They may be simply a review of the agency's, and the brand's, performance: this will occur perhaps quarterly, perhaps less often. A regular formal review is, however, valuable for both sides, and should certainly be planned into the operation of every significant account.

The meeting may take the opportunity to examine the state of the client's business and its markets, and to develop strategic thinking about how to move the business forward. This could involve the first briefing about new products in the pipeline, or a move into new geographical markets, for example.

Sometimes, too, there is a case for a more open-ended, creative type of meeting—what the ad business tends to call an 'away day'—when both sides meet away from their offices and set out to develop new and imaginative ideas about the shape of the future business. To square this particular circle, there are one or two—mostly small—agencies that like to use this sort of meeting to develop creative ideas specifically for the client's required communications campaign. Playing on the fact that most people in the agency, not just the creative team, and, indeed, on the client side are quite capable of being creative, they spend a day in a team brainstorming session, focused on solving the communications problems for the campaign.

The budget

Organizing the agency is all very well, but you get nowhere without money. How do you decide how much to spend, and what to spend it on? Setting marketing and advertising budgets is difficult,[2] and practice tends to lag well behind theory.

We have to start from a brief consideration of a company's revenue and costs. As shown in the Figure 3.2, a firm sells 20 million units at £1.50 each, giving ex-factory sales (often called 'net sales value' (NSV)) of £30 million. Taking away from this the cost of making the product—raw materials, factory expenses, packaging, etc., gives a gross margin of 55 per cent, leaving £16.5 million. Out of this, the company has to pay for marketing the product (selling, physical distribution and communications), and allow a profit. This last is usually called the 'profit contribution', and will in turn be reduced in the company's accounting system by overheads and some other central expenses, but it is a realistic basis for looking at the brand's profit

[2] The classic book on the subject remains Simon Broadbent's *The Advertising Budget*, NTC Publications, Henley-on-Thames, 1989.

	£000	%
Net sales value (20 m × £1.50)	30 000	
Less		
Cost of goods		
(materials, packaging, production)	13 500	45
= Gross margin	16 500	55
Less		
Marketing costs:		
Advertising	1 500	5.0
Sales promotion	1 400	4.7
PR	350	1.2
Point of sale	200	0.7
Market research	150	0.5
Selling + discounts, etc.	1 955	6.5
Physical distribution	545	1.8
Total	6 100	20.4
= Operating contribution	10 400	34.6

Figure 3.2.   Cost structure of a typical fmcg brand

performance, because everything above this line is, in a sense, the responsibility of the brand.

Historically, most advertisers have tended to look at advertising as an expense to be taken out of the margin available after manufacturing costs have been incurred. It has been assumed, often on the basis of the brand's or the company's history, that, say, 5 per cent of the NSV should be taken for advertising, or 20 per cent for distribution, sales, promotion and advertising. In the example given this would give a profit contribution on NSV of 35 per cent, which is quite high, but by no means impossible.

But *why* should advertising take 5 per cent (or 10 per cent or 15 per cent)? There have been a variety of answers to this, but the most popular one is, and remains, judging from research being done in the US by the AAAA,[3] 'This was what we did last year', or 'That's what we always do'. In defence of this, it is probably fair to say that the one way in which marketing management can expect to get their budgets through 'on the nod' is to refer to precedent and to established company practice: that way no one asks them too hard to justify the budget. But this, and the related practice of allocating so many pounds per case or per unit to advertising, is a

---

[3] See P. Root and M. Naples, 'How should advertisers budget?, *Admap*, September 1998.

UK (as % of consumer spending)		US (as % of NSV)	
Shampoo	19.9	Sugar/confectionary	17.4
Cinema	13.7	Watches and clocks	15.9
Cold treatments	11.9	Dolls, stuffed toys	15.3
Breakfast cereals	8.4	Soap and detergents	9.7
Washing powders/liquids	7.7	Perfume/cosmetics	8.5
Female fragrances	7.7	Processed foods	7.8
Deodorants	7.5	Beverages	7.6
Electric shavers	6.7	Cigarettes	5.9
Watches	5.4	Ice cream	5.1
Cosmetics	5.1	H/hold electrical goods	4.1
Condoms	4.5	Restaurants/fast food	4.0
Dog food	3.7	Photog.equipment/supplies	3.3
Video games	3.2	Men's clothing	2.6
Cars	2.5	Cars	2.4
Chocolate confectionary	2.2	Dairy products	2.0
Carbonated soft drinks	1.5	Computers	1.7
Toilet tissue	1.5	Tyres	1.7
Beer	0.7	Personal credit institutions	1.2
Cigarettes	0.4	Grocery retailers	1.0

Note different methods of calculation

Figure 3.3. Selected advertising-to-sales ratios UK (1996) and US (1997): in rank order (Source: UK: *AA Advertising Statistics Yearbook 1998*, US: *Advertising Age*, 30 June 1997)

mechanistic and irrational approach. It takes no account of the brand's specific marketing communication needs and little account of the competitive situation.

It should be noted, too, that advertising-to-sales ratios (A/S ratios) vary widely between markets—often for no very evident reason—and that, for the most part, larger brands within a market are able to get away with lower A/S ratios than smaller brands. This is both because the larger brands are more established and do not have to 'work' so hard and because the smaller brands may find that the threshold costs of making progress in their market are relatively high in relation to their sales or market share. Figure 3.3 shows some representative market A/S ratios from both the UK and the USA.

Clearly, what the competition is doing should affect what you yourself decide to do. It is possible to establish from available research data what your competitors are spending: you can identify exactly what they are doing and achieving on TV through the BARB service (p. 164) and there are two UK services, with approximate equivalents in most other major advertising markets, that collect detailed expenditure data for all main media. In the UK, these are A.C. Nielsen–MEAL and MMS.

Both services calculate expenditures by ratecard costs, and then adjust these for approximate discounts: the figures are not, to be honest, very precise. What the services do provide, however, is the basis for comparative calculation of what their expenditure delivers, in terms of coverage and frequency against target audiences that can be defined from the media research.

This means, therefore, that you can calculate quite precisely what your share of consumer opportunities to see (OTS) (see p. 131) in any media group is, even if the estimates of your share of expenditure are a trifle uncertain.

This can provide the basis of a set of benchmarks for establishing a budget in relation to competition. If you have a share of voice (share of impacts, share of expenditure—however you are best able to measure it) below your share of your market, it is likely that you will start to lose that share. Similarly, if your share of voice is significantly higher, you ought to be increasing your market share. It is not, in practice, quite as simple as that, because big brands achieve economies of scale, through distribution, consumer experience and sheer familiarity, so that they can get away with underspending, relative to their market share; while smaller brands may have to overspend against their market share in order to survive, let alone gain share of market.

What matters, therefore, for market dynamics, is how you change your share of voice from one period to the next (this type of analysis, developed at Unilever in the 1960s, is known as 'dynamic difference'). In general, an increase should help you, while a decrease may see your share slipping. (In spite of this fairly obvious fact, it is surprising how often you will see marketing plans in which an increase in share is planned in conjunction with a decrease in marketing expenditure. This can be achieved, certainly, but only where the brand has considerable momentum, or if you are clever—or lucky—enough to come up with a particularly powerful campaign.)

Obviously, planning budgets in relation to the anticipated marketplace activity is an advance over simply sticking to an arbitrary percentage of NSV, however hallowed by history and market practice this may be. The problem, of course, is that while you know what happened last year, you cannot with any confidence predict what will happen next: a leading competitor may decide to invest a lot of money in building market share, and your planned share of voice may be reduced accordingly. This is unavoidable, but it does mean that—ideally—budgets are never set in tablets of stone.

Further, there is, at least in theory, a better way of setting budgets. This is the so-called 'task' method. As you plan your campaign, you identify a range of specific objectives that your communications programme will have to achieve. You can then—sometimes—put a price on what is needed to achieve these objectives and use this process to build up a budget request. There are two obvious problems: first the sum of the tasks, as costed, may be far more than you can afford; and it is often difficult either to put a cost on achieving a specific objective or to be certain that achieving this objective will actually have the desired effect on sales.

The most sophisticated methods of setting budgets involve the building of mathematical models. This is in itself a valuable learning process, and can look extremely convincing: but you have to recognize that the models are only ever theoretical constructs, and that within them the causal relationships are not always clear-cut.

A very brief schematic summary of the various methods is given in Figure 3.4 (see p. 40) which draws heavily on Broadbent's analysis.[4]

Summary

- Working with an agency should be a professional business relationship and structured accordingly.
- This requires a formal contract, with especial attention paid to the thorny question of how the agency will be remunerated for its efforts. The contract should also cover a range of other details.
- The agency will aim to tailor its account team to fit with the client's structure, with the main contacts going through the account management team and the client marketing department. This should not preclude direct contact between the client and other departments of the agency.
- The relationship will—inevitably—revolve around a series of meetings, which need to be call reported to provide a record of the decisions taken.
- The budget will be central to the relationship. Setting a budget is difficult, but the difficulties are often avoided by using simple rules of thumb.

Questions for consideration

- You are the account director of an agency that has just won a major account from a high street bank. The bank expects the agency to provide a service covering media advertising (but not the media buying), including a major TV campaign to build the brand; press advertising to provide information about specific products and to get response to a freephone number; and the creation and production of the bank's consumer direct marketing campaigns.
  (a) What specific headings should you put into your draft contract with the bank?
  (b) How would you like the agency to be remunerated, and why?

---

[4] Simon Broadbent, *The Advertising Budget*, NTC Publications, Henley-on-Thames, 1989.

Method	Pros	Cons
A/S ratio	Easy to use	How to set the ratio?
	Easily justified and defended	Ignores sales effects
	Helps stronger brands	May be too small
		Not related to margin
A/M ratio	Easy to use	How to set the ratio?
(advertising to margin)	Easy to defend/justify	Ignores sales effects
	Supports high margin brands	May be too small
	Inflation built in	
	Affordable	
Case rate	Easy to handle	How to set the rate?
(or other volume-linked	Supports high volume brands	Ignores sales effects
calculation)		May be unrealistic
'Inertia'	Simple	Ignores media inflation
(what we did last year)		Takes no account of
		objectives
Media inflation multiplier	Supports success	Different inflation rates may
(used in conjunction with		lead to distortions in
e.g. case rate)		overall budget
		Why compensate media for
		inflation automatically?
Competitive comparisons	Easy to use	Assumes competition is right
	Easy to defend	Ignores sales effects
	Supports stronger brands	May be too little
	Focuses on competitors	May overplay larger brands
Task	Focused on tasks, results	Ignores affordability
	Encourages clear thinking	Tasks may be wrongly set
Affordable	Affordable, by definition	Ignores sales effects
(residual)		May be too small
Brand history	Realistic	May provide few clues
Dynamic difference	Improves understanding	May not really work
(share of voice and	Helps realism	May be misleading
market)		
Modelling	Aids learning	Theory may be too limited
	Provides a framework for	May appear infallible
	judgement	
Experiments	Aid learning	Rarely genuinely
		representative
		Often stopped too early
		Easily disrupted by
		competition
		Seldom show dramatic
		effects

Figure 3.4.   Setting ad budgets: Pros and Cons of Main Methods (Source: Based on S. Broadbent, *The Advertising Budget*, Ch. 5 (q.v.).

- There are several different ways of remunerating an agency. Which of these appears to be more advantageous to (a) the client, (b) the agency? In each case, why?
- You are the account manager in charge of a newly won account for a retailer who has done little advertising. They have asked for your advice on setting a budget. What factors would you take into consideration, and what principles would you propose to justify your recommendation?
- Figure 3.3 shows two sets of A/S ratios, based on different sources and methods of calculation. How could you set about comparing them, so that you could be reasonably sure that you were comparing like with like?

4   How advertising works

Advertising is the whip which hustles humanity up the road to the better mousetrap

E. S. Turner

Advertising, of course, sells. Advertisements inform, persuade, remind, influence, change opinions; they may even alter attitudes and feelings. Advertising changes society, makes people buy things they do not want, enables multinational capitalist monopolies to batten on the working classes.

Well, doesn't it?

Before we start looking at the process of planning, creating and placing advertisements, it is important to understand what advertisements can be expected to achieve, and how they do this.

It may seem somehow obvious that ads persuade people to buy things; and, indeed, it is frequently claimed by people who want to control or suppress some form of advertising (to children, or for tobacco, or fast cars) that advertising 'forces people to buy things they don't want'.

Things are not as simple as this, and there is considerable argument about just what ads can and cannot do, and how they do it. The fact that this argument exists is important for anyone involved in advertising, because our assumptions affect our expectations of what an ad campaign can achieve, and the way in which we set out to measure the results (or to pre-test the ads, in order to try to establish that they will work).

In practice, most people who work with advertising do not think very hard or often about these questions. They carry built-in assumptions, based on their experience, or on something they may have read or been told, and which direct their thinking in ways which may not be inappropriate. It is assumed that ads can do, basically, one or more of the following: create awareness of the brand, inform people about it, encourage—or even persuade—them to try it and create some sort of emotional or attitudinal bond between consumers and the brand that will lead to regular purchase (brand loyalty). The ways in which ads can do this are seen through a variety of different theories.

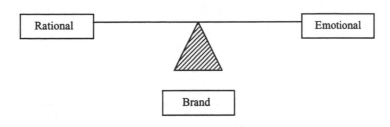

Figure 4.1.   The brand

Advertising and brands

We should recognize from the start that most advertising (with the possible exception of some public service campaigns and the occasional generic campaign for a commodity) is concerned with *brands*.

A brand is the way in which its owner sets out to identify and differentiate a product or service from those of competitors. This is done both by exploiting the brand's functional qualities (its taste, texture, efficiency, quality, etc.) and by endowing the brand with an attractive set of emotional associations or 'values'. The combined effect of this process is to make the brand more or less unique in its market, with recognizable advantages over its competitors and a positive relationship with its users. As a result, the brand can be maintained in its market, even if competitors achieve functional parity and it may well be able to hold a price premium over the market as a whole.

Stephen King, JWT's planning guru, said: '*A product is something made in a factory: a brand is something that is bought by customers. A product can be copied by a competitor: a brand is unique. A product can be quickly outdated: a successful brand is timeless.*'[1] A brand is, in fact, a combination of what the brand owner has fed into it, through the marketing mix, and how the consumer has perceived this, rationally, emotionally and—above all—through experience of the brand. As Figure 4.1 suggests, all brands have a balance of rational and emotional elements. These are built up by the brand owner's various inputs, especially advertising and other communications (see Figure 4. 2). When the brand touches the consumer, this input is processed—not always exactly as the brand owner wishes—and the consumer's knowledge, attitudes and experience combine with the rest to create the brand's real-world position (see Figure 4.3). (Note that the brand only really exists as a set of images and associations *in the minds of consumers*.)

Advertising's job is to help to communicate to consumers the relevant information about the brand, and the emotional values that the marketer wishes to associate

---

[1] Stephen King, *What is a Brand?* J. Walter Thompson, London, 1970.

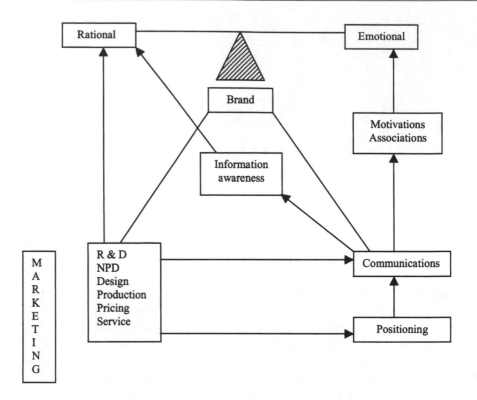

Figure 4.2.   The marketing input to the brand

with it, so as to make the brand as strong and attractive as possible. This involves informing, persuading and motivating, it also involves maintaining the established reputation or image of the brand, once it has developed its position in the market. Over time in the life of the brand, the role for the advertising shifts from an aggressive search for new customers to a more defensive stance, to protect the ground won.

The traditional view

For many years, most people in advertising thought that an ad worked in a tidy, structured, linear way: the ad attracted the consumer's attention, then created interest in the brand, which led, in turn, to the desire to buy it and, hence, to a purchase. The first 'model' of this kind was formulated by Elmo St J. Lewis in 1898 and was called 'AIDA': Attention–Interest–Desire–Action. This type of model of how ads work is called a 'hierarchy of effects' model, and many people still act as if this is how they think ads work, even today.

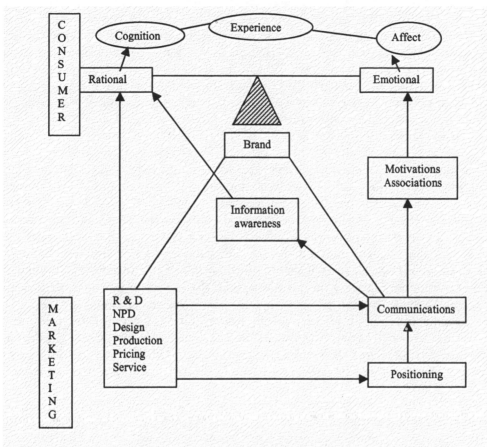

Figure 4.3.   The brand and the consumer

AIDA, and a number of more refined successors, is now really a museum piece. It doesn't fit the facts, in terms of what actually happens in the marketplace; it does not fit what we know from psychology, which tells us that whatever happens in people's minds, it certainly does not follow the orderly sequence suggested; and it takes absolutely no account of the fact that most ads, most of the time, are seen by—and indeed targeted at—people who have already bought the brand at least once. Furthermore, it makes the fundamental assumption that ads do things to people.

People using ads

Modern analysis shows rather clearly that people do things to (or with) ads: they are not the passive recipients of messages from people who want to sell things. Rather, people decide which ads, from the thousands they are exposed to every day, they will take any notice of. They pay attention only to part of the ad. Some people are quite resistant to looking at ads at all, especially on TV. Others treat ads as a subject for derision or discussion in the pub—or even, sometimes, as information to be remembered. What's more, people very rarely take any immediate action on seeing an ad, except sometimes for direct response ads. Whatever they do as a result of seeing the ad will happen when they next go shopping, or when they next run out of the product category advertised, which may be weeks or months later.

What this means, therefore, is that ads depend on what sticks in people's memories. This raises further technical questions, because it is easy to assume that it is essential that people should remember as much as possible of your ad. This is not, really, the important thing (though it can be reassuring). What matters is that they remember enough about your *brand*, so that when they are next in the market, your brand is the one they choose. A lot of research about the effects of advertising has concentrated on the recall of the advertisement: what it said about the brand, what the story was, who the star actor in it was, the slogan at the end. While this can tell us something about the memorability of the ad as such, it says little about its effect on the brand. Indeed, Gordon Brown, founder of market research agency Millward Brown, which is the world leader in advertising tracking research (see Chapter 8), concluded that the only important measure of recall of the advertising was, quite simply, that it had been advertised recently.

What is important is that consumers take out of the advertising enough memorable associations with the brand, so that when faced by a brand choice in a store (or wherever), they will tend to choose the advertised brand, because of its favourable associations. In other words *it is not what the advertiser puts into the ad that ultimately matters: it is what the consumer takes out of the ad.*

Frameworks

In 1992, two market researchers in the UK, Mike Hall and David Maclay,[2] set out to find out how the people who planned advertising thought their advertising would work. They questioned people in ad agencies and on the advertising and marketing side of advertiser companies, and came to the conclusion that there was no single model of how advertising worked. Rather, there were four, which they called frameworks (see Box 4.1)

---

[2] M. Hall and D. Maclay, Science and Art: How Does Research Practice Match Advertising Theory?, MRS Conference, 1991.

Box 4.1   'Frameworks': Different ways in which advertising is expected to work

Framework	Expected effect	Typical examples (UK 1998-1999)
Sales response	Immediate action	Direct response ads Store sales ads
Persuasion	Rationally-based interest, further enquiry	Virgin One Volvo
Involvement	Enhanced emotional bond with brand	Coca-Cola Peugeot 306
Salience	Interest in ad itself—increase brand's importance	Most fragrance ads Tango

---

While every ad will use at least one of the frameworks, many will use more than one—it is a matter of balance.

This formulation at least seems to recognize the fundamental reality: that it is most unlikely that all advertising should work in the same way. This is, let's face it, pretty improbable—and yet a whole subsector of the market research business is dedicated to the belief that one single system and the theory underlying it is sufficient to pre-test any ad. Indeed, for many years there were essentially two competing theories: one based on recall, which goes back to two researchers, Daniel Starch and George Gallup, in the 1930s, who worked with press advertisements; and one based on persuasion, developed by Howard Schwerin in the 1940s to test TV ads. While the recall school has largely disappeared, persuasion, in one form or another, continues to dominate quantitative pre-testing of ads, especially in the USA.

By contrast, research systems based on the frameworks analysis have made some progress in the UK, but are not widely accepted elsewhere: perhaps people find it too difficult to define in advance how their ads are meant to work, and the interpretation of the findings is less simple; persuasion systems give you a nice, simple, single key score.

Strong or weak force?

The original hierarchy-of-effects models and the thinking that went with them assumed that advertising is a powerful force that could virtually compel people to buy a product. Advertising is the means to build strong brands and to create unshakeable consumer loyalties to the brand. The job of competitive advertising is, indeed, to seduce one brand's loyal users and to persuade them to become loyal users of one's own brand. It is possible that this was once a valid analysis of what happened in the marketplace, in the days when there was far less advertising, far fewer brands, and consumers were far less experienced in dealing with advertising than they now are.

One can find what look like examples of this sort of thing, at least in the short term, in the response of consumers in the former Soviet bloc to the influx of western brands and advertising since 1989. Mary Goodyear, a qualitative researcher with vast international experience, has suggested that most countries' markets go through a series of stages in the development of sophisticated responses to advertising (see Figure 4.4).

It has been convincingly shown by Professor Andrew Ehrenberg and his colleagues, over a number of years, that the idea of advertising as a strong force is not in line with the facts of the market—especially those of established fmcg markets. They have demonstrated, first, that in most markets consumers buy from a repertoire of brands—true brand loyalty is quite rare, and mainly found among lighter users of the category. Then, the proportion in which these brands are bought can be predicted by quite a simple formula (the Dirichlet model) from the brand shares of the individual brands in the market: within consumers' repertoires of brands, the brand bought at any single purchase appears almost random, but the total purchases will reflect the brand shares in the market.

From this, Ehrenberg concluded that the role of advertising in these markets must be quite limited: too much of what goes on in the market is effectively dictated by what has gone before in effect, by people's experience. What advertising does, therefore, must be merely to keep the brand in people's minds (Ehrenberg calls this 'salience', which is used in a slightly different sense from that used by Hall and Maclay). Ehrenberg has summarized his view of how advertising works in his 'ATR & N' model: Attention , Trial, Nudging and Reinforcement.[3]

John Philip Jones, in his important book *When Ads Work*,[4] has argued that in fact ads can have quite a strong short-term effect, but that this is eventually watered down by the counter-effects of competitive activity, over the longer term.

The typical advertising practitioner, and the typical marketing director, find it quite hard to believe that advertising is not a powerful tool. After all, they spend a great deal of money on advertising, and it seems unlikely that this should all be being wasted. (There is a famous and much over-quoted remark, attributed in the UK to the first Lord Leverhulme, founder of Unilever, that 'I know that half of my

---

[3] A. S. C. Ehrenberg *et al.*, *Justifying Our Advertising Budgets*, South Bank University, London. For journal references, see Ehrenberg and Scriven, *Admap*, September 1997.
[4] Lexington Books, New York, 1995.

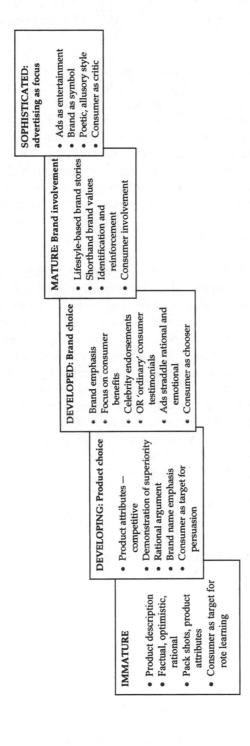

Figure 4.4. Five stages of advertising sophistication (Source: Based on M. Goodyear, 'The five stages of advertising literacy', *Admap*, March 1991)

advertising is wasted, but I don't know which half'.) The problem in all this is twofold.

First, there is ample evidence, for example from the IPA Effectiveness Awards papers, published in a series that dates back to 1981 under the title *Advertising Works,* that demonstrates clearly that for some brands, some of the time, advertising undoubtedly has a powerful effect on the brand's performance, right down to the bottom line—profit. Ehrenberg would argue that these examples are sufficiently rare to be considered exceptions to the general rule; but the evidence is enough—on its own—to encourage marketers and their agencies to keep trying to achieve radical change in the marketplace with the aid of advertising as their primary weapon. They have to recognize, however, that the circumstances that make this possible, which depend on both market forces and product development in their own market, are rarer than most marketers imagine.

The second problem is more complex. As we shall see in Chapter 8, it is possible to use the mathematical techniques of econometrics to measure with some precision the effects of different types of marketing activity on brand sales. To do this, however, and to use the learning from the process to fine-tune the deployment of the marketing budget is a costly and complex procedure, and relatively few advertisers have access to the skills and the scale of operations to use these techniques to the full. The situation is complicated by the fact, of which Ehrenberg makes a great deal, that for most established brands, the realistic objective of marketing activity in general, and of advertising in particular, is to sustain the level of sales and market share: it is essentially defensive, rather than offensive. The advertising acts as a sort of flywheel to keep the brand engine running: if it slows down, eventually the brand will suffer, but it is quite difficult to measure, in advance, when this may happen.

Consumer expectations

We can look at advertisements from the point of view of consumers to start to shed further light on the whole process. What do people want from an ad—always assuming that they are remotely interested?

Information

One of the key functions of advertising is to provide information (which includes, of course, reasons for purchase—'persuasion'). In fact, for many years, this was the only value that economists were prepared to attribute to ads, and this led, logically, to calls from left-wing economists and politicians to restrain or tax advertising that was not providing information in support of new products. This, of course, failed to recognize the need for advertisers to keep competing, by reminding their customers of products that they might already buy, in the face of the clamour for attention from new competitors.

Consumers, certainly, look to ads for information, sometimes. In general terms, this can be seen from the relative success of ads that offer what we now describe as 'new news' about a brand. If you run an ad that tells people something new and relevant about a brand, the ad will score well in various forms of research. More specifically, there is a whole class of products, in particular durables and financial services, that demand a great deal of understanding by consumers if they are to make a sensible choice. These 'high information' products can be effectively advertised with advertisements that carry a great deal of information: people in the market will make the effort to attend to a commercial or to read a long-copy press ad.

The converse of the need for information for 'high-information' products is, of course, that it will always be difficult to keep people's attention if you try to provide a lot of information about a low-information brand or category. This is why most fragrance ads, for example, carry almost no information. It can be argued, indeed, that most perfume ads are quite simply saying 'Here I am', and that they are purely announcements. A look at a variety of perfume ads would tend to confirm this, if we want to take it literally. However, it is equally clear that most of them embody an attitude or character which is inviting a specific type of consumer to identify emotionally with the idea of the brand and, hence, to try it.

The agency FCB has developed an approach to analysing markets and brands on their information dimensions—the FCB Grid shown in Figure 4.5—and has pointed out that very often low-cost, low-information brands, which are by

	Response	
	THINK	*FEEL*
HIGH INVOLVEMENT	Economic	Psychological
	Learn-feel-do	Feel-learn-do
LOW INVOLVEMENT	Responsive	Social
	Do-learn-feel	Do-feel-learn

Figure 4.5. The FCB Grid (Source: McDonald, *How Advertising Works*, p. 117)

definition low-risk purchases, are bought first and thought about afterwards; only after some experience do people begin to develop attitudes to these brands. FCB describe this process as 'Do-think-feel'. By contrast, a more considered purchase may work in a different way: 'Think-feel-do', or perhaps 'Feel-think-do'.

Support and confirmation

An important use to which consumers put ads, which is not readily recognized by commentators outside the industry, is to use ads as an endorsement of a purchase or purchase habit already established. There is plenty of evidence to show that car buyers will read ads for the car they have just bought, some time after the purchase, looking for reinforcement of their decision. Even for quite trivial grocery brands, the knowledge that the brand is popular, that it is putting out advertising with which the consumer feels in tune, is support for its continued use.

This, of course, underlies the massive use of advertising in support of established brands: it also underlines the risk inherent in radically changing the nature of a brand's advertising. If a set of users of the brand is contented with the product and happy with the image that the brand conveys in its advertising, a major change may start to undermine this confidence and identification with the brand.

Entertainment

One of the most surprising research findings of recent years for much of the advertising community was the discovery, in a 1991 project mounted by the US Advertising Research Foundation,[5] that the best research predictor available in pre-testing of ads that were proven to be successful in the market was whether consumers liked the ad or not. This was, in fact, a formal recognition of academic research dating back some 10 years earlier, but it ran heavily counter to existing research thinking.

Ad liking does not necessarily entail the ad being, literally, entertaining. This may help, but if it is also irrelevant to the consumer, the ad will not be liked. Liking, in fact, can result as easily from the provision of necessary information in an accessible and helpful way as from a magical song-and-dance routine. A growing body of research shows that ad liking can be successfully related to other measures of advertising effects, such as recall and sales effectiveness.

Attention

There is rarely any very good reason for a consumer to pay any attention to an ad. The only time that ads may be deliberately looked for is when a particular purchase

---

[5] R. I. Haley and A. L. Baldinger, 'The ARF copy research validity project', JAR, April–May 1991.

is planned and the consumer is actively seeking information. Then, ads may be seen as one place to look, along with others. Other ads are typically only attended to if they have something that actively attracts the consumer's attention. Even then, they may well get a good deal less than full attention. This does not mean, however, that they will have no effect. Modern analysis of the processes of attention and memory shows that memory works by the stimulation of the neural networks in the brain, and each time a stimulus activates the relevant set of neurons, the memory trace is strengthened. This can happen virtually subconsciously: in fact, we operate like this all the time in our daily life. No one sets out deliberately to learn the layout of their living room, but it takes little use of it before we can walk through it in the dark without bumping into anything or knocking things off tables.

This is, in fact, a learning process, but one which is unlike the active rehearsal that goes into school learning. Nonetheless, as we see, over time, several ads for a brand, and perhaps buy the brand to try it, this all strengthens the memory traces in the brain, so that, when faced by an in-store display, we recognize the brand as familiar and, perhaps, desirable.

From the advertiser's point of view, there is a massive and obvious temptation to do everything possible to get noticed: to achieve what the business calls 'cut through'. The reason is simple enough. We are exposed to a massive range of advertising stimuli every day. Various estimates suggest that the average Briton may have the opportunity to see or hear—in some sense—some 1300 ads per day, and the figure is higher in the US. Clearly, we are able to screen most of this noise out quite effectively, even if some of it does get through almost without our noticing, as has been suggested above. (Equally clearly, only a small proportion of it is going to be in any meaningful sense relevant to us at any one time, so for most ads this really does not matter.) The result of the analysis, however, is the belief that it is essential, not just to include an 'attention-getting device' in every ad, but to make this loud, dramatic, startling, aggressive.

From what has gone before, there is clearly a conflict between this kind of attention-seeking and the need for an ad to be likeable. Consumers like ads to be likeable: one of the things they tend *not* to like about ads is when they force themselves upon their attention.

Attitudes

It has long been believed that advertisements work, ultimately, by their effect on people's attitudes. This is what persuasion is all about. So, we ought to be able to measure changes in people's attitudes to our brand and its competitors, and use this information to forecast changes in the relative market shares. Similarly, if we can identify the key attitudes in our market, we can seek to strengthen our brand's position in respect of these.

Unfortunately, this raises problems. First, there is now a lot of evidence that, in many markets, changes in attitude—whatever they can be attributed to—follow purchasing behaviour, rather than preceding it. Ehrenberg, again, has pointed out that attitude differences between brands among a population of all users of the category can be accounted for almost completely by the relative market shares of the brands. (This argument looks less good if the research is done so as to separate out users of each individual brand.) Finally, it appears to be quite difficult to get attitudes, as measured by standard research techniques, to change at all.

Quite recently, a new way of looking at attitudes has started to become popular. Rather than focus on particular aspects of the brand, researchers are asking questions to determine people's relationship with the brand: are they committed, loyal users, or are they merely using the brand because it's there? In the UK, two companies in particular, Taylor Nelson Sofres with their Conversion Model and Millward Brown with Brand Dynamics, are actively promoting this approach, with the aid of case studies that seem to demonstrate the ability of this type of measurement to predict market share movements.

It seems to me reasonably clear that, whatever else advertising can or cannot do, successful advertising does involve, at least over time, some form of shift or strengthening in consumers' attitudes. The only problem is how to measure it both satisfactorily and sensitively enough. We need to recognize, too, that attitudes interact with brand experience as well as with brand advertising. Just because we have been advertising, and an attitude changes, it is not necessarily safe to assume that the advertising is responsible.

Summary: what's needed for success?

From a very wide range of research, going back many years, there seem to be a number of elements that are essential for a successful ad campaign:

1. It has to catch the target audience's attention, enough—at least—to create a relevant stimulation of the right neurons in the brain. It is often assumed that this attention-catching has to lead to tightly focused, full attention and detailed, in-depth 'processing' of the ad by the consumer. In practice, this seems to be unnecessary, because all that is needed is . . .
2. An adequate and relevant link between the ad stimulus and the brand: this may be almost anything, from a visual mnemonic of the packaging to the use of a well-known slogan. It is likely to be the core idea of the ad—and there is an obvious problem if the idea is a strong one but it is not connected to the brand, because the memory of the idea will dominate.

3. The ad should contain sufficient information to satisfy the consumer's likely needs: if it cannot contain enough (a 30-second TV commercial has room for at most two pieces of 'hard' information, if it is to give the viewer any chance of assimilating them), then it needs to provide the consumer with guidance. ('Call this number'; 'Read our ad in *Radio Times*'; 'Pick up a leaflet at any Post Office'; 'Visit our web site'; 'Clip the coupon'.)

4. The ad should be likeable. This means that it should provide useful information and/or pleasurable entertainment: and, generally speaking, that it should not shout or hector, nor contain gratuitously ugly or distressing images.

5. The ad should have the potential for strengthening or modifying one or more key attitudes about the brand.

6. There needs to be a clear understanding of what the ad is actually trying to do, and how it can be expected to achieve this. What is the appropriate framework for the ad? What is the target audience expected to think, feel or do as a result?

7. Ads work over time: it is at odds with reality to believe that one exposure to an ad does anything much to a consumer (except simply act as a reminder).

Within all this, it is important to recognize that advertising is, like it or not, a fashion business. Styles in advertising come and go in different countries. Since 1995 or so, there has been a small but very noticeable trend for British advertising to be very 'in your face': brash, aggressive, noisy, asking to be noticed for itself, rather than for what it is selling. Give it a couple of years and this may appear totally old-fashioned.

Questions for consideration

☐ Get a selection of ads, from different media, and decide how they are meant to work, in terms of the Frameworks theory.

☐ Find an advertiser who is using a multimedia approach: see how the different media are used to provide information, to attract attention, to motivate.

☐ Many advertisers focus their research on accurate recall of their advertising. What can this usefully tell them?

☐ 'Persuasion' is a task for advertising. How could you decide whether or not an ad is persuasive? What different meanings can you attach to the word in an advertising context?

5 Planning advertisements: the strategy

In war, let your great object be victory, not lengthy campaigns

Sun Zi, *The Art of War*

Advertisements do not usually spring fully-formed from the fertile brain cells of an agency's resident creative genius. They are derived—often painfully and laboriously—from a careful process of strategic analysis. The client and agency team work together to identify precisely what the advertising is intended to do, to what target audience or audiences; what information it must convey; what emotional values or associations it needs to ally with the brand. Only when all this has been done do the creatives get let loose on the project, and the strategy agreed between agency and client provides the guidelines and the control mechanism for the creatives' work.

As a client, you may be impatient to see ideas from the agency: that's what you hired them for. As an agency, you may be anxious to develop ideas; particularly for a new client and a new brand, you may be bursting with half-formed thoughts that look as if they may turn into valuable, indeed sensational, ads.

If you succumb to these temptations, you are liable to be wasting your time. Unless you have a very good idea of where you are trying to get to, you will find the whole process very frustrating.

It's for precisely this reason that most large- or medium-sized agencies, in the UK at least, have a planning department (see page 13): in some agencies, especially smaller ones, the job of developing strategies belongs to the account director. It should be recognized, however, that planning is too important to be left to the planners: a good planner will work with both agency and client teams as the strategy is formulated, and the fine-tuning of the detailed creative brief may well be discussed with the creative team before it reaches its final form. As ever, good ideas may come from anyone: the number 3 on a player's shirt does not preclude the odd successful shot on goal.

Strategies and objectives

First, we need to distinguish between objectives and strategies, as these still seem to be regularly confused in marketing documents. Objectives are, simply, targets: what

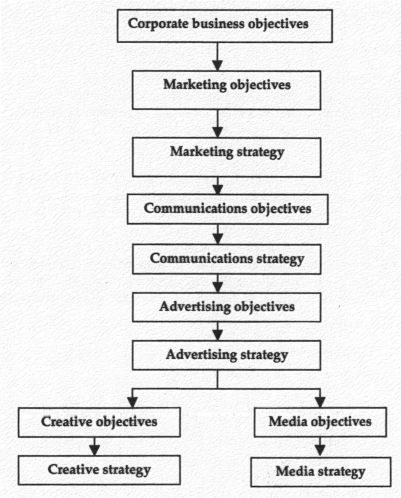

Figure 5.1.   The hierarchy of objectives and strategies

we wish to achieve. These may be set in terms of sales, market share, consumer penetration (the proportion of the target audience buying a brand), brand awareness, etc. The *advertising* objectives will be a subset of the overall *marketing* objectives for the brand (see Figure 5.1).

Strategy is the means by which we aim to achieve the objectives. Our marketing strategy will cover all the main aspects of the marketing mix. While it may be prefaced by an overall vision statement ('We will continue to lead the market in quality, innovation and customer service'), it will define elements such as: the overall brand positioning and any desired changes; distribution strategy; pricing strategy; range policy; communication strategy (which includes advertising, but also other forms of communication); service standards; and so on.

The development of the marketing strategy and the marketing objectives sets the framework for developing the advertising strategy. Advertising strategy development starts by identifying specific objectives that can be met by the advertising, and which will enable advertising to fulfil its role in the overall marketing mix.

Advertising *objectives* are more or less specific statements of what is to be achieved by advertising, in terms of (for example) increased awareness, or improved scores on certain attitude scales, or increased liking of the ads, or response rates for direct response campaigns.

Advertising *strategy* is a statement of how the objectives are to be achieved, in terms of creative content and media deployment. These two elements—specific objectives and specific strategy—provide the basis of the brief to the creative department.

It is easy to labour this point, but I have seen far too many advertising briefs that put marketing objectives (such as 'to increase our share of the market by 5 per cent') into the advertising objectives, or even the advertising strategy. This is sloppy thinking and misuse of language, and will lead to problems later, as a result.

Developing the strategy: the planning cycle

The advertising strategy may be a lengthy document, which has, in turn, to be translated into a creative brief; the latter, ideally, should occupy no more than one or two sheets of paper, and will present a tightly refined summation of the strategy. I will go into this in more detail in the next chapter.

The planner's aim is to provide the answers to two deceptively simple questions:

- ☐   Who do we want to talk to?
- ☐   What do we want them to get out of our advertising?

To arrive at the answers, you have to go through a more or less logical process of analysis, based on a combination of the advertiser's and the agency's knowledge of the brand, market research and experience. Then, to turn the answers into a creative brief that will genuinely inspire the creative team, there is a need for imagination and creativity on the part of the strategists.

What the planner needs to know can be viewed as a cycle of information and analysis. It is a cycle because marketing and advertising are continuous processes, and the knowledge gained from one campaign can be built on as we develop the next. The planning cycle is illustrated in Figure 5.2. (Different agencies may use slightly different versions of this, but they are all broadly similar.)

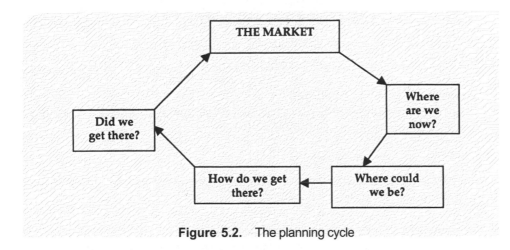

Figure 5.2. The planning cycle

This version starts at the top with an examination of the marketplace, and the various terms used in the figure cover the following areas:

The marketplace

The market in which our brand competes: trends in sales, market share, consumption, distribution; the state of product development and innovation; patterns of consumption—who are the heavy and light users of the category, and why? This material can provide us with the basis for an understanding of how our brand stands in the marketplace.

The present—where are we now?

This is the next area for examination. We describe the brand's position in the market: brand shares and trends in brand share; product advantages and disadvantages over the competition both in physical terms (lab tests and blind consumer tests) and in terms of consumer attitudes and opinions; planned and possible product improvements; recent marketing activity, together with that of competitors. This stage can usefully include a SWOT analysis (Strengths, Weaknesses, Opportunities, Threats) (see Box 5.1).

Box 5.1   SWOT Analysis

This is a useful technique for summarizing the situation a brand is in. It needs to be quite carefully put together, because it is all too easy to throw in everything, including the kitchen sink, to make the analysis look impressive. It is better to be rigorous about selecting factors that are genuinely important to the brand, in its market, and to have only two or three factors under each heading. You then have—with luck—identified the areas where action should be focused.

A fairly typical SWOT analysis is this one, for a producer of frozen chicken products:

Strengths
- Ready access to supplies of high-quality, low-cost chickens.
- The latest processing technology.
- Growing reputation with the retail trade as a source of commodity products.
- Access to ample investment funds for marketing.

Weaknesses

- Crowded and competitive market with two major, branded competitors and substantial share for retailers' own label.
- Lack of consumer awareness or reputation for the brand.
- No clear branding or brand positioning, as yet.
- Lack of experienced marketing management to drive the development.
- Limited distribution among key multiple retailers.

Opportunities

- Lack of effective consumer branding by all but two competitors.
- Growth market, particularly for further processed, frozen products.
- Scope for product innovation.
- Retail interest in the sector.

Threats
- Retail development concentrated on own-label lines
- Need to develop a range of products, relatively quickly, to achieve sustainable weight in the market: this is expensive and requires extensive NPD (New Product Development) work.
- Rapid competitive imitation of successful new lines.

This is, clearly, a *marketing* analysis, but it begins to delineate some of the areas where advertising will have to make a contribution—and to indicate the limits to what advertising might be able to achieve, unless adequate attention is paid to the rest of the marketing mix.

For an established brand, the analysis would usually be focused more on the relationship between the brand and consumers, which is closer to the advertising task.

The future—where could we be?

Here we are looking initially at the marketer's ambitions for the brand, as expressed in the marketing objectives: what are the targets for sales, brand share, consumer penetration and consumer usage of the product? This immediately focuses attention on two things: whether the targets are realistic (or ambitious enough), and what is going to be required to attain them. The first of these can usually be answered, to an extent, by looking at recent market history. But the answer will ultimately depend on the availability of the required resources, and the successful use of the resources to influence the target audience in the right way. (It may be, for example, that the market share targets are unrealistic unless retail distribution is significantly improved. It is better for the agency to point this out in advance than to find itself blaming the client's sales force for a failure that is being attributed to the advertising.)

Objectives and strategy—how do we get there?

The marketing objectives can be translated into a series of communication (and other) objectives. The communication objectives are where advertising fits in, but it is important to recognize the role of other forms of communication—PR, point of sale, direct marketing, staff communications and so on. As we have seen, (Chapter 1) all these different items ought to be integrated in a way that ensures that together they build up the brand's communications in the right way. Each of the possible elements in the communications plan can contribute something rather different (see Figure 5.3), and for an individual brand the pattern may have its own variations on the general picture provided by Figure 5.3.

In defining specifically the role of advertising, we need to be aware of what advertising can and cannot do. It cannot, for example, do the *complete* job of selling a product, in most cases. It cannot usually do the job assumed by much retail advertising, of providing consumers with a list of prices that they will then remember: this is done much more efficiently at the point of sale—but what such ads do achieve is to put across the idea that here is a store with a wide range of interesting products at what must be competitive prices, or they would not bother to advertise them.

Things that we can realistically list as roles for advertising are set out in Box 5.2.

Box 5.2   Possible roles for advertising

Roles for advertising, not mutually exclusive:

- □ To increase awareness of the brand.
- □ To increase awareness of key characteristics of the brand.
- □ To encourage non-users to try the brand.
- □ To strengthen the loyalty of existing buyers.
- □ To develop specific beliefs and attitudes to the brand.
- □ To announce changes to the brand's specification or range.
- □ To generate requests for information.
- □ To raise staff morale.
- □ To encourage the retail trade to stock the product

Activity	Awareness	Image	Brand building	Direct response	Sampling/ trial	Repeat purchase	Loyalty	Information gathering	Measurability	Customer service	Distribution
TV	X	X	X	X					X		
Outdoor	X	X	X								
Press	X	X	X	X	X	X		X	X		
Direct mail				X	X	X	X	X	X	X	
Door to door	X			X	X			X	X		
Telemarketing				X			X	X	X	X	
Sales promotion	X	X		X	X	X					
Sponsorship	X	X	X				X	X	X		
PR	X	X	X				X				
Trade promotion	X		X								X

Figure 5.3. Appropriateness of communications activities for different roles (Source: Based on *Royal Mail Guide to Integrated Communications*, Post Office, 1995)

Advertising objectives and strategy

From this analysis, we can begin to develop specific objectives and strategies for advertising. I will return to these in a moment.

Effects—did we get there?

Your advertising, if it is well-planned and works together with the rest of the marketing mix, should have an effect! It is clearly essential, within the planning cycle, to measure the effects of the advertising, because this provides a key part of the input for the start of the next planning cycle. Measuring advertising effects is discussed in Chapter 8.

Planning the advertising: objectives and strategy

Objectives

Once we have identified the role for advertising we can often translate this into quantified objectives, which can then be monitored through appropriate research. Thus, we might set a range of objectives for an established confectionery brand as follows:

1. Overall, to develop and strengthen the brand's position as a leader in the quality informal gift market, especially at Christmas
2. To raise spontaneous brand awareness from 80 per cent to 90 per cent
3. To raise advertising awareness from 37 per cent post- Christmas to 45 per cent
4. To increase the proportions of category buyers describing the brand on key attributes as follows:

	Now	Next year
–A favourite gift:	30%	35%
–Excellent value for money	32%	40%
–Top quality ingredients	35%	40%

5. To increase the proportion of the advertising aware who say that they like our ads from 45 per cent to 60 per cent.

As can be seen, the sort of objectives that we can reasonably set for the advertising are to do with understanding of attitudes to the brand and specific responses to the advertising. If we are using one of the commitment types of research (see p. 54), we might well set as one of our objectives an increase in those of our users who are more strongly in favour of the brand.

Objectives will differ in detail and character according to the market and the stage of life of the brand. Well-established brands' objectives are likely to be essentially 'maintenance' in character, while newer brands will be looking to expand their horizons, and objectives will concentrate on raising awareness, developing consumer knowledge and encouraging new users to try the brand.

Turning Objectives into Strategy

Setting the objectives should be fairly straightforward. The difficult part is translating what we know about the brand and its virtues into a strategy that can deliver the objectives that we have set, and can give the creatives the required stimulus to develop the right advertising to fit the strategy. This process goes back to the two questions raised earlier (page 58). Who do we want to talk to? And what do we want them to get out of our ads?

Who do we want to talk to—the target audience

If you are a salesperson, an important part of the job is to find out as much as possible about the person you are selling to. The more you know about their fads and foibles, their strengths and weaknesses, the better you can adapt your pitch to them. It is exactly the same with advertising, except that you are not talking to one person across a desk or in a store: you are talking to thousands or millions of people, in their homes or their cars or trains or buses.

All the same, you are not going to be talking to the entire population (unless you are running a major government campaign, and even then the campaign will have its priorities). You are talking to the one in 100, or 50, or whatever, who might buy your product. Almost invariably, the core target group for a given brand is surprisingly small as a percentage of the population. Because your target is that one in a hundred—or, rather, lots of them—that one is going to be different, to stand out from the crowd, in some way or another. How do you spot them? Well, since one in a hundred Britons means half a million people, you are talking about quite a large group, who must have *something* in common if they all buy your product.

If you can define what this something is, it will make it much easier for everybody to begin to understand who they are and how to talk to them. This is an important use for the market research that has been analysed in the first three stages of the planning cycle. If you think about large groups of people, there are numerous ways of dividing them up into groups that have something (or a lot) in common. Looking for groups like this is called 'market segmentation', and there are a number of ways of doing it (see Box 5.3), using either your own market research or such publicly-available surveys as the *Target Group Index (TGI)*,[1]

---

[1] Published annually by the British Market Research Bureau Ltd.

Traditionally, marketers and their agencies have relied on demographics—age, sex, social class, income group, educational attainment, regions of the country—as the initial basis for defining a target audience. This has had the value of relying on readily available and familiar information that can be easily tied in to a variety of market and media research.

Box 5.3   *Market segmentation*

Segmentation is the essential basis for targeting advertising and other communications. There are a number of ways in which more or less readily available research sources can be used to segment markets, and research companies are constantly trying to develop new and better ones. *Demographic* segmentation has come to be recognised to be very broad-brush, and more refined analyses have come into play:

1. Geodemographics: Originally based on TGI, these systems identify small geographic areas where consumers have common characteristics, in terms of buying behaviour, attitudes, media exposure, etc.
2. Lifestage: This is an extension of demographics, which recognizes that as people go through life, their circumstances, especially their work and family situation, change quite dramatically, and similar stages in life tend to lead to similar needs and purchasing behaviour.
3. Attitudes: Based on research surveys designed to discover consumers' attitudes to the market concerned and the brands in it, cluster analysis allowed marketers to split their market into groups of people with similar attitudes to the product category and to target these through their creative approach.
4. Psychographics: the use of so-called 'values and attitudes' surveys enables researchers to divide whole populations into a number of groups of more or less like-minded people, and these groups can be shown to have different purchasing habits in different markets.
5. Lifestyle: there are research companies that use postal surveys to accumulate very large databases of consumers and their interests and buying behaviour in various markets. These provide the basis for segmenting markets on the basis of 'lifestyle'.
6. 'Holistic': Most segmentation studies start out by deciding what sorts of factors to segment on. It is possible, however, to structure the research so that any of the types of factors already listed could be used, singly or in combination.

These more elaborate forms of segmentation all rely on cross-referencing different groups of data, to provide a more powerful analysis. They depend, therefore, on researchers' ability either to provide 'single source' data such as *TGI*, which covers brands, demographics, media exposure and some psychographic data, or to use sophisticated 'data fusion' techniques to combine information from a variety of different research sources.

Most of the demographic factors are readily intelligible, and the divisions can be found in most standard British published research sources, from government surveys to commercially-available data such as *TGI*, industry-syndicated media research such as the *National Readership Survey* or *BARB,* and published market reports like *Mintel*[2] or *Retail Business*.[3] In the same way, any quantified survey that you have carried out on your own behalf will routinely collect demographic data as the basis for analysis.

The only one of the factors that may be unfamiliar (and possibly incomprehensible to non-UK readers) will be social class, or social grade. The British have long been obsessed with class, which pervades much of our social attitudes, and for many years researchers have used a standard system of classifying people into six social grades, which are based, for ease of data collection, on the occupation of the head of the household.

This system is—clearly—a gross over-simplification, and the market research industry has devoted a great deal of brainpower to trying to find an adequate substitute, without much success. At the same time, the use of this sort of system has spread internationally, and ESOMAR (European Society for Opinion and Marketing Research) has developed a standardized methodology that parallels the UK system, but is different from it, in an attempt to aid international comparisons.

The UK classifications, and the approximate proportions of each class in Britain, are shown in Figure 5.4.

It is worth noting that the proportions are by no means constant. Increasing prosperity and changes in employment patterns mean that the A and B groups, for

A	3.0%	Higher managerial, administrative and professional
B	17.8%	Intermediate managerial, administrative and professional
C1	27.5%	Supervisory, clerical, junior managerial, administrative and professional
C2	21.9%	Skilled manual workers
D	18.2%	Semi- and un-skilled manual workers
E	11.6%	State pensioners, widows, casual or lowest grade workers

Figure 5.4. Social grade, definitions and proportion in the GB population, 1998 Source: *National Readership Survey*

---

[2] Published monthly by Mintel Publications Ltd.
[3] Published monthly by Corporate Intelligence in Retailing.

example, have increased their combined penetration by virtually three percentage points since 1985. Traditionally, the C2 and D groups represented the 'mass market', and they accounted for over 60 per cent of all adults until the late 1970s.

It used to be the case that, by knowing reasonably precisely someone's age, social class and location, you could predict quite well how they would think, where they would shop, what sort of holiday they would take, whether they had a bank account, and so on. In the last 30 years or so, however, many of the predictable distinctions have either blurred or disappeared entirely, and marketers and researchers have tried to develop more sensitive ways of analysing populations into meaningful clusters or groupings. As a result, what used to be a good, but by no means infallible, guide to spending behaviour seems to be of limited value, in spite of its continuing widespread use. (It remains an essential element of the media buying system, because target audiences defined primarily by age and class are the basis of the 'currency' in which media deals are negotiated.)

Geodemographics, lifestyles and values

In the attempt to improve on simple demographics, researchers in the 1970s lit on the idea of combining the massive range of information on product and brand purchasing and media usage contained in the *Target Group Index* with geo-graphical data derived from the 10-yearly census and the (then quite new in the UK) postcode system. The first of these systems, now marketed by CACI Ltd, is ACORN (A Classification Of Residential Neighbourhoods). CACI have analysed the data so as to break down the population into, in the latest format, 17 groups comprising 54 types of area, with no type accounting for more than 4.5 per cent of the population.

A rather similar system was developed by a company whose business was to collect information on the credit-worthiness of individual households. This system, called MOSAIC, is now marketed by Experian, a company with substantial interests in marketing databases. MOSAIC has 12 main groupings, and, like ACORN, some 50 sub-groups. Typical descriptions from the two systems are shown in Figure 5.5.

As can be seen, the two systems use rather different typologies, ACORN talking primarily about people and property ownership, MOSAIC using a mix of personality types and descriptions of housing. While these two are arguably the most familiar of the geodemographic systems, there is another, Super-Profiles, which is also used quite widely, and appears in the classification material on the *National Readership Survey*. Both ACORN and MOSAIC have specialized versions that have been developed for the financial services industry.

The value of geodemographics comes in targeting of marketing activity at a local level. Because any postcode can be translated into a type or subgroup, it is possible

ACORN			MOSAIC		
Group	Type	% of population	Group	Sub-group	% of population
5. Well-off workers, family areas	Home-owning family areas	2.6	L2 Suburban semis	Green belt expansion	3.6
	Home-owning, older children	3.0		Suburban mock Tudor	3.0
	Home-owning, younger children	2.2		Pebble-dash Subtopia	4.2
10. Skilled workers, home owning	Established home-owning	4.5	L3 Blue collar owners	Affluent blue collar	3.0
	Owners in older property, younger	3.0		30s industrial spec.	3.8
	Home-owning, shiftwork With skilled Workers	3.1 3.1		Lo-rise right-to-buy Smokestack	3.0

Figure 5.5. Examples of ACORN and MOSAIC groupings (Source: CACI, *Experian*, 1997)

to select specific small areas for door-to-door marketing or mailing; or as a guide to the location of a new store designed to appeal to certain sorts of people; or to map the distribution area of local newspapers being considered for an advertising campaign.

Another promising direction, which has been pursued by some large advertisers and agencies, is so-called 'lifestyle' research. This involves regular, extensive surveys asking people questions about all sorts of aspects of their attitudes to life. The aim is to identify groups with underlying systems of values that can affect their approach to shopping and consumption. With the aid of quite complex statistical analysis, you can look at the consumers of any product field or brand on which the survey has collected data, and define them in relation to the values revealed by the survey. These systems, of which VALS (Values and Life Styles) and RISC (The Research Institute on Social Change) are probably the best known, are available internationally, and this is valuable for anyone who is trying to market a brand internationally or globally, because all the material can be reduced to a common framework.

RISC, for example, develops a 3-D 'map' of a population, divided into 10 segments, on 3 key axes: the north–south axis is basically a measure of modernity or traditionalism; the east–west axis reflects open or closed social attitudes and the back–front axis distinguishes a local focus from a more global one (see Figure 5.6).

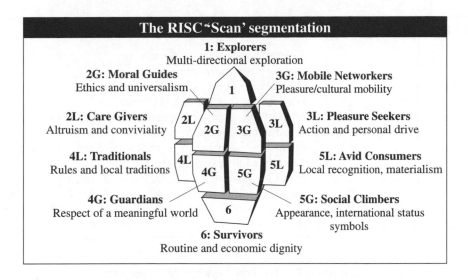

Figure 5.6.   The RISC 'Scan' segmentation (Source: *Admap*, June 1998)

The users of any brand covered by the survey can be located on this map, and this, combined with data about weight of use and brand loyalty, can be used to identify the brand's areas of strength and weakness.

Brand usage

This last example brings into focus a vital element in identifying a target group: their familiarity with, and use of, the brand. Our interest as advertising planners lies in identifying the people we can best influence (or whom we most need to influence) to achieve the advertising and marketing objectives. Are we trying to get new users to try the brand, or are we trying to get existing users to stay loyal, or perhaps use more of it?

A brand's users can be plotted on a spectrum, from non usage of the category and total ignorance of the brand at one end to heavy category usage and almost total loyalty to the brand at the other (Figure 5.7). Clearly, what we are trying to do with the advertising will vary, depending on which of the various groups we most want to influence.

Readers should be aware that there is a substantial debate in progress about brand loyalty and how, if at all, it can be strengthened. It used to be assumed by marketers that people used either Brand X or Brand Y, and that the object of marketing and advertising was to convert users of Brand Y to Brand X, or vice versa. In fmcg markets, it is clear that most consumers in fact have a repertoire of brands from

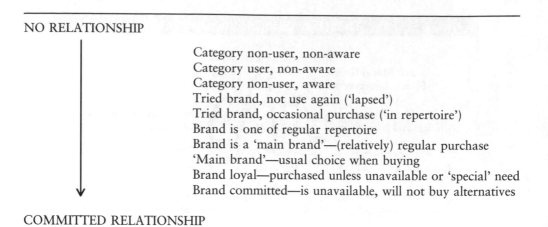

NO RELATIONSHIP

Category non-user, non-aware
Category user, non-aware
Category non-user, aware
Tried brand, not use again ('lapsed')
Tried brand, occasional purchase ('in repertoire')
Brand is one of regular repertoire
Brand is a 'main brand'—(relatively) regular purchase
'Main brand'—usual choice when buying
Brand loyal—purchased unless unavailable or 'special' need
Brand committed—is unavailable, will not buy alternatives

COMMITTED RELATIONSHIP

Figure 5.7. The brand relationship 'Spectrum'

which they buy, and Professor Ehrenberg[4] has demonstrated that this process can be analysed to show that it is largely dictated by the size of the brand: the bigger the brand's share, the larger, virtually automatically, will be its share of the average buyer's repertoire. He goes on to argue that brand loyalty is in fact pretty illusory, and that few, if any, brands have any real strength beyond their size.

The logical conclusion of this, for advertising, is that it is misguided to try to do much more with an ad campaign than to remind people of the brand's existence, in as creative a way as possible.

This view is quite extreme in its implications for advertising planning, and it is, I believe, misleading. There is no doubt, from qualitative research, that consumers can distinguish very clearly between different brands, even where they are physically very similar, in terms of personality, character and likeability: people do identify, more or less strongly, with some brands, and not with others. Similarly, various research companies have developed systems for looking at markets that can separate out the degree to which consumers are committed to particular brands in a market. What's more, and this is the important factor, they can use changes in levels of commitment to make predictions about changes in brand shares: the level of consumers' involvement with brands does matter.

This means that there is a genuine purpose in setting out to move consumers further up the metaphorical ladder from non-interest to enthusiasm for your brand.

---

[4] e.g. A. Ehrenberg, and J. Scriven, Added values or propensities to buy? *Admap*, Sept. 1997.

Now, if you accept that, it is quite important for the person creating the ad to know whether the target group of consumers is rather ignorant (or totally ignorant) about the brand, or whether they have used it a number of times already. The ignorant have to be informed and given reasons to try the brand. The knowledgeable have to be involved and encouraged, and given—usually—emotional support for continuing to use the brand. (Or, in some cases, given suggestions about new uses they might find for the brand, so that they buy more often.)

What should the target group get from our ads?

Every marketer's dream is the product that meets some fundamental human need, perfectly, and does this in a way that no other product can match. In today's competitive markets, very few—if any—products are like that, and, if they are, you can bet that pretty soon someone will have either matched it at a lower price or introduced something even better.

This means that any brand you find yourself advertising is going to have to compete, and compete against other brands that, by and large, deliver exactly the same benefits to buyers, in much the same way, to much the same standard of quality.

As a result, advertiser and agency are going to have to work hard to sort out what has to be said about the brand to ensure that enough consumers buy it, or go on buying it, regularly. The object of the exercise has become to try to *differentiate* your brand effectively from its almost identical competitors (think of Coke and Pepsi).

Deciding what should be said about the brand has to start from two related points:

1. The brand itself and the product it embodies; and
2. The way in which the brand is—or is intended to be—*positioned* in people's minds and in the market.

A good brand positioning, which can be hard to develop, should be true to the brand and its products, distinctive, relevant to consumers and competitive.

Interrogating the brand

A discipline established by a number of leading agencies is to start the process of strategy development by interrogating the brand—finding out everything there is to know about the product, its history, how it is made, what it is made of, and so on. The underlying assumption behind all this is that there will be buried somewhere in the brand's make-up some key truth or truths that can be used as a hook on which to hang an ad campaign—or at least some individual advertisements.

A classic example of the process being translated into a well-known ad campaign is the UK campaign for BMW, developed over more than 15 years by WCRS (see Box 5.4)

Box 5.4   BMW: *The Ultimate Driving Machine*

BMW's agency, WCRS, went through an exhaustive process of consumer research and discussion with BMW engineers, before identifying four core, linked values that were fundamental to the brand: Performance, Exclusivity, Quality and Advanced Technology. Each of these has evolved in character over the last 15 years, as consumer attitudes and the standing of the brand have developed and changed. The campaign has used a very large number of individual ads, and, usually, each has focused on a single aspect of the car's engineering as a demonstration of one or more of the core values; and while the cheaper 3-series cars make up the majority of sales, advertising has been spread over all four models (3, 5, 7 and 8-series), so that the prestige of the more expensive models rubs off on the others.

The result of the advertising (allied to on-going product development and dealer development) has been a dramatic increase in sales, share and brand standing, and has enabled the brand to maintain a significant price premium while it has moved from a niche brand selling under 15 000 cars a year in the UK to an admired leader in the more expensive sector of the market, with sales over 60 000 a year.

Source: *Advertising Works*, 8, ch. 1

In the days when most advertising was for fmcg products, and competition was less intensive than it now is, agencies, led by Ted Bates's Rosser Reeves, aimed to identify a Unique Selling Proposition, or USP, that could be used to differentiate a brand from the competition, and usually appeared as the sign-off or slogan in advertising. Ideally, these USPs were physical characteristics of the brands concerned, but they could be more psychological: 'Guinness is good for you' and Colgate's 'Ring of confidence' are examples of the latter, M&Ms' 'Melts in your mouth, not in your hand' of the former.

It is still occasionally possible to find a genuine USP for a wholly new product, but they are pretty rare in established markets. (There is a tendency for marketing people to produce advertising briefs which list a brand as having 'These seven USPs'. On closer inspection, this means that the brand concerned has two or three good selling points, plus another three or four features to which it would be nice if the ad could draw attention. None of them, in practice, turns out to be a genuine USP.) If you find a brand with a real USP, this is usually because it is a very small, niche brand.

This means that advertisers have had to become altogether cleverer in picking the things to communicate about their brands. They have come to recognize that what consumers get from buying the brand is not—for example—food, but the satisfaction of having a convenient, well-presented dish that can be prepared in minutes and leaves no washing up: the benefit of being able to cater without effort at the end of a gruelling day at work. Brands, in fact are not just physical products, but a bundle of satisfactions and benefits—some physical, to be sure, but some purely psychological.

Positioning the brand

Brands exist, for the most part, within markets—even if the boundaries of the market are not always clear: it is often necessary to define, rather carefully, your brand's 'competitive set' of brands, in order to know what market you in fact compete in.

The implication of all this, however, is that your brand has to be differentiated from its competitors in ways that will influence consumers' preferences in your favour. To do this, you have to understand how competition works in your market: the chances are that there are a number of rather similar brands, but that they are all trying to compete in slightly different ways. They are *positioned* differently in the market.

Positioning is the definition of how and where the brand is going to compete. What particular virtues has it? What particular benefits does it offer? What special circumstances can it best be used in? If you consider the UK market for mints, this is a small and dynamic market with a considerable number of brands. Polo is far and away the leader, but there is plenty of competition. As it is an impulse-purchase market, the brands cannot be elaborately positioned. Polo is, essentially, everyone's friend: a brand with a neat sense of humour, an ability to poke fun at itself and the world around it, and a ubiquitous presence. Tic Tac, a much smaller brand, cannot compete in this area: its owners, Ferrero, have decided to concentrate on the small fact that each mint has less than two calories, allied to the particularly fresh taste of the product. Tic Tac is advertised as offering two hours' freshness for less than two calories. An older, and now little advertised brand, Murraymints, is a traditional type of product that is large enough to be sucked or chewed for a long time. For years, Murraymints were the 'Too good to hurry mints'. These are all, in effect, positionings. A more elaborate and complex example is given in Box 5.5.

Box 5.5   A choice of positionings

The Bank of Scotland has an extremely flexible mortgage called Personal Choice. Personal Choice, which is not the cheapest mortgage on the market, gives people the opportunity to vary their payments, to take 'payment holidays', or to pay in large lump sums, so as to shorten the life of the mortgage. Once you have paid off a bit of the mortgage, you can borrow more money, up to the original total, or pay bills with the aid of a cheque book linked to the mortgage account. In other words, you can, for example, buy a new car with it—at rates well below the rates charged for normal personal loans. Less obviously, you can use it as a very good savings vehicle; if you pay money into your mortgage account, you are effectively 'earning', tax-free, an interest rate equivalent to that which you are paying on the mortgage—this is highly competitive, but something people find it rather hard to understand.

Given a product like that, you are faced with a positive cornucopia of possible positionings for Personal Choice. For a start, is it a mortgage, a savings vehicle, a way of borrowing, a bank account? Or is it simply too complicated to be credible and comprehensible? A couple of ads illustrate how the Bank has, in fact positioned the product: they have preferred to take the straightforward approach of positioning the product as a highly flexible mortgage, that offers ways of saving money.

Like most press ads for financial services the main messages are in the headlines

A positioning, then, is a way of describing what is really important about the way in which the brand is meant to fit into its market. It must, obviously, represent a truth about the brand, and it must offer benefits to its potential buyers that are strong enough to make them interested in buying. And it needs to be a means of differentiating the brand, in a relevant way, from its key competitors.

Summary

- A clear and defined strategy is an essential prerequisite for advertising development.
- The process of defining a strategy is essentially logical and analytical. It goes through a series of steps—the planning cycle—which are, in fact, a continuous process through the life of the brand. The strategist may use a variety of tools, such as SWOT analysis.
- The aim is to establish realistic and attainable objectives, and to identify appropriate strategies to achieve them, with the aid of market research and other information available about the brand and its market.
- For advertising, the focus of analysis is the consumers: who are they and how do they relate to the brand and its competitors?
- The key output of the analysis, providing the basis for creative strategy, is the definition of the target audience and of a competitive and distinctive positioning for the brand.

Some issues to consider

- Take a brand that is very familiar to you (perhaps you use it every day). How would you describe its strengths and weaknesses in its market? Which of these strengths or weaknesses lend themselves to, or require, action that might involve advertising?
- Consider two very different cars: Nissan Micra and Vauxhall Omega. How would you expect the target audiences for these cars to differ from each other and why? How might this effect the way these two sub-brands might be positioned?

6 Planning the advertising: the creative brief and creative briefing

Write the brief with the intention of changing the world

Steve Henry, HHCL, in *Excellence in Advertising*

It is one thing to sort out the strategy. It is another to turn it into something that the creative team will respond to with enthusiasm and imagination—and the better the creative team, the more demanding they are likely to be. This chapter suggests some of the ways in which a creative brief can be designed both to meet the demands of the strategy and to turn on the creatives.

It is important to recognize two things about creative briefs: first, that they are not the same thing as briefing the creative team: it is no good distilling the strategy into two carefully crafted pages of A4, and then throwing it to a team and telling them to get on with it. We will come back to this. Secondly, there is undoubtedly room for the creatives to contribute to the development of the brief: while they may want to argue with the original version simply because something else appears to be easier to execute, they may also have more positive contributions to make. The brief can often be sharpened through a dialogue between the planner and the creatives.

Creative briefing forms

Nearly all agencies of any size have a 'creative briefing form'. This is a short series of headings that the planner has to complete, together with various administrative details, such as the media to be used, the dates of key meetings and presentations—and the first insertion or airdate—and the signatures of key people who have to sign off the brief before it can be given to a team to work on.

Most of these forms follow pretty similar formats, though there are variations. In all of them, however, there are three key elements that define the way in which the brief will work: the description of the target audience and its relationship with the brand, the 'proposition' and the supports for the proposition. Some would say that the tone of voice of the communication is also a key ingredient (see Figure 6.1).

Bartle Bogle Hegarty	Conquest	Duckworth Finn Grubb Walters
1. The role of Advertising –What do we want people to do as a result of our ads? –How do we believe the ads will work to achieve this?	The product is: What is the brand personality? Who is the target audience?	What is this brand called? Who do we want to buy it? Why should people buy this brand?
2. Who are we talking to?	What are we advertising for?	
3. What is the single most important thing the ads should convey?	What is the proposition?	
4. Why should people believe this?	What is the support for this?	
5. What practical considerations are there?	What do we want people to think or do?	

All three briefing forms also include details of timings, media to be considered, etc.

Figure 6.1.   Creative briefing forms: main headings (Source: adapted from L. Butterfield (ed.) *Excellence in Advertising*)

Describing the target audience

As we have seen, there are many ways in which a planner can look at market data to identify the target audience for a campaign. But the audience still needs to come alive in the minds of the creative team if they are to find it at all easy to write ads that will get over the barriers that lie between an ad and success.

The planner has to put into the brief enough information to define the audience, to identify its existing relationship with the brand, and to bring it to life. So, a marketing plan may talk about the target audience in almost purely demographic terms: 'Younger families with children: CIC2 housewives aged 25–40, especially occasional users of Brand X'. But an advertising strategy and the brief that is based on it will say something more like this (for a confectionery brand):

☐   Women, aged 25–40, who love—but may feel guilty about—eating chocolate. A bit self-indulgent, and able to afford little luxuries. They enjoy most forms of pampering.

☐   They are well aware of [our brand], but buy it (or several of the direct competitors) infrequently, and for special occasions: they do not see it as a day-to-day, casual eat.

- □ They think of the brand as special, and like eating it, but they don't know what the product contains, and they rarely think about how nice it is.
- □ They see it as being a bit distant—aloof, stuck-up, probably foreign.
- □ They are reluctant to buy [our brand] for themselves, but they like being given it.

This definition is, clearly, based on quite detailed research and specific decisions about which people to target (most boxed chocolates have an older age profile than that of the target), and the sort of things that the planner is hoping to achieve.

In a different sort of market—say cars—the target might be specifically defined in terms of owners of particular competitive models that could be seen as susceptible to switching makes at their next purchase. It would need, in addition, the sort of psychological characteristics mostly used in the chocolate example, in order to show how the target group look at cars and approach buying them. There's a great deal of psychological distance between buyers of, say, a Suzuki Swift and a Mazda MX5. Think about it.

More generally, it is quite important to be clear about what sort of relationship the target consumers have with the brand to be advertised: are they very familiar with it? Are they current light users, who we wish to encourage to use our brand more often? Are they lapsed users, who will, we hope, respond to news of a relaunch or reformulation by trying the brand again? Are we hoping to attract people who have never tried—or perhaps never heard of—our brand?

Why this matters should be fairly obvious: if we are trying to get new users, we are going to have to work hard to attract their attention, and give them good reasons (rational or emotional, or both) to try the brand. In 'Framework' terms (Box 4.1), this requires a combination of salience and persuasion—perhaps with a bit of involvement thrown in. If, on the other hand, we are aiming to make sure that our heaviest users keep taking the juice, what is needed is going to be almost pure involvement, wrapped round a gentle reminder of all the things that—we hope—make them love the brand.

The strategy: what should the target group get from our ads?

As can be seen, the analysis to define the target group has gone into some detail about who uses the product, how they use it, what they think of it, and so on. This provides the basis for deciding what the advertising has to achieve. This starts from studying the brand itself, in order to identify its strengths and weaknesses (part of the material for a SWOT analysis—Box 4.1): a list of the sort of questions a planner might want to ask is shown in Box 6.1.

Box 6.1   Some key questions for understanding and defining a target group's relationship with our brand

- □ Who uses the product category?
- □ What do they use it for? Are there different groups doing different things?
- □ Which brands do they use? Do they use different brands for different purposes?
- □ How often do they buy, and use, the product?
- □ Where do they buy it? And in what sort of mood or frame of mind? Is this a casual, routine purchase, or something more interesting and important? Why?
- □ When and where do they use it? Why?
- □ How do they judge between brands? (Taste, colour, size, technical features, durability, reliability?)
- □ What do they think is good or bad about our brand?
- □ What about the competition?
- □ Is our brand any better than its competitors (a) in blind-test terms, (b) in reputation among consumers and (c) scientifically/objectively?
- □ Have they actually heard about our brand? Have they ever tried it?

The task of the advertising is likely to be to try to strengthen the brand's good points, or to bring these points to the attention of a new audience. Equally, however, it may be to try to redress a weakness. From the target audience description for our chocolate brand, it is easy to deduce that whoever is doing the thinking about the brand believes that it is too 'special' for its own good: the idea is to try to get people to loosen up about it, to buy it and eat it for more casual occasions. To do this, it looks as if the brand has, somehow, to become friendlier and more accessible. Further, targeting it at a younger audience than the majority of regular eaters of boxed chocolates suggests that someone has identified either a weakness in the brand's user profile or the opportunity to influence a more susceptible and less habituated group of women.

We have, in fact, applied behavioural, attitudinal and demographic segmentation to our search for the target group.

We are also beginning to get towards what we would like them to get out of our ads. Why do I put it like this? Why not 'what we want to tell them about our brand'? The answer goes back to what actually happens to ads when people see or hear them. Ads are not something that people especially want to take any notice of. They intrude into our lives, sometimes noisily and aggressively; they get in the way of what we are reading; they interrupt our favourite TV programme. So we very often switch them off altogether (mentally, or physically, by 'zapping' with the remote control on the TV): we are very good at this. Or, when we do attend to an ad, our response to it is filtered through a whole range of diversions and mental barriers. We very often only take notice of part of an ad, and succeed in ignoring the key points that the advertiser really wants to get across. It is rather as if people are involved in a game of 'Chinese whispers' with the ads.

We also, very often, get far more out of the visual clues in the ad than the words, because our eyes are quicker, usually, than our ears, and memory tends to be more efficient at preserving visual stimuli than absorbing verbal material. So much so, that research has shown that a radio commercial that picks up on key elements of the sound track of a TV campaign can easily stimulate visual images from the TV commercials—a process known as 'visual transfer'.[1]

What this means is that we need to be very careful about how we think about the communication process by which our ads will work. Communication is not a simple, one-directional stimulus $\Rightarrow$ response process: between the sender and the desired recipient of a message, there is a great deal of distortion and noise, rather like lots of short-wave radio; and the recipient can decide—voluntarily or instinctively—to accept only part of the message. Increasingly, too, people are coming to recognize that communication should, ideally allow for the chance to reply: people like dialogue. At its simplest, this means that ads with a response mechanism—a coupon, and address to write to, a telephone number to call, a web site to visit—are often more attractive than ads without.

It is easy to exaggerate the importance of dialogue, and the direct marketing industry does so consistently. As many people have now pointed out, it is only pretty sad people who really want a dialogue with a brand of baked beans—and, indeed, Heinz, the market leaders in baked beans in the UK, have recently dismantled most of a very ambitious programme of direct marketing, in which they diverted much of their large TV advertising spend to database building and the distribution of a promotional magazine.

Box 6.2   Heinz and direct marketing

Heinz is one of the leading food manufacturers in the UK, with a number of market-leading lines and a very large string of smaller products. In 1994 they announced that they would be taking a large part of their substantial advertising budget, and devoting it to the development of a direct marketing programme. This they did. The visible outcome of this became a customer magazine, *Heinz At Home*, that was mailed regularly to people on their substantial database, which eventually totalled some five million: this magazine consisted largely of coupons and other offers, and reportedly achieved quite significant uplifts in the sales of the promoted lines.

---

[1] Unpublished research by Initiative Media, which repeats work done by Radio Luxembourg in the early 1970s, also unpublished.

Then, in early 1998, Heinz announced that they were returning to substantial TV advertising and that the direct project was, to all intents and purposes, over. What appears to have happened is that although the direct programme was able to deliver specific sales increases for individual lines, the overall Heinz brand—the umbrella that sustained all these products—was being starved of oxygen. The brand needed sustaining, through the broadscale communications that the direct programme could not—and was not designed to—deliver.

The point, however, is that we cannot take for granted that if we say—for example—'Beanz meanz Heinz' to our target market, they will necessarily limit their reaction to a belief that there is no other brand of beans worth buying. Indeed, the message was never designed to elicit only that response. The aim was to give people a very warm, familiar feeling about a brand that had the standing, the confidence and the self-mocking wit to play with the English language in this way. Ultimately, the take-out should, probably, have been: 'I like Heinz: they're a friendly brand that's really part of my life—and I know my family will enjoy them'.

Thus, a key question that needs to be answered in any creative brief is 'What do we expect to happen as a result of people seeing this advertising? What do we want people to think, to feel, to do?' The way this question is formulated goes back to analysis done at J. Walter Thompson in the 1960s, which suggested that ads could or should be looking for three types of response: a rational reaction to the information in the ad; an emotional reaction; and some form of action. And, since people are rarely able to act directly as a result of seeing an ad (you can't easily drop everything when you see a commercial in a late evening TV programme and go out and buy the product), 'action' may well mean no more than making a mental note to look for the brand on the next shopping trip.

But what about the proposition?

It is all very well to concentrate on people's desired responses, but we still have to decide what it is we actually want to say about our product. Any salesperson knows that it is very difficult to sell a product unless you are quite clear what it offers, how it does it and what the arguments are that can back the story up. What's more, no client is going to be happy about the agency going off and starting to make ads without having a clear idea of how the brand is supposed to be sold.

So, what many agency briefing forms call the 'single-minded proposition' is a core element of the brief. The idea is that it should be possible to describe the key selling features of the brand in one succinct and compelling sentence or phrase. This is not easy, and has become a lot more difficult as the physical differences between brands have been reduced, and brands have proliferated in many markets. Back in the 1950s it was possible for Rosser Reeves of the US Ted Bates agency to propose the idea of the Unique Selling Proposition (USP). This is a statement of a brand's characteristics that embodies an important truth about the brand and is also important to buyers of the category. The brand, by using its USP aggressively in its advertising, comes to 'own' this key characteristic of the market sector.

USPs tended to be based on physical product features, such as Polo's 'The mint with the hole', but many were (and are) more emotional, such as 'Good food costs less at Sainsbury's' (which is emotional because it is only sustainable if the emphasis comes on 'good'), or 'The world's favourite airline'. (As I have said earlier, USPs often double as straplines in ads.)

If a brand *has* a real USP, you are, these days, very lucky. (You can be sure that it will not have, as a lot of brand planning documents tend to suggest 'several' USPs— these are merely selling points where the brand has, perhaps, a slight edge over the main competition.) Competition is too intense, and competing brands tend to be very similar on the important factors that influence consumers' choice.

Furthermore, the development of advertising regulation and controls has made it in some cases impossible to sustain even long-established USP statements. Examples are 'Persil washes whiter': Persil did this for about 50 years, but eventually the claim was judged unsustainable, and was certainly unacceptable to the regulators; and 'A Mars a day helps you work, rest and play': here, although the claim is sustainable in terms of energy, it became unacceptable to modern rules about nutritional claims.

Propositions, then, are these days rarely 'unique' and exclusive in the traditional USP sense. What they can be—and have to be—is distinctive, relevant and competitive. Distinctive, in the sense that they can separate the brand in some way from its competition; relevant, in that the distinction is based on factors that matter to consumers of the category; and competitive, in that what is being put forward has the effect of making the brand appear superior to its competitors.

Because of the parity that has been reached in terms of technical performance in most product categories, propositions increasingly have to be at least partly emotional in character: they aim to connect the brand more powerfully to its target audience than its competitors can. Thus, although Nike trainers have, arguably, at least some technical points of superiority over competitive brands, the brand's proposition is all about achievement: originally 'you can do it', and now 'just do it'. Competitor adidas, by contrast, has a proposition that is much more about professionalism and leaving nothing to chance.

Box 6.3   Some propositions

Diamonds are for ever	De Beers	Primarily emotional
Intel Inside	Intel	Emotional
United Colours	Benetton	Emotional
Kills 99% of known germs–dead	Domestos (bleach)	Factual
No *FT*–No comment	*Financial Times*	Fact + emotion
Exceedingly good cakes	Mr Kipling	Primarily emotional
The listening bank	Midland Bank	Emotional
Committed to responsible use of funds	Co-op Bank	Fact (+emotion)

Supporting evidence

The creative team will want to know—reasonably enough—what it is about the brand that justifies the proposition. What are its key characteristics? What is better than the competition? What is physically unusual about the product? Do people have a special relationship with the brand? What is special about the people who use it?

It is easy to put down a long list of things that might conceivably be important, without too much thought about how the information could be used. There is a real need to be disciplined about the quantity of material here: you are not producing a product manual, you are providing a stimulus to the creative team and a focus for their work. This is one of the areas where discussion between creatives and planner is very useful: the need is to end up with material that the creatives can really use—and, at the same time, to avoid committing yourselves to the use of a whole range of information in the ads that will actually get in the way of communication. A 30-second TV commercial can only expect to put across successfully perhaps two pieces of factual information. If we start out by trying to include five facts, we will end up with a mess.

Creative briefs

Creative briefs, then, are not easy to write. Potentially, they can lead to great advertising, but to do so they have to start out with that aim. As Steve Henry, creative director of HHCL, one of the top creative agencies in the UK, has said, you should write the brief to change the world. This is, obviously, easier to do for an exciting product and a client who is committed to great things. One of the advertising world's great problems is that it is too easy to produce routine creative briefs and routine advertising—and that both agency and client are often happy with that: it's safer.

Boxes 6.4 and 6.5 present two briefs that take a more ambitious view of things, and the ads that resulted.

Box 6.4   See the aroma

Appletise is a high-quality carbonated apple juice, made with no added ingredients. It competes in a sector of the soft drinks market loosely described as 'adult'—which means that people under 20 are not the primary drinkers. This subcategory is more a manufacturers' definition than a consumers', but it defines a group of drinks with relatively sophisticated tastes, which tend to be used as substitutes or accompaniment for alcohol, and to be drunk either in pubs or clubs or with meals.

The problem facing the agency was to find a way to revitalize Appletise in a crowded market, with a limited budget. The brand was well known, and many people have tried it, but it is quite a small brand, and showing no dynamic progress in the market.

A programme of research showed clearly that the brand's greatest strengths lay in its taste, which is very 'appley', and in the little-recognized fact that it is a pure, natural product. The difficulty, for advertising, is that everybody is saying things like 'pure', 'natural', etc , in the food and drink markets, all the time. It is not news.

So, the agency looked for evidence that could demonstrate the facts about Appletise, and realized that, when you open a bottle, you literally get hit by the smell of ripe apples. The proposition became: 'Appletise: you can smell the apples'.

From this, the brief developed:

The product is: 100 per cent pure, sparkling apple juice, made from apple concentrate, with no artificial colourings, flavourings or additives.

The brand personality: the 100 per cent pure alternative. Confident in its inherent qualities of healthiness, simplicity, quality, sophistication and naturalness.

Why advertise?: To regenerate awareness and trial of Appletise.

Who are we talking to?: Relatively upmarket adults, aged 20–40. They tend to have busy, stressful lives, and are aware of the need to be 'healthier' but they are not freaky about it. They may have shifted to a healthier choice in snacks and drinks that are fruit or diet based. This is a bandwagon crowded with competitors, and choice can be daunting. While trial may be promiscuous, re-purchase depends on quality. Carbonated drinks have traditionally carried sugary, junk food associations. In contrast, Appletise is pure, refreshing and naturally sweet.

What do we want to say?: You can be sure Appletise is good because you can smell the apples.

Justification and support: 100 per cent pure apple juice that smells as fresh as it tastes. It is extremely refreshing, and provides a range of health benefits that you expect to get from apples.

How should people react?: 'I didn't realize Appletise was really pure apples. I must try some (again)'.

The resulting commercial succeeded in raising awareness of Appletise significantly, and in shifting consumer attitudes. Sales and market share rose, too, but were hampered by packaging changes that affected distribution.

30″ T.V. SCRIPT
APPLETISE
'BLOKE'

Open on Jonathan Meads sat on a merry-go-round horses ride.

JONATHAN M: As we career toward the next millennium, people are actually claiming that they can see an aroma, of freshly cut apples.

This is shot as though a documentary/reconstruction crew have found our main character, 'Bloke' a happy lad in his mid twenties stood next to a wall, with a friend (Tony) leaning next to him.

BLOKE: You know, I could smell apples, we all smelt apples, and erm Tone said he could see it, see the smell, it was like, yeah, you can't see a smell, but thats what he said.

Ripple-fade into a beautifully shot bottle of Appletise next to a glass of lightly sparkling Appletise.

Ripple-fade to Jonathan Meades with a bottle of Appletise.

JONATHAN M: Can we really see the aroma of Appletise? Open a bottle and keep an open mind.

Four stills from one of several Appletise commercials

Box 6.5 *When Harry met Molly*

In the UK grocery market, Safeway is one of the 'big four' chains, but in 1994 the brand lagged a long way behind leaders Sainsbury and Tesco in reputation. It had an undistinguished image and no real brand heritage on which to draw—at best, the store was an 'overgrown delicatessen'.

Analysis of the brand's situation showed that Safeway's main strength was among young singles and couples, and fell off sharply among families—and the demographics were moving strongly against this pattern: the store had to find new users among mothers of—especially—young children. It was decided to go out for this market, recognizing that hitherto the brand had seemed to have little to offer to this group, who had, accordingly, deserted in droves.

This finding led first to changes in store provision of mother-and-baby facilities, and in product ranging. The need then was to find an advertising approach that could deliver the new focus.

The resulting campaign was built on the proposition that Safeway is 'the best ally a mother with young children can have'. To interpret this proposition effectively, the ads had to be able both to attract and charm and to persuade; they had to achieve action—a genuine change in consumers' behaviour. To do this, the TV campaign—and it was an early decision to concentrate the spend on TV, in contrast to the usual big grocer split between TV and press line-and-price ads— had to have the flexibility to both create favourable, relevant image for the store, but also to carry quite specific messages about merchandise and facilities.

The result was a campaign that saw the world entirely through the eyes of a two-year-old boy, Harry, and subsequently those of his (presumed) sister, Molly. They became nationally famous, and well loved, as research showed, and the effects on sales and attitudes to the store were dramatic.

Briefing

It is not enough for the planner to write the brief, get it signed off by the account director and—probably—the creative director, and then drop it off on the desk of the designated creative team. This is fine for a minor job within an on-going campaign, though even then it is probably worth a few minutes' discussion.

For a major new campaign, more is needed. The creative team needs to emerge from the briefing both knowledgeable and inspired with enthusiasm. This means that they have both to become immersed in the brand and be given a direction and momentum towards it. At some stage in the process, they need to go round the factory, visit the shops or restaurants, apply for the bank account or the loan, fly the airline ... They need to meet the people who make the products and run the business, the people who have to handle the customers (and their complaints and queries) ... They should get a chance to talk to consumers about the brand, or at least to be exposed to videos of consumers describing their experiences. They will need to have available the fact sheets, the brochures, the technical specifications.

Much of this is part of the pre-planning process, and it can produce the sort of insights that can be crucial for the eventual campaign. As the team absorbs the brand experience, the shape of the brief is being developed, and rough ideas are being developed in (at least) the back of the team's minds.

This all becomes crystallized in the actual brief, and what is then needed is to create an event that will reestablish the key points in everyone's minds before they go off and start the hard work. There are, obviously, an infinity of ways in which a briefing session can be made into an event. Certainly, it will be helped by a bit of 'theatre'. This can involve simply the use of the agency's presentation facilities to show video clips, display the product, and so on; but it could involve a carefully structured visit to one of the client's outlets or branches, or an 'away-day' in an unusual location.

Summary

- The creative briefing process is designed to guide and stimulate the creative team to produce brilliant advertising. The planner and the team should, ideally, work together to agree the brief.
- All agencies have creative briefing forms. These vary, mostly in fine detail, but are designed to be succinct and precise.
- A brief should bring the target audience to life, as literally as possible, and show how the audience is expected to relate to the brand and respond to the advertising.
- The core of the brief is the proposition: this defines the essence of the ad, and evolves from the brand positioning. Propositions may be rational or emotional, but frequently combine the two.
- The brief should provide the creative team with enough supporting evidence to back up the proposition—but not too much.
- Briefing the team can be a crucial factor in stimulating their enthusiasm. A good briefing can, and sometimes should be, theatre.

Questions to consider

- Take an advertising campaign you admire. Deconstruct it to arrive at the brief. Who are the target audience? What are their attitudes to the brand? What is the advertising trying to modify or strengthen in these attitudes? What is the proposition? What evidence do we find in the ads to support the proposition? What are the audience expected to do as a result of seeing the ad?

- Do the same thing for a campaign you dislike. Put yourself into the place of (a) the client, (b) the agency. What factors led to the eventual result? Are you still right to dislike it? Why did the client buy it?

- Take a brand—any brand. What questions do you need to answer before you can start to formulate a creative brief? How does this differ between, say, a packaged grocery brand, a savings account from a bank and a personal computer?

7 Creating the ads

Only connect ...

E.M. Forster

There used to be an agency on the west coast of the United States that had a statement about how to make good advertisements. It went:

- Rule 1. There are no rules.
- Rule 2. There may be exceptions to rule 1.

I do not intend to try to tell you how to create an ad. If you look at all that has been written on the subject over the years, most of what has been said concerns rules of style and form, not of content—simply because the best ads are, by common consent, those that are new and original, and no one has any very good rules for being new and original. Arthur Koestler discussed creativity (rather well) for some 600-plus pages in his *Act of Creation* and reached little more of a conclusion than that creativity involved unexpected leaps and unpredictable connections.

There are, however, a number of principles that can usually prevent the creation of positively *bad* advertising, and a substantial number of guidelines that may help refine the details of individual ads and enable them to work better. Since the world is full of very ordinary advertising, this may help to reach at least a good average standard. The problem is always to do better than that, and that is where creativity and imagination, rather than any rules, have to dominate. Much of the material in this chapter is based on research summarized in Giep Franzen's book *Advertising Effectiveness* (see Bibliography). Many of these principles are more or less general, others are specific to individual media.

General principles: Essential Elements

Branding and category identification

Any ad needs to make it clear what is being advertised—the product category and, most importantly, the brand. As Professor Ehrenberg has suggested, an important role for advertising is to enable the brand to say 'Look! Here I am'. It is possible, of course, to play a bit of a guessing game, and this is quite common on TV, where brand names are often not revealed until the end of the commercial; and in postmodern Britain, there is a small fashion for creating ads which take the conventions of one market sector, and turn out to be for another. Quite a good example of this during 1998 was the commercial for Vauxhall's Network Q Used Car programme, which was ostensibly about a man undergoing a fitness check.

Research evidence quoted by Franzen suggests that suppressing the brand name can be counter-productive: the earlier the brand name appears in a commercial, the more people will correctly make the link between ad and brand. You have to trade off this fact against the possible benefits of giving viewers a 'reward', in terms either of guessing the brand before it is revealed or of satisfying their curiosity towards the end. Equally, there seems small justification for the policy of a now-retired ad controller of a very large multinational who used to examine every new commercial, frame by frame, and reject automatically all those where the brand name failed to appear by frame 11.

Similarly, in press ads, there is a well-known desire among agency art directors to reduce the size of the client's logo or other branding devices, and a corresponding requirement among clients to have it as large as possible. It seems reasonably obvious that there is no point in being anonymous, though there may—just may—be some point in playing a bit of a 'guess the brand' game in some circumstances.

> *When the client starts to fret, make his logo larger yet.*
>
> *If he still remains refractory, show a picture of his factory.*
>
> *But never in the direst case show a picture of his face.*
>
> Anon, 1950s

Attention-getting devices

Advertising has to attract attention, somehow, in order to penetrate the divided interests of the audience. There are far too many commercial stimuli fighting for our attention, and most are ignored. So, ads have to find ways of breaking through the noise.

This leads, frequently, to excess. Loud music, hectoring voices, the over-use of what are believed to be key 'trigger' phrases: 'new', 'don't miss this', 'listen', 'free', 'now'—frantic speed of delivery of voice-overs, funny voices, press ads full of starbursts and bold print, fast-cut TV commercials, flashing lights, the use of provocative headline words ('sex', swear words), exploitative sexy pictures . . ., and so on. The list is almost endless, though disappointingly predictable.

Looking constructively at the problem, it is clear that the keys to effective attention getting lie in a combination of the media context and the brand concerned. You stand a better chance of getting attention in a medium if what you are saying stands out in contrast to the programme or editorial in which it appears, *or* if it tunes in so closely with its context that it becomes almost seamlessly part of that context, and the reader or viewer is simply carried into the ad by the flow. Bearing in mind, too, that you are often going to be among other ads, a distinctive tone of voice—quieter, perhaps—may make the difference.

Then again, if the brand carries its own interest, because it has something new or fascinating to say, this is a far better way of getting attention—in its own right—than standing up and shouting. What's more, it has a better chance of working for the brand than a 'bolt-on' attention-getting device that can actually divert attention from the brand; you then get an ad that people notice, at least superficially, but no benefit for the brand.

It is notable that a significant proportion of UK ads in the 1990s have aimed to gain attention by being aggressively 'in your face' in one way or another. While this has worked positively for some, such as Tango, which appeals to precisely the young target market for which this sort of thing is often appropriate, it is a limited and limiting solution to the problem, since it risks alienating the target audience, or at least a large part of it.

In practice, it is probable that visuals are more important as attention-grabbers than words, especially for print ads: it is the ability of the advertiser to create fascinating, compelling, unusual—but relevant—pictures that will often make the difference. We are, psychologically, more responsive to pictures than words, and we can take them in much more quickly.

Analysis of factors in ads that attract attention, reported by Franzen, shows that attention can be influenced by size, colour, sound, intensity (loudness, bright colours), movement and directional signs. In terms of the qualities in a stimulus that help attract attention, novelty, surprise, uncertainty, unusualness and complexity (up to a point) all seem to encourage our interest.

Likeability

American research in the late 1980s (see page 52), since widely confirmed elsewhere, identified the likeability of an ad as a key factor in its effectiveness. People respond better to ads they like.

Likeability is a complex concept: it does not simply mean that an ad should set out to be humorous or to entertain. It means that the audience should feel that it is useful, informative, helpful, pleasing, constructive—and, perhaps, entertaining and/or humorous.

As should be apparent, this tends to run counter to many of the ways in which ads seek to attract attention, and emphasizes the problems associated with the more obtrusive attention-getting devices, since these can induce irritation.

By now, likeability is a common element in many TV strategies, and almost essential for cinema, but is less consistently aimed for in press. Part of the reason for this lies in the severely functional and informative nature of much press advertising, especially newspaper ads for retailers and financial services. It is notable, however, that press advertisers in these fields who do try to make their ads more palatable seem to do well; examples are Sainsbury's old magazine campaign featuring recipes, and the 'advertorial' ads run by a number of financial services companies.

Simplicity

In general, people are not particularly interested in what ads have to say. This means that ads have to have a straightforward, concentrated message, and to avoid confusing this message with extraneous matter.

On the face of it, this is a recipe for very boring ads—which will fail on the grounds of both attention getting and likeability—so it has to be recognized that simplicity on its own is not enough. What it does mean, though, is that the number of points that an ad tries to make has, in general, to be limited. This depends, ultimately, on the medium used and the nature and purpose of the ad, but it is a reasonable generalization that a single point made well and strongly will always be more effective than several different points, almost however well they are put across. Ideally, every ad should feature *one* key point, and this applies just as much to a long-copy press ad for a financial service or selling a complex product off-the-page as to a 30-second TV commercial or a poster. Posters, of course, are the ultimate discipline, because the maximum number of words that you can hope to use successfully is reckoned to be seven, and even fewer are better: quite simply, the amount of time available for scanning a poster as you drive past it limits the number of words you can take in. (In special situations—e.g. cross-track ads in the Underground—this rule does not apply, and people may read quite a long ad as they wait for the next train.)

The problem this raises lies in the fact already mentioned that one of the factors that encourages our attention is complexity: there is a quite difficult balance between the complexity that involves and attracts and that which alienates and irritates. The message is that it is all right to wrap up a simple thought in a relatively complex format, but that over-complication is risky.

Have an idea: be original

Implicit in the importance of novelty for getting and retaining attention is the need for originality. Ads that work tend to contain original ideas. The use of the word 'idea' here is important: it is not especially difficult to present a brand in a way that is novel—more or less. It is a lot more difficult to present it through the medium of an original idea, that says something new and interesting to the target audience and wraps it effectively around the brand. In the classic Heineken campaign, 'refreshment' is the basis of the brand's proposition, but the idea that the brand 'refreshes the parts other beers cannot reach', and the many ways in which this was executed over the years, is what made it a great campaign.

Heineken's new campaign, with the less immediately compelling line 'How refreshing. How Heineken', has, on first viewing, succeeded in taking the idea of refreshment a step further, quite successfully. The concept revolves around the appearance of new and practical solutions to long-standing problems—such as the habit of British utilities of digging up the same street in series, rather than joining together to use the same trenches. The only question, to my mind, is whether it has the potential flexibility, and hence long life, of the preceding campaign.

Offer the audience real benefits

One of the great—and true—advertising cliches is 'Sell the sizzle, not the steak'. In other words, make people salivate by offering them the rewards (or the anticipation) of the product, not the product itself. This heightens the desire for the product.

Mostly the benefits you offer should be those conferred by the product: the results people can expect to obtain by buying or using it. These are mostly fairly generic to the category (see Box 7.1), but the necessary trick is either to appropriate to the brand a key category benefit that no-one else is exploiting, to concentrate on psychological benefits that can be linked closely to the brand (as in most fragrance ads), or to create benefits for the advertising itself. The *category* benefit approach is, obviously, akin to the USP approach (page 81). By *advertising* benefits, I mean making the advertising itself so attractive and 'more-ish' that people will get a benefit from it. The classic example of this from recent years is the Nescafé Gold Blend 'soap opera' campaign, which attracted a large following for a number of years, as people watched the progress of the mini-romance between the two protagonists. In the same way, beer marketers often say that consumers 'Buy the ads, not the beer'.

Box 7.1   Product benefits: some examples from different categories

Fast-moving consumer goods
Tea: Relaxation, pick-me-up (Tetley), sociability/entertaining (PG Tips).

Cheese:	More interesting sauces, quick and nourishing snack (Philadel-phia), easy sandwiches (Kraft Slices), traditional country nourishment.
Canned soup:	Warmth, quick simple meal(Cup-a-Soup), homeliness (Baxters), comfort, reward, relaxation.
Perfume:	Sexiness (So), attract opposite sex (Impulse), impress friends (Red), fantasy (Chanel No 5), escapism (Amarige).

Durables

| Microwave: | Quick and easy catering, new kinds of recipes, quick defrosting, easy to use up leftovers = less wastage. |
| Car: | Very wide range—status (Lexus), family transport (Megane Scenic), 'Be a rally driver' (Subaru), freedom (Discovery), security (Volvo), sexiness (Peugeot 306, Megane, Alfa Spider). |

Services

| Insurance: | Peace of mind (BUPA), reliable assistance (CU), quick and easy purchase (Direct Line). |
| Fast food: | Quick family meal, trust, cheap good food (all McDonald's) |

Be careful with humour

Some of the great figures of advertising, such as Claude Hopkins and David Ogilvy, have been extremely scornful about the use of humour in advertising. No one, they have said, buys from a clown. This may be true of their special field of expertise direct-response, off-the-page press advertising but it is manifestly untrue in general, even in terms of straight salesmanship. Go to London's Petticoat Lane market on a Sunday, and see for yourself how humour sells.

Nonetheless, there is a need to be a careful with humour. Obviously, there are some product categories where humour is clearly inappropriate, if not actually in bad taste (which may be seen as a recommendation for it in some circles!). Equally, humour can get in the way of an advertising message, unless the proposition and the brand are very carefully integrated into the joke. Finally, of course, you come up against the ultimate problem of all humour. Some jokes are simply not very good, and some people don't get them even when they are good. (And, of course, if you want to use a humorous campaign internationally, you run straight into the well-recognized problem that national senses of humour differ very markedly: a rib-tickling joke in Japan may go down like a lead balloon in China or France, or wherever.)

A number of analyses of the contribution of humour to advertising, including Franzen's, show that humour tends to contribute to advertising recall and liking, but may be slightly less good at persuading or modifying attitudes. Humour can get in the way of an argument. Overall, however, it is clear that there are benefits to be had from getting humour right, and its ability to be liked is an important incentive to try.

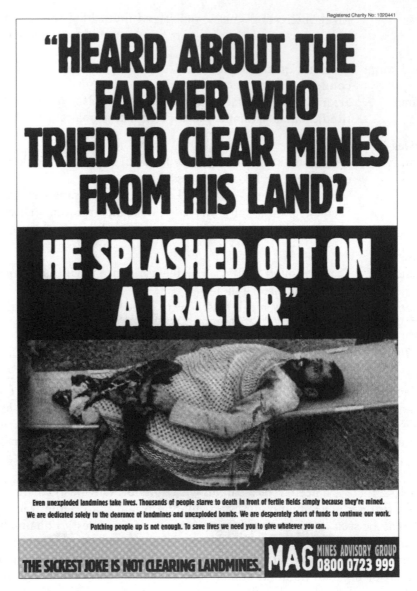

Charity ads often use sensational images to attract attention

Sex sells

Well, yes, it does, but then so does almost any other powerful emotion. What's more, you have to be careful with sex (just as in real life). Political correctness and the industry's self-regulation system (Chapter 15) combine to restrict the uses of sex to the subtle or the relevant—it makes perfectly good sense to use sex to sell a fragrance (the Impulse *Art School* TV ad is a recent classic), but the Advertising

A humorous, appropriate use of sex in an Impulse commercial

Standards Authority (ASA)'s monthly reports regularly carry complaints about car parts firms and office equipment suppliers using near-naked women as attention-getting devices (or worse) in totally inappropriate settings. Yes, sex sells, but really only in the right media, to the right audience, for the right product.

Include a response opportunity

It is perhaps a small exaggeration to say that *every* ad, in any medium, should include a means for the consumer to contact the advertiser—a telephone number, an address, an Internet URL, a coupon or whatever. Increasingly, however, ads do include response devices, and this reflects two things: the rapidly growing recognition among brand owners that establishing, or at least facilitating, direct contact with customers and prospects is a good thing, and the apparently growing desire among consumers to make such contacts. (I say 'apparently' because the growing body of reported evidence for this[1] seems to me to be so closely tied to the rather evangelical approach of the direct marketers I am by no means convinced that the research is as objective as it should be.)

At the very least, the inclusion of an address or phone number can be interpreted by the consumer as a sign of willingness on the part of the advertiser to be open and approachable. More constructively, as distribution channels change and become more complex, it is likely for most brand owners that a more direct relationship with their end-users will become desirable, so that the start of accumulation of a database of interested customers or prospects can never come too soon. (The important thing, of course, is to be sure that you do something with the responses, if any, when you get them.)

---

[1] From, e.g. D. Peppers, and M. Roger's, *The One-to-one Future*, Piatkus, London, 1993, onwards.

Box 7.2   Response devices and their uses

Response devices in approximate order of effectiveness (varies by category)

- ☐ Address in copy
- ☐ Coupon
- ☐ Phone number in copy—not freephone
- ☐ Phone number in copy—freephone
- ☐ Website/email address
- ☐ Phone number as baseline/headline/feature—not freephone
- ☐ Phone number as baseline/headline/feature—freephone

Using response

- ☐ Make a sale
- ☐ Send information—follow up by (e.g. mail or phone)
- ☐ Collect addresses for future mailing
- ☐ Collect addresses and customer/ contact details for analysis and future contact
- ☐ Collect addresses and details for cross-analysis with other data sources, to facilitate market understanding and marketing planning
- ☐ Develop resulting database to establish regular, interactive contact ('dialogue') with customers.

Individual media

The principles listed above apply pretty much across the board, though exactly how they do so may vary slightly according to the medium used. What I want to do now, though, is to consider creating ads for different media, since the process does vary between them. It essential, too, that when the original creative thinking for a campaign is being done, the team are aware of the different ways in which the campaign idea may be used. There are undoubtedly campaign ideas that *only* work in film, in press or even on radio, but as the practice grows of looking for integrated campaigns that operate across several media and also below-the-line and in support materials, it becomes vital to think in this way.

Press

We all recognize a press ad. It has a headline, a picture, some body copy—perhaps with subheads—and, at the bottom, possibly a coupon and the company or brand logo. Maybe there is a slogan or footline, too. Sometimes there is no picture, and the amount of the copy may vary from very little to what seems like half a book.

Exactly why it looks like this (usually) has good reasons behind it. We are used to books and newspapers being laid out in this way, and the layout feeds the 'natural' way in which our eyes will tend to scan the ad—for the 0.3 seconds we allow ourselves before we may decide to turn over.

What this is, however, is basically a formula. And a formula goes right against the guidelines that have been suggested for attention getting. So, what can we do about it?

Clearly, we have to be able to inject originality and ideas into our ad somehow, or it will be just another flipped-over, unseen ad.

Words or pictures?

Pictures can speak to us more quickly and powerfully than words, so, if we can produce a powerful, relevant picture, we may have started to crack the problem. Much good press advertising relies very heavily on imaginative or evocative or quirky pictures for its effect. If you use pictures as the key, they should reveal something about the brand and the story you want to tell, but, ideally, not all of it—you do want people to read the words (however few) as well. (A possible exception here is fashion advertising, where the picture can usually say all that is needed.)

To take a recent example, Sanatogen Gold ran the ad shown in Plate 14 in a men's magazine. The hunky gold body looks pretty good—but why is it gold, and why is the man carrying two foil boxes? You have to read the copy to find out—and, if you do, there is at least a good reason to think about a product you may find relevant.

Pictures, of course, do not have to be photographs. They can be drawings, paintings, cartoons, collages, computer graphics or whatever. It does not, in principle, matter what technique they use, as long as they fit the product and the message the ad is trying to convey. Before 1960, for example, almost all fashion ads used illustration, but nowadays they are mainly photographs—which suggests a possible advantage for anyone who thinks of going back to illustration . . .

But it's not always easy to find a good visual idea, and press ads have traditionally relied heavily on words. Words in the headline to seduce the reader into the ad, and words in the body copy to put across the product story. When ads are approached like this, any illustration often becomes pretty much a bolt-on addition—something to help the reader identify the product category. Somewhere, there's a list of the commonest words appearing in headlines: it consists of short, punchy, magical words like 'new', 'free', 'now'. You can argue whether this betrays a paucity of imagination—bearing in mind that the vast majority of ads are, at best, pretty ordinary—or, perhaps that these words have great power, and should therefore be used.

Thinking back to what I have said earlier, they score on simplicity and relevance, but they certainly score zero for originality. What they are, of course, is a valuable shorthand, which may be useful when the message is essentially promotional. They say little when the ad is supposed to be helping to build a brand, or even selling an expensive item off the page.

The English language is a rich, evocative flexible tool, that cries out to be used more imaginatively than is implied by the suggestion that every headline should include one of the most-often-found headline words. If you have not got a picture, use the words to paint one. It can even be done for a promotion: for example, '*The swallows are heading south, El Nino's creeping east and the wrong kind of leaves are starting to fall. Relax. Why not winter in a Rover 200 with 0% APR from just £8,995?*' as John Meszaros said in an article in *Admap*,[2] 'Poetry, that'.

This cuts across one of the classic 'rules' of direct response advertising: 'put the proposition in the headline'. In other words, do not mess about with clever plays on words or allusions to obscure corners of English literature. If you are offering people 'This Magnificent Hand-crafted Figurine for only £37.99', put it in the headline and get on with it. As the best textbook on direct marketing, Drayton Bird's *Commonsense Direct Marketing*, makes clear, this is, like all rules, a good one but not infallible.

Size and shape

Research shows that larger ads are more effective than smaller ads—though not directly in proportion: a page is only some one and a quarter times as effective as a half page (Figure 7.1). It may be perfectly adequate to use a series of smallish ads to achieve the same effect as a few large ads, and, as we shall see in Chapters 9–12 on media, there are some good arguments in favour of this.

Agency creative directors will always tend to favour large spaces—whole pages or double page spreads (DPS)—because these both feel more important and provide more room for a layout with space and scope in which to work: smaller spaces can very easily become crowded and unattractive, and 'white space'—often anathema to the client—enables the ad to breathe and look attractive. Ultimately, it all depends how much information or material you wish to put into the ad; you cannot expect to run a direct response ad for a music club or a book club, offering a whole range of titles, in a half-page ad.

Sheer practicality suggests that, at least in newspapers, there is often a strong case for using what we call 'page-dominant' sizes: a 38 cm × 6 cols ad in a broadsheet paper, or a 25 cm × 4 cols ad in a tabloid. Using these spaces means that the ad will

---

[2] Car wars: does size matter?, *Admap*, February 1999.

Ad size	% recognition	Index
<250 mm	24.5	49
250–562 mm	29.8	59
563–937 mm	38.8	77
938–1312 mm	42.2	84
1313–1625 mm	44.5	88
1625–2000 mm	45.8	90
2000–2250 mm	48.7	96
2250–2750 mm *	50.5	100
2750–3375 mm	54.8	109
3375–5000 mm	56.7	112
>5000 mm	63.0	125

* Full page size.
Note: These Dutch data replicate 1960s UK studies, and are closely paralleled by more recent UK studies—e.g. Cardillo and Walker, *Admap*, January 1998.

Figure 7.1. Ad size and ad recognition percentage of readers (Source: NIPO studies of *Het Paroel* newspaper, 1972, in G. Franzen, *Advertising Effectiveness*)

normally appear as the only ad on the page, and be set into editorial material. This enhances the chance that the reader will look seriously at the page concerned, and find it quite difficult to avoid your ad.

A similar consideration is the shape of the ad. Publications do not, on the whole, like 'funny' shapes, (see Mercedes A class ad, page 102) though it is sometimes possible to negotiate special arrangements, and from time to time one or two magazines have offered incentives to advertisers to find new and original shapes for their ads. There is some evidence, however, that, for example, a *horizontal* half-page or third of a page is more effective than its vertical equivalent, presumably because it works better with the way we read a page. It's also possible, of course, to run your ad in the 'wrong' direction on the page, like Cadbury's long-running series of cartoon strips for *Time Out*, which is run vertically on its side. However, this can irritate readers, rather than attract them, and is usually a device of desperation.

In magazines, you can play more complex constructional games, with gatefolds and fold-outs and scratch-and-sniff patches, and the like. Or, if you are a computer wholesaler, you can fill the pages of *What PC?* or *PC World* with a 16-, 32- or even 64-page catalogue ad, which is, of course, simply using the magazine as a relatively efficient way of distributing a catalogue to a well-defined target group.

A distinctively shaped ad for a novel car design.

Colour

Colour attracts. It creates or enhances moods and emotions. It provides contrast or emphasis. It can become a brand 'property'—think of Marlboro and red, or, in the UK, Cable & Wireless and yellow (Plate 16) (except that two or three other advertisers are using the same yellow ...). It can become associated with quality, but that depends on the colour and the quality with which it is reproduced. And, of course, as ever, you can create a contrast, and so stand out, by being wholly or predominantly black and white in a mainly colour environment.

The poor man's version of full colour is, of course 'spot' colour—the use of a single colour to highlight or enhance some elements of the ad. This is common in retail ads in newspapers, and can help the ad to stand out—or to look extremely tacky! (see Plate 1).

Formats and genres

There are a wide range of more or less standard types of press advertisement. Look through a few newspapers, and you will quickly recognize them. A few examples are shown in Box 7.3.

Box 7.3

- The retail sale screamer: loud headline, lots of products, starbursts, exclamation marks, big prices, heavy use of a close-out date—Allied Carpets, Dixons, Currys.
- The financial services comparison: a table of apparently comparable product features from competitive products, carefully selected to demonstrate our brand's superiority—Direct Line.
- The advertorial: heavily used now by more complex financial services products—Bank of Scotland, Plate 10.
- The pseudo-quiz. Always a good attention-grabber—Virgin One, Plate 15.
- The brand icon—common for fragrance, fashion—Estée Lauder, Plate 12.
- The classic off-the-page, long-copy, every-detail-you-could-ever-want-to-think-about, including many you never ever thought of ...—Plate 5.
- The move-the-metal car promotion—Fiat.
- The topical opportunist—Guinness.
- The celebrity endorsement—Nike.
- The cartoon strip—*Time Out*.
- The recipe ad—Uncle Ben's, Sacla (Plates 3, 4).

Television and cinema

Most agencies like TV. It has large budgets. Most agency creatives like TV, because the opportunity to play with moving pictures, music, sound effects, special effects, a whole variety of styles and genres, is exciting and stimulating. Their peers respect it. What's more, there is plenty of evidence to show that TV delivers—just so long as you can afford to use enough of it. The problem, of course, is that simply because TV is so powerful and versatile, it is often quite difficult to reconcile the creative potential of the medium with the hard-headed need to sell the brand advertised.

As TV has developed, too, the techniques and methods of using the medium have evolved, and the range of technical possibilities has proliferated. In particular, the suite of electronic special effects available to the film-maker has become enormous, varied and very exciting.

The secret of creating good TV commercials lies, therefore, in never forgetting the brief: what we are advertising, what we have to say about it , and what sort of people we want to say it to. Whatever the flights of fancy that may be encouraged by the medium, its use has to remain anchored in the realities of the brand and the marketplace.

There are two ways in which we can meaningfully think about TV in the abstract: in terms of genres of commercial and in terms of techniques.

Commercial genres

If you watch enough commercials, it becomes clear that there are, in practice, a quite limited range of commercial formats or genres that are in common use. (see Box 7.4)

Box 7.4   *TV Commercial genres:*

Typical formats	*Example(s) (1998–UK)*
□ *Product-based*	
Demonstration	Land Rover, Ronseal
Product story (manufacture, ingredients,etc)	Tetleys Tea, BMW
Competitive contrast/challenge	The Pepsi Challenge, Daz
□ *People-based*	
"Slice of Life"	Detergents, frequently
Mini-drama (series,even)	Nescafe, NatWest, Stella Artois
□ *Borrowed fame*	
Endorsement	Nike, Egg (Prudential)
Parody/pastiche (of film/ads/sitcoms)	Boddington's
□ *'Using the medium'*	
Drama	AA, Commercial Union
Song-and-dance	Halifax, Nationwide
Cartoon	Tetleys Tea, Bud Ice

Different genres tend to become associated with particular product categories—which may be a useful way of letting the viewer know what sort of product to expect, but can lead to over-conventional thinking. Most car commercials, for example, involve a substantial element of product demonstration and product story, though there's sometimes at least an element of drama or slice of life in them as well. Think of the Peugeot 406 launch film, which combined product, drama and song-and-dance, or the Peugeot 306 commercial with Kim Basinger, which has endorsement, a mini-drama, a fair amount of sex and a little product demonstration, or Renault's long-running Clio campaign, which eventually received massive PR coverage when Nicole got married in the final ad in the series.

As these examples show, within a slightly longer-than-standard film, it is possible to mix-and-match genres, and still tell a coherent story. Nonetheless, if you stick, as the majority of mainstream UK commercials do, to 30 seconds, there is a strict limit to what you can get into a film. (For the Japanese, who have a 15-second 'standard', the problem is worse still.) For a start, the number of words that can be spoken coherently in the 26 or so seconds actually available for speech in most films is no more than about 70 to 80 (though a race commentator in full flow could certainly fit in nearly twice that, and one or two retail sale ads seem to be doing the same).

Then, again, you have to think of the 'essential' ingredients: the product itself, and—usually—some reasonably clear pack identification; very probably some words 'supered' on the screen, to provide information (perhaps a contact phone number), or to satisfy legal requirements (which is why financial service ads contain so much statutorily dictated illegible small print); the brand's slogan or standard endline; perhaps some music associated with the brand … and so on.

Just as press ads have a standard 'shape' to their layout, which fits well with the way we are accustomed to scan a page, so a TV film has, usually, a more or less coherent order and sequence to it. It tells, in one way or another, a story—however implausible or unlikely. It has a beginning, a middle and an end. If it does not, it risks losing a large part of its audience, very quickly. By all means build in a joke or a surprise, but if you mess about with the more or less logical sequence of a commercial, you will usually be in trouble.

Techniques

Go to film school, or spend enough time in the cinema, and you can imbibe an immense range of techniques with which to embellish, enhance or—if you get it wrong—wilfully damage a commercial. In particular, modern electronic editing suites and equipment enable the film-maker to achieve an amazing blending of materials and scenery, without ever leaving the studio. You want a tropical beach? Shoot your scene in the studio, and we'll put in the beach, footprints in the sand and all, later.

This means, of course, that Ford can make a commercial for the Puma featuring a long-dead actor; that the old Holsten Pils campaign could insert the brand into a variety of ancient movie scenes. It enables commercial directors to imitate the innovative techniques of films such as *Who Killed Roger Rabbit?* and *Toy Story*. It makes possible, and wholly convincing, the instant-replay sequence in the Orange Tango commercial, or the dazzling series of effects in the Smirnoff cinema campaign (Plate 6). It offers every possibility of turning the most unpromising material into a nearly worthwhile commercial.

But not, really. Technique is no substitute for an idea. And all the window-dressing in the world won't sell the unsellable. So techniques like these are there to assist the message of the commercial to get through—by clarifying the story, by adding that magic likeability that, research shows, makes a commercial more likely to be effective, by helping to attract, intrigue and involve the viewer in something that, if the truth be known, is of very little real or pressing interest.

Similarly, techniques are quite capable of getting in the way of comprehension and attention. A classic TV technique, available and in use since the 1960s, is the use of unnaturally quick cuts from one scene to the next. Directors love it, because it speeds up the flow of the commercial and enables them to cram more scenes into their 30 seconds. Consumers, whenever a researcher asks them, mostly hate it: they find it confusing and irritating. And that's true even of the younger generation of consumers who have grown up with it—the 'TV-literates' who are supposed to be so clued up on ad techniques that they can deconstruct the most obscure piece of commercial film-making into its objectives, strategy, etc., without breaking sweat.

Music

Music, guessed Shakespeare's Orsino, is the food of love. For the commercial-maker, music is, perhaps, the food of love for the brand. Few commercials are without music—and those that are are usually charmless hard-sell face-to-camera exhortations to visit a retailer's Blue Cross Special Sale. (In the UK, unlike the US, Blue Cross has nothing to do with suffering animals ... unless we include the bargain-hunters.) There is surprisingly little published analysis of the effects of music, either in general or of different kinds, on the effectiveness of commercials. I know of one recent pioneering article by Alan Branthwaite and Rosie Ware,[3] which formed the basis of a subsequent ESOMAR presentation, and one unpublished dissertation. Franzen, as far as I can see, does not mention the subject.

Yet, to both the professional and the viewer, music is central to a substantial proportion of the commercials on TV, and there are clearly specific criteria in the creators' minds for the choice of the 'right' music to enhance the film and,

---

[3] A. Branthwaite, and R. Ware, 'The role of music in advertising', *Admap*, July/August 1997.

especially, to create an appropriate mood. In some cases, the music is an established part of the brand's advertising; however it got there in the first place. This tends to be classical music, which is seen, rightly or wrongly, as timeless. Hovis is inextricably linked with the first movement of Dvořák's *New World* symphony; until finally banished from the screen, Hamlet cigars relied heavily on Bach's *Air on the G String*; Ferrero Rocher has used the same, specially-composed, rather tinkly music for nearly 15 years. In some cases, too, someone has asked for 'a bit of background music', and then someone else has suggested, yet again, 'Spring' from *The Four Seasons*, which is probably the most used ad-music of all. Pop, or mainstream, music may be more dynamically used. M People's *Hero* provided an excellent track for the launch of the Peugeot 406, and Levi's has used a string of hits, selected to fit the mood of their ads, while Allied Dunbar's *There May be Trouble Ahead* seems to have had an influence on the rediscovery of classic hits of the 1930s and 1940s.

Ideally, the objective should be quite subtle and specific. It is to use music that will—with luck—be familiar to the target audience, and will have appropriate associations (or even lyrics) to fit the brand. The late Bob Peyton developed a theory when he was at JWT in the late 1960s that the ideal tunes for selling to anyone— especially a housewife—were pop songs current in the target group's late teens, since this was the age at which they would be most involved with pop music, and it was likely that the music would carry powerful emotional memories.

Then, of course, there are jingles: little songs about the brand. They used to be very popular, but are now mainly seen as old-fashioned and rather silly. The available evidence suggests, in fact, that jingles get in the way of comprehension and remembering of the ad message.

Voice-over and dialogue

Virtually all commercials include at least a few words. These may be dialogue between characters, a voice-over commentary, or a combination of the two. In many cases, the voice-over will be a 'famous', recognizable voice—Joanna Lumley and Penelope Keith are two that seem to crop up everywhere. At a guess, the benefit to the advertiser comes more from the 'voice's' sheer professionalism, rather than audience recognition, but there may be some benefit from the celebrity association.

Dialogue—so long as it is well written—is likely to make an ad more interesting and involving, but raises a major problem in international advertising: how do you translate it or adapt it? For a British audience, at least, dubbed commercials are a major turn-off: people are sufficiently sophisticated to want lip-sync, and object to anything cruder. Other countries, used to dubbed US films as staple TV fare, may be less critical, but there is still the inevitable problem that different languages work out at different lengths for any but very loose translation, and a well-crafted script needs precision in its transfer to another language.

Writing the script is an art in itself. It's an art where economy of expression is key, and rhythm is important. The only way to learn this is to watch and analyse a lot of commercials, and to practise, practise, practise.

Commercial length

TV commercials tend to be 30 seconds long. That happens to be the unit we all started with, at least in the US and UK, and it is the unit that pricing and thinking about TV advertising works from. What's more, all the evidence suggests that, except in some special cases, it is a pretty good length, too. Franzen suggests that 30 seconds is more effective than either longer or shorter lengths; and there is now US sales modelling evidence showing that the recent fashion for using cut-down versions of 30-second films (in the US, 15 seconds, in the UK 20 or 10 seconds) to increase frequency and reduce costs is not very effective.[4]

One area where longer commercials are not only common but almost essential is the growing market for direct response TV (DRTV). If you are going to sell a product or service sufficiently effectively on TV to get a positive response from viewers—even if it's only a request for more information—you need more time and elbow-room than a 30-second ad allows. DRTV ads are usually at least a minute long, and some of the specialist shopping channels on cable TV carry so-called 'infomercials' that are a good deal longer. These are the TV equivalent of fact-laden long copy ads in the press.

Radio

Radio is just like TV, but without the pictures. Unfortunately, that seems to be the way most creatives treat it. To be fair, there is good evidence for what the researchers call 'visual transfer', when a radio commercial based on the sound track of a TV ad can be shown to bring to the minds of listeners the visual scenes from the TV ad.

The Radio Advertising Bureau has published an illuminating critique of a sample of UK radio ads,[5] which describes the various ways in which radio ads are created, in terms of genre and format and a good deal of their content. Much of this is very similar to TV practice, with two major exceptions: radio has a much larger element

---

[4] See, e.g. M. von Gonten, 'Tracing advertising effect: footprints in the figures', *Admap*, October 1998.
[5] C. Wilson, *The Grammar of Radio Ads*. Radio Advertising Bureau, London, 1998.

of straight 'pitch' advertising; a very high proportion of the rest is–or tries to be—humorous. An astonishingly high proportion of the humorous ads are poking fun at other ads or ad genres. The RAB book makes clear that this self-referential approach is evidently very popular among agency people, but considerably less so with the clients who are big spenders on radio.

What appears to be happening is that radio ads have become locked into stereotyped thinking, and that there is a need to break the apparent 'rules'—as ever, the recommended route to potential success.

Summary

□ Creating good ads depends on creativity: having ideas. This cannot really be taught, though a good creative director can help the process develop and improve, by example and by advice and constructive criticism.
□ Correspondingly, the 'rules' that exist for helping create ads are, at best, guides to possible formats, suggestions as to how to organize the ad, lists of elements that should be included. While we have looked at these, and discussed a little why they should be so, this is not going to turn the reader into a top creative.

That is why the suggested task for this chapter is rather different:

Suggestions for development

1. Take a press ad, preferably for a brand that is being sold on its merits, not as part of a promotion. Analyse what it is trying to do—its target group, the key sales points of the brand, the benefits being offered, etc. Using this informa-tion—and anything else you may know about the brand—as a brief, write a script for a 30-second TV commercial for the brand.
2. Do the same thing for a TV commercial, converting it into a press ad.
3. What are the constraints—or opportunities—presented by these two different processes? Which is easier to do? Why do you think this is?
4. Could you now create a better ad than the originals you used, in either medium? Is this because you have had a better idea, or simply that thinking about the techniques used leads to better ways of doing the same thing?
5. Do you think either of the original ads you worked on was especially good? Why?

8 Evaluating advertising: How do you know it's any good?

It is not possible to make a realistic test of the effectiveness of a commercial ... in advance of real-life exposure

Alan Hedges, *Testing to Destruction*

If you manage a substantial brand, and the agency is developing a new campaign, you want to be reassured, before spending perhaps several million pounds behind the ads, that what you are doing will work. Moreover, your senior management will take a dim view of a campaign that invests large sums and then bombs. So, you will want reassurance, preferably from consumer research, that what the agency is recommending is right. What's more, because you are probably a numbers person, and your management, especially the finance director who has to sign off your budget, certainly are, you would prefer this evidence quantified. Indeed, since a new commercial may cost £300 000 to produce, and a series of them a good deal more, it would be nice to have this evidence *before* the investment in production takes place.

Even if you have not taken this precaution, you will certainly want evidence from the marketplace that the campaign, once running, is meeting its objectives—and, ideally, you would like early warning of success or, more vitally, failure.

We are, then, talking about two things: in the jargon, 'pre-testing' and 'post-testing'. As we shall see, post-testing now includes a variety of complex and sophisticated considerations, while pre-testing raises a number of difficult issues.

First, though, it is worth thinking about how you should set about judging an ad.

Is it a good ad? Why? Why not?

If you are involved with advertising, you will find yourself, all the time, looking at ads and asking yourself these questions. When you are the client, or the agency account director, faced by the creatives' latest gem, it is your job to do the same thing. How should you go about it?

Basically, there are just three questions that are fundamental:

- Is the ad on strategy?
- Is there a real idea here?
- Is it fresh and/or original?

There is, also, a fourth, which inevitably intrudes. It should, ideally, be ignored, but rarely is:

- Do I like it?

Is it on strategy?

Assuming the strategy is clear, it should not be too difficult to answer this. You do have to remember, though, and it can be difficult, that the ad is usually designed to appeal to someone very different from yourself. You need to remember, too, that it is what people get out of the ad that matters—and that this will depend as much on the way it is said as on what is said. Further, a fact about the brand does not have to be spelled out if it is abundantly apparent from the visual—and vice versa.

Is there a real idea here?

How do you recognize an idea, or at least a relevant one? Arguably, it has two key features: it is at least slightly unexpected; and it works indirectly, through metaphor or simile or analogy, as well as directly. And, if it is any good, it is absolutely appropriate to, and tied in with, the brand. An idea enhances and expands the brand: it goes beyond the mere words in the strategy, and adds something to them.

Is it fresh and original?

You will find that creatives set great store by being original, and that the snidest criticisms in—for example—*Campaign*'s feature *'Private View'*, where creative directors review half-a-dozen new ads each week, are of ads that use recognizably borrowed ideas. This is fine and dandy, but, as someone once pointed out, there *are* only a few ideas available. What's more, the chances that a punter in Scunthorpe has seen the Japanese ad that is the basis for your new campaign, or even the cult movie that you have so cunningly pastiched, are slim. Consumers set no store by originality for its own sake: creatives do. What grabs consumers is what is to *them* a new, fresh, exciting, enjoyable way of looking at a brand or product category. So, does your new campaign provide this? Does it redefine the rules of your competitive marketplace in some way? If so, is it *relevant* to the consumer? Then, you may have a winner on your hands.

Do I like it?

The most difficult decision you will ever take is the one that says 'I hate it: but if you tell me it's right for the market, I'll run it'. Unless you are slap in the middle of the target group for your campaign, it really doesn't matter whether you like it, or not. It does matter whether they do: as we have seen, likeability is a key characteristic of successful ads. But remember, you will have to defend the ads to your colleagues: so be prepared!

Few people, however, are prepared to rely solely on their own judgement where large sums of money are concerned. Corporate cultures are all against it. So what can you do to use research to guide and confirm your decisions?

Pre-testing and creative development research

You will notice that the title of this section is more complex than the simple concept implied by the first paragraph of this chapter. This is because there are no easy answers to the problems involved, although the advertising business, and the market research industry with it, have devoted endless work-years trying to create them.

There is, of course, a simple philosophical problem: in spite of all the astrologers, prophets, forecasters and tipsters in the world, no one can predict the future. OK, it is possible to suggest a range of probabilities, in many cases, but, in essence, you prophesy at your peril. However, since all management relies on forecasts of one kind or another, this should not prevent us from trying. But we have to recognize that, somewhere along the line, our skill, experience and judgement are going to have to be the final arbiters.

The key, advertising-specific issue is that to try to predict what an ad might achieve in the marketplace, we have to have a very clear view of how advertising in general can work and of how the specific campaign under consideration will or should work. As I have made clear in Chapter 4, there are several different ways in which advertising may be expected to work, in terms of how the ads are conceived and the tasks they are expected to perform. It follows logically that any form of pre-test must be designed to reflect the way in which the ads should perform, and be carried out among the specific target audience that the ads are intended to influence. It is highly unlikely that a single test format can meet all contingencies.

But there is more to it than this. Most ad campaigns work, in real life, through a process of attrition and over time: the idea that a consumer will see an ad, and instantly go out and buy that brand, instead of their usual brand, on one viewing of the ad, is, objectively, nonsense. People are not like that. Alan Hedges, quoted at the head of this chapter, has a wonderful—though abbreviated—account of how a housewife is exposed to, and interacts with the ads for a group of competing fmcg brands, over a period.[1] This makes it vividly clear that, in the same way that we 'learn' a neighbourhood, sub-consciously and in parts, over time, so we gradually accumulate (and 'learn') thoughts and associations about a brand from its various forms of advertising—again, over a period of time. Eventually, we may even try a new brand because of this.

Pre-testing

In spite of this, many research agencies operate pre-testing systems that involve recruiting an audience to watch, in a typical example, a film show in a theatre. Into this a commercial or a series of commercials is inserted, much as in a TV commercial break. Before the show, they are asked a number of questions, more or less carefully masked, about the product category concerned in the test, and these questions include a form of brand choice designed to discover their preferences among the main brands in the category. After the film show, further questions are asked, which show how reported attitudes to the various brands may have changed after exposure to the commercial and, in particular, whether the brand choice has moved in favour of the advertised brand.

This enables the researchers to provide a measure of 'preference shift' or, as it is often called, especially in the US, 'persuasion', and of 'attitude shifts'. In each case, the percentages of respondents who choose the brand, or agree with a statement about it, before the test showing are subtracted from the percentage doing so after, to provide a plus (or minus) score.

These scores can be compared with accumulated 'norms' from previous tests, for the brand concerned, or for the product category, or—at worst—for similar product categories. 'Hey fellas, we scored a +5.4: it's a goer!!' A nice, single number that says it all.

Or not.

Obviously, what is being measured here bears no direct relationship to real life. But does it manage to separate sheep from goats, good ads from bad? The US research company rsc The Quality Measurement Company, who are the largest international marketer of this type of system, have devoted much effort to trying to demonstrate a correlation between high positive 'persuasion' scores and marketplace success. The arguments are complex, but I do not believe they have conclusively made their case. There are too many ads in their voluminous data that get excluded (often for good reasons) from analysis, and they have, of course, absolutely no idea what might

---

[1] A. Hedges, *Testing to Destruction.*, 2nd ed, IPA, London, 1998.

have happened if the ads that never ran as a result of rsc testing had done so. All they are managing to do is to show that where an ad scored reasonably well on their tests, *and* subsequently ran, *and* the advertiser allowed them to see the results, there is a fair chance that its marketplace performance was quite good. While this may be good enough for the play-safe manager, it leaves a lot to be desired as a universal testing system. You have to recognize that, at best, you are sub-optimizing.

Of course, rsc (and others) have worked hard to counter these criticisms, and, also to make their research more helpful to the advertiser and agency. In particular, they have developed more detailed questionnaires to help determine how or why an ad appears to be succeeding, or failing, to communicate (what we call 'diagnostics').

The rsc's form of straight preference-shift testing is not the only system around. Other research firms have developed approaches that are more focused on the how and the why of what the ad is achieving in terms of communication. Millward Brown, for example, has developed a system called the Link Test, where the 'link' has two meanings. The more important of these is based on the theory that successful ads have a core creative idea that is strongly linked to the brand: unless this is so, people will remember the ad and its associations, but not the brand, so that the ad is effectively wasted. The second meaning is that the results of the Link Test can be used to predict, with reasonable confidence, the key score, the Awareness Index , on Millward Brown's ad tracking studies (see below, page 121). In the same way, other researchers, such as Hall & Partners, have adopted the 'frameworks' analysis (page 46), and tailor their questionnaires to the objectives of the advertising, very specifically.

Nonetheless, it is clear that Alan Hedges' comment is, objectively, true. So, what use is there for 'pre-testing'? And, more importantly, at what stage in the development of the advertising can research be applied to help to ensure that we are indeed on the right lines?

Creative development research

Obviously, the first essential use of research for creative development is to ensure that the strategy is developing on the right lines. At a very early stage in the creative process, it makes sense to talk to real consumers about how certain ideas and ways of looking at the brand grab them—or fail to. A variety of very rough stimulus material—scrap art, snatches of music, rough drawings, tentative headlines or endlines for ads—can be used in qualitative research to confirm hunches about what may make a campaign work. Indeed, you can formalize even this stage of the exercise and carry out quantified research to rank in order of apparent attractiveness a range of appeals, concepts, product features, possible celebrity endorsers for the brand, and so on, though this will usually be more appropriate later in the process.

The aim of this sort of research is essentially 'creative': it is there to rule out obvious dead ends, but it is also intended to encourage new hypotheses and directions. It should, as far as possible, involve the creative teams directly, because contact with the target audience will improve their understanding of the task and the restrictions that people's sophistication and knowledge (or lack of them) may impose. On the basis of the research, the planner and the creatives can improve the brief and even the underlying strategy, and build a more rounded picture of where the brand can go, and how to steer it there.

The next stage is to develop ideas for advertisements. These will be debated within the account group and, ideally, with the client. Although some agency creative directors prefer not to show the client anything until there is a fully-fledged recommendation on the table, I believe that the process works best when the client is involved in creative development from quite an early stage. For this to happen, however, there has to be a high level of confidence in the relationship, on both sides.

Then, there is room for a further round of research. Again, this will usually be qualitative, and designed to find out primarily how well the ad ideas are communicating to the target group. Do they understand, quickly and easily, what it's all about? Are they interested? What personality for the brand is projected by the ads? Are there specific elements in any of the ads that seem to be especially intriguing/exciting/confusing/ new/strange, etc.? Does what is being put in front of them fit their idea of the brand or at least come close enough to be a realistic point to aim for? Do any ideas really grab them? Again, the aim should be to increase our—and particularly the creatives'—understanding. To help find out which words, which images, which thoughts carry resonance with the target audience, and can be used to build the brand. The whole process is illustrated schematically in (Figure 8.1).

Finally, we have the finished product—or, perhaps, a couple of alternatives. Ads that have been worked out in detail, and are ready for production. Can they be researched? What can research tell us? Is it valid to research them as (for TV) storyboards or animatics ('filmed storyboards', where the frames of the storyboard are filmed so as to give the illusion of movement, and music and voice over may be added to increase verisimilitude)? Or as roughs, for press ads? What type of research makes sense?

By this stage in the development process, we should have a pretty good idea of what may go wrong with the advertising when it is exposed to consumers. There will be issues of clarity and tone of voice; issues of emphasis; questions about particular characters in a commercial; concerns about the location or setting; and so on. Assuming that everybody is still on board with the strategy, the choice between commercials, if there is one, is likely to be one of style and personality, rather than of the ingredients in the message.

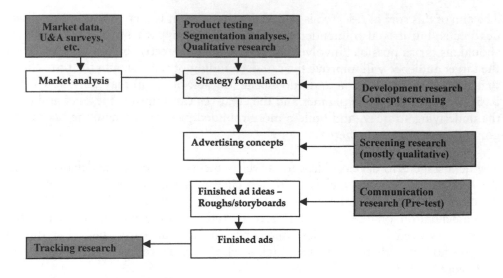

Figure 8.1.   The development research cycle

The key questions will be about the ads' ability to communicate effectively with the target group, in the way the ads are meant to work. Given a choice, we need to find out which approach appears likely to do this better, and why this is so. If we have one single candidate ad or campaign, we will want to know whether there are things in the ads that can be improved, and perhaps which of a group of ads would be the best to launch the campaign.

Either way, this is a stage at which we would be justified in carrying out a quantitative study: research that can confirm that consumers do—in the hot-house and artificial conditions of research—get the message and respond favourably towards it. We look, especially, for comprehension and liking, and for involvement with the ads.

There is an ongoing debate, especially within ad agencies, about whether it is possible to do this more or less final research on anything less than a finished ad—which may mean spending large sums on TV production, or photography for a press or poster campaign. Creative people will argue strongly that 'production values' are essential to the success of their film: I would argue that if the film depends so much on production values it will, usually, be inadequate for its task. In the UK at least, people are quite capable of accepting a rough ad or a storyboard, especially if they are given a simple explanation in advance. The only exception to this is where there is a use of special effects that is absolutely central to the idea—and even here it is surprising how far verbal explanation can take you. I bet that it would have been possible, for example, to research the Volvo 870 launch commercial, where the car morphs into a horse, without making the film first.

You will notice that even here, I am not suggesting that the aim of this research is to 'evaluate' the advertising against some numerical benchmark. Here I am with Alan Hedges. You can find out if the ad communicates, and you can use the research to check whether there is anything wrong with the way the ad is put together. If you've done the rest of the development work carefully enough, that should be sufficient to tell you whether you have a good campaign or not. And a score on a 'pre-testing' system will not help you. It is merely a comfort blanket.

Post-testing and campaign evaluation

The central buzz-word of the advertising business in the last half of the 1990s has been 'accountability'. Not just 'Does my advertising work?' but 'Can you prove that it not only works, but is worth it, in terms the financial director will understand and accept?' In a world where Lord Leverhulme's alleged remark that 'I know that half my advertising is wasted but I don't know which half' is still trotted out at every opportunity (there, I've done it again), this is challenging stuff. So much so that the latest trend in thinking on the subject is that it is too simplistic to look at the advertising in isolation, but we should be looking at the ROI (return on investment) on the whole brand marketing spend. (For the really advanced thinkers, this goes one step further, to looking at the ROI customer by customer.)

This is an important, and very complex, debate, which is beyond the scope of this book. Readers should, however, be aware of it, and recognize that the measurement of Brand Equity, which relates closely to the measurement of ROI on brand marketing investment, is an important, rapidly growing and controversial field.

Here I want to be more simplistic. We need to recognize that, as has already been made clear, advertising is only part of the marketing mix, and that its effects are likely to be enhanced (or, occasionally, diminished) by other forms of marketing communication investment. Nonetheless, it is perfectly possible to demonstrate that advertising, *per se*, works: the IPA's Advertising Effectiveness Awards programme has assembled over the years around 1000 case histories that demonstrate the fact, in a variety of different ways.[2]

There are many ways to assess the success of an advertising campaign. All of them require at least some market research, and some are complex and expensive. The

[2] Various editors, *Advertising Works*, 1–10, IPA, London/NTC Publications, Henley-on-Thames. 1982–1999.

experience of the IPA Awards programme suggests that, increasingly, the award-winners, who presumably represent the state of the art, are using several different approaches to demonstrate success—and, to meet the conditions of the awards, to rule out the influence of other parts of the marketing mix.

How do we know our advertising is working? A few suggestions:

- Sales have increased (beyond reasonable expectations).
- Market share has increased.
- More consumers are aware of the brand.
- More consumers have tried the brand, or are using it regularly ('trial' and 're-purchase').
- Consumers' attitudes to the brand have improved significantly, in ways that the advertising was aiming for.
- Consumer responses (coupon replies, telephone calls, etc.) have increased.
- Conversion rates from responses to sales have increased.
- The retail trade is willing to stock more/more retailers are stocking the brand.
- Our brand's price is higher relative to the market, with no loss of market share.
- Traffic ('footfall') in our stores has increased.
- People's behaviour has changed—more use of rear seatbelts/fewer teenagers taking drugs/more safe sex (public service campaigns).
- The media liked our ads so much/were so shocked by our ads that we obtained the equivalent of another £10 million in free advertising space.
- Brand profits increased over time by five times the advertising investment.

These, and more, can be found in any volume of *Advertising Works*. Which is right for you? And, more importantly, which will top management believe or accept?

And, anyway, how do we go about measuring them?

Box 8.1   *Time scales: realism in measurement*

Stock markets in the US and, increasingly, the UK, expect their member companies to report results quarterly. So, big companies' accounting practices revolve around quarterly reporting periods. Advertising is not, in most cases, a quick-return investment: effects of a single burst of advertising decay over anything up to nine months, and a campaign may have effects over years. It is therefore unrealistic to expect advertising results to look at all impressive on a quarterly basis, without a very sophisticated form of accrual accounting—which is not in place, anywhere. By contrast, most sales promotion techniques (money off, couponing, etc.) produce immediate and substantial short-term sales effects, which can look very good in a single quarter's figures. The only small, niggling problem is that there is a growing body of evidence to suggest that sales promotion, especially price reductions, can, unless very carefully handled, actually undermine a brand's longer term position: it encourages brand pro-miscuity, increases price elasticities, and can even affect brand image in negative ways.

One part of the solution, for advertising, lies in John Philip Jones's observation that ads that work over the longer term always appear to work in the short term: but this is a quite sophisticated argument, and may not impress non-marketers— evidence of short-term effects, even if they do not appear to pay back, would, however, be better than nothing. All the available evidence shows that ad campaigns rarely, if ever, actually pay back (cover their costs in terms of extra *profit*) in the short term.

Marketers have available a variety of tools—some of them distinctly expensive—to monitor the performance of their brands and, specifically, of the advertising. What follows covers just the main ones.

Sales and market share data

Sales can be measured, at their simplest, by ex-factory deliveries—but then you have to know a lot about the distribution chain to be sure that sales from the factory have any close relationship with sales to end-users or consumers. So, fmcg companies have for many years used *retail audit* services, where researchers check on a sample of shops, to measure consumer sales. In recent years, at least in the grocery sector, as electronic scanning (EPOS) has become almost universal, it has become possible to collect scanning data. In the US, this is widely and broadly available through specialist research firms, but in the more concentrated UK market it has proved less easy to obtain scanning data from the main players. Scanning is a key measurement factor, since it enables analysts to look at sales through grocers, or individual chains, on a weekly basis, and so to detect the effects of advertising, promotions, etc., very sensitively.

As an alternative to retail-based measures, research firms have established large *consumer panels*. Here, they are able to collect substantial volumes of demographic and psychographic data about the panel members, and purchases are registered by applying electronic scanners to the shopping as it enters the house. In some cases, these purchaser panels have also been used to collect media exposure data, and this has made possible the expensive but extremely powerful analysis of 'single-source' data (a current example of this is the TVSpan operation being run in the UK by TNSofres in conjunction with Meridian TV.[3] Purchasing information can be

---

[3] See, e.g. A. Roberts, 'Recency, Frequency and the sales effects of TV advertising', *Admap*, February 1999.

directly linked to media exposure, enabling the researcher to compare the brand purchases of people who have or have not been exposed to the brand's advertising. This has been the basis of the work of John Philip Jones[4] and others, which has shed considerable light on the relationship between advertising and brand purchase behaviour.

Box 8.2   *Market testing and test marketing*

The principle of market testing is simple. Instead of running a marketing programme in the whole country, you run it only in a small region, and compare the results with what happens in the rest of the country, where you do nothing, or continue with your normal activity. In the UK, this normally means using a TV region (Chapter 10), since research facilities are geared to these. In the US, one or more major marketing areas (DMAs—defined marketing areas) can be used. Obviously, assuming all other things are equal, the results in the test region can be compared directly with those in other areas, and provide a measure of the success or failure of the advertising (or whatever). There are, however, a number of problems involved in this procedure:

- The test region should, ideally, be statistically typical of the country as a whole. This is, in practice, often difficult to achieve, especially in the UK. 'Typicality' ought to cover not just the population demographics, etc., but also the retail trade, the quality of the sales operation on the ground, etc.
- It has been shown that results are much easier to read if not one, but several test areas are used. This is easy in the US, but difficult in the UK.
- Competitors may recognize that you are testing, and set out to disrupt the test, through special promotions or other activity.
- Your own salesforce may interpret their role as being to make the test succeed at all costs, and put in extra effort—or the regional sales manager may have a breakdown, and foul things up ...
- It may require quite a lengthy period before the results of the test can be read with confidence. By this time, the market may have moved on, competitors have taken counter-measures, and so on.

Nonetheless, major fmcg marketers, such as Unilever and Procter & Gamble, still use market testing extensively—though both may now use a whole country as a test area for Europe, or even the world.

Of course, if sales go up, this need not be due to the advertising, or to the advertising alone: and, for many brands, marketing success may be simply to keep sales at the same level, in a mature or declining market where competitive

---

[4] J.P. Jones, *When Ads Work*, Lexington Books, New York, 1995.

pressures are increasing all the time. We will need to be able, somehow, to separate out advertising effects from other influences. Nonetheless, positive sales movements when we have been advertising are—at least—encouraging. One way of getting a fix on this is by using a market test (see Box 8.2).

Market share data can be derived from the same research sources as sales: but panels are likely to provide more accurate data, especially for brands sold through a variety of types of shop. A gain in market share is likely to be a more positive result than a shift in sales, because this takes into account the state of the market. Again, however, it cannot automatically be attributed to the ads: other factors may be helping. It is a truism—often ignored by senior management—that you are unlikely to increase your share of a market by decreasing your share of the market's advertising effort (your 'share of voice'). If competitors have cut their expenditure sharply, a market share gain may be attributable more to this than to anything you have done yourself.

Consumer feedback

Apart from specific purchasing behaviour, information on how your target consumers are behaving, and how they are thinking about your brand and its competitors, is likely both to provide evidence of your advertising's direct effects and the potential means of diagnosing problems and refining future strategy. More or less regular consumer research is therefore a highly desirable part of post-campaign evaluation.

There are basically two ways of going about this. Traditionally, advertisers used to carry out an appropriate consumer survey before launching a new campaign, and then repeated the process, either at the end of the campaign or, if they were rich enough, at intervals throughout it. The latter makes most sense, because it avoids the possible problem of measuring what appears to be success, but is actually an incipient decline. Figure 8.2 shows what could happen. A measure is taken of brand X in January, before the campaign breaks, and in June, when it has finished. The score is clearly a lot higher: everyone is happy. But if a measure had also been taken in April (the plain bar on the chart)) it would be clear that the campaign had had a splendid initial effect, but that this was now wearing off.

This led to the modern practice of running so-called 'tracking studies', in which a relatively small sample of consumers—perhaps 100 or 200—are interviewed every week, and the results accumulated on a rolling basis. This has the effect of smoothing out the more or less random short-term fluctuations that will occur, usually purely as a result of sampling factors, and of providing a sensitive, continuous monitor of the brand's progress.

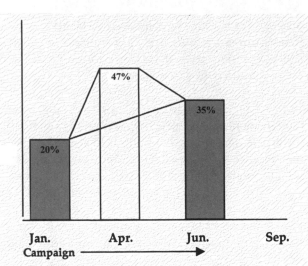

Figure 8.2.   The risk of infrequent measurement

By far the best-known tracking system, especially in the UK, is Millward Brown's. A Millward Brown survey can, of course, ask any sort of questions, but the key measure of advertising effectiveness that they have developed is the *Awareness Index* (AI). This provides a measure of the impact of the campaign, and can be compared against scores for a very wide range of other brands. MB start from the premise that the important thing about advertising is that it should be noticed and attributed to the right brand: they are not concerned with whether people remember any details of the ad itself, although they do normally ask questions to establish this, too. The key question is 'What brands of . . . (detergent, life assurance, small car . . .) have you seen advertised on TV lately?' (TV, usually, because this is the main medium for most major advertisers).

This question has proved to be sensitive both to the volume of advertising activity behind a brand and to the quality of the advertising. Given a percentage of the target group who say they have seen an ad for the brand, MB go on to calculate the amount by which this advertising awareness increases per 100 Gross Rating Points (GRPs).[5] For a new brand, the initial index will be, simply, the percentage aware divided by the 100 GRP weight of the campaign—23 per cent aware, from a campaign of 450 GRPs, gives an AI of 5.1, which is quite a good average score. For an established brand, however, things are more complicated, because the accumulated effect of advertising for the brand produces a steady level of claimed awareness, which MB call the *base*. The base changes over time: for a successful brand, with successful advertising, it will increase, over time. Then, to calculate the

[5] GRPs: one GRP represents 1 per cent of the target population having been exposed to an advertising campaign, so 100 GRPs is equivalent to the entire group being able to see the ad once. This is not, in fact, the case—see page 158.

AI at any one time, it is necessary to subtract the base from the total awareness figure, in order to arrive at the AI.

While the AI is a valuable indicator of the campaign's prowess, in its own right and in comparison with competitors, it is not, of itself, very informative. It provides no clues to advertiser or agency as to what is going right (or going wrong), and how to improve and develop the campaign. Any tracking study will, therefore, collect a range of data about people's claimed use of the brands in the market and their attitudes to them; and it will probably, also collect some information about the advertising itself; details of what is remembered, whether people like it or not, and so on.

Although Millward Brown can point to quite a good correlation between high AIs and increased market share, researchers are still trying to refine their understanding of what consumers are thinking about brands, to try to predict future shifts in brand shares. The model that a number of firms, including MB, are developing is based on the idea of brand loyalty or brand commitment. The idea is simple. In any market, especially competitive fmcg markets, most users of a category have a repertoire of brands that they buy or are prepared to buy—if their store is out of stock, has not got the right size, or whatever. If you ask people the right questions about how they view the brands in the market, you can place them on a sort of 'ladder', from complete rejection of a brand to almost religious enthusiasm for it (see Figure 8.3). From inspection of this ladder, or its equivalent, depending on the research company, you can divide the market into groups in terms of their relationship with your brand, and see how you stand against the competition. One object of marketing then becomes to push people up the ladder towards ever greater commitment to your brand; and you can analyse the data to identify which brand's less loyal users represent the best prospects, so as to target your advertising messages and media choice accordingly.

It is claimed that changes in this pattern of attitudinal loyalty appear before any change in more orthodox attitude measure of the brand, and in advance of any change in behaviour. A favourable shift in commitment to the brand should presage

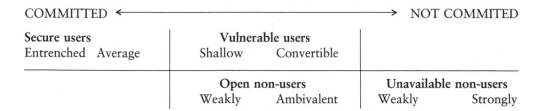

Figure 8.3.   The commitment spectrum (Source: R. Heath, 'Brand commitment as a predictor of advertising effect', *Admap*, April 1997)

an increase in brand share. This is in contrast to orthodox attitude measures, where experience suggests that changes in attitude are just as likely to *follow* a change in behaviour (for some reason you try a brand, and are then surprised how good it is) as to precede it (you come to think it might be worth trying the brand because you think it is good in some way, and then you try it).

Econometrics and modelling

All these measures are valuable. But they are mostly fairly imprecise, and they find it very difficult to separate out the effects of the advertising—specifically—from those of promotions, PR, point-of-sale displays, an increase in in-store shelf-space, and so on.

The only techniques that can begin to do this are those of econometrics—the building of mathematical models of the market, that can be manipulated to separate out the effects of advertising and other activity from each other. I will not go into any great detail about this. It is a technical subject, and needs considerable skill to do well: it is, still, part art, part science, even though its output is in the good scientific language of numbers. Essentially, modelling relies on analysis of a stream of data on the market over a period of time. The data need to include not merely sales and advertising expenditures, for the brand and its competitors, but also other marketing activity in as much detail as possible, together with information on prices in the market and—perhaps—measures of seasonality or the weather, of the progress of the economy or of consumers' confidence, and so on. Once the data have been assembled, they are statistically analysed to tease apart the relationships between them, typically through the use of multiple regression analysis, though other techniques are also used.

A very good, practical, but quite detailed account of how an advertiser might use modelling to measure the success of the advertising is given in Simon Broadbent's book *Accountable Advertising*.[6]

This kind of modelling can be quite depressing for the advertising person when first seen. It is usual for price to be far the most important factor in changes in market share in a market, often accounting for as much as 70 or 80 per cent. Advertising, by contrast, rarely accounts for more than 10 per cent, except for very short periods of time, and various forms of promotion can be considerably more potent in the short term. As Broadbent makes clear, it is necessary to carry out considerable experimentation with the data, in order to establish the best fit between the model and the real world. In particular, it is necessary to arrive at a workable estimate of the rate of decay of the advertising. There is plenty of evidence that a large part of

---

[6] S. Broadbent, *Accountable Advertising*, NTC Publications, Henley-on-Thames, 1998.

an ad's effect will occur as soon as it is exposed. But there is no doubt that even an individual ad, and certainly a campaign, will have an effect, of sorts, that carries on over time. If, therefore, we attribute all the effect of a burst of advertising to the period in which it occurs, our calculations will almost certainly be wrong. However, as Broadbent points out, we can learn a lot from gathering data systematically about the progress of our brand in its market, and using the data to plot relationships between our brand and competitors, and between the different factors we have measured for our brand.

Without going as far as modelling, we can use the analysis of the available data to develop the beginnings of a detailed picture of brand progress, which can be used to ask precise and focused questions of the model-builders.

Is there ever enough data?

Someone once defined management as 'decision-making under conditions of uncertainty'. Marketing is a field fraught with uncertainty: consumers are quirky and idiosyncratic, and the variety of the variables that can affect a market is huge. Few, if any, companies can afford to gather, on a regular basis, enough data to give them a perfect picture of their market—almost by definition, someone, somewhere, is going to introduce a new factor that the research system fails to capture and account for.

A reading of any volume of *Advertising Works*[2] will show how real-life managers and marketing analysts approach the evaluation of advertising campaigns, with whatever tools are available. It just sometimes needs a bit of imagination.

Summary

- Advertisements can be judged purely subjectively. A good ad: is on strategy; contains a real, relevant idea; and is fresh and original (to its target market).
- Commercial pressures dictate that ads should be researched, both before they run, to be sure they will work; and after they have run, to see how they have worked.
- Pre-testing should, ideally, be designed to improve the ads, and ensure that they communicate effectively. While theory says that you cannot test ads to predict their effects, much pre-testing sets out to do this.
- Post-testing, or tracking, aims to establish both that the ads have had the desired effect and to identify changes in consumer behaviour and attitudes that may be attributed to the campaign and/or provide clues for future development. This research is best done more or less continuously.

□ To fully understand the effects of the advertising, it is necessary in most cases to undertake mathematical market modelling, using the techniques of econometrics.

So, can you judge?

To begin to apply the lessons of this chapter, try the following:

1. Take the first ad in a magazine—any magazine. Is it any good? Why? Why not? What factors have you used in arriving at a judgement? Are you being objective or subjective? Have you looked at the ad from the target consumer's view-point?
2. Take the same ad. You have had this presented to you by the agency as the recommendation for the new campaign. What questions would you ask them about it? Why?
3. When you've heard their answers, you think you need some research. What factors will you take into account in planning the research? What do you expect it to tell you? Are there particular issues that you would want to explore?
4. You are responsible for advertising a new brand of ready meals. What market and research information would you hope to have in place to measure the success of the campaign? Realistically, how long do you think it would be before you could judge success or failure? Why? What factors are likely to affect this?

9   The media: where should we put our ads, and why?

Never mind the quality—feel the width

Vince Powell and Harry Driver: title of 1960s UK Sitcom

All advertisements appear in the media—or at least one medium (to be pedantic, but accurate). Nowadays, 'meeja' is a study in its own right, and within advertising it is the most technically complex and most rigorously researched part of the industry. As we have seen (Chapter 2), media as an ad agency function is rapidly being separated from the creative side of the business, and handled by specialist agencies. This seems certain to continue. The reasons are simple: media planning and buying are becoming ever more sophisticated, in the face of burgeoning volumes of research data about an increasingly extensive and fragmented range of media. What's more, there is a growing business for specialist media auditors—companies who advise advertisers on the quality and efficiency of their media planning and buying.

The available choice

An ad can appear almost anywhere. In all developed countries, and most of the South, too, by now, there are five main media available: TV, the press, outdoor, cinema and radio. These are rapidly being joined by the World Wide Web. They are important in different proportions in different countries, largely as a result of historical development, but it is generally true that the press (in total) is still ahead of TV (the most dynamic growth medium over the last 30 years or more), and that other media are considerably smaller.

In addition to the main media, there is a swarming host of other possibilities open to the advertiser. These are often described, in the UK at least, as 'ambient' media—because you meet them in unexpected places, unlike the (relative) formality and predictability of ads in the main media. Examples range from the traditional 'sandwich board' on someone walking in the street to railway signboards, public toilets (everywhere from the mirrors to the floors to the urinals themselves), cows beside motorways and railway lines, postcards on racks in cinema foyers and in restaurants and cafes, telephone kiosks (in London at least, in spite of the telephone companies' displeasure, an intensive medium for the sex industry), floors in

Media	1987	1989	1991	1993	1995	1997
Print	80.0	94.5	101.4	102.9	125.9	132.5
	57.7%	56.3	54.6	51.3	50.5	49.0
TV	41.7	52.3	60.6	72.1	92.0	103.3
	30.1%	31.2	32.6	35.9	36.9	38.2
Radio	10.5	12.8	14.0	15.9	19.4	22.1
	7.6%	7.6	7.6	7.9	7.8	8.2
Outdoor	6.1	7.7	9.1	9.3	11.5	11.9
	4.4%	4.6	4.9	4.6	4.6	4.4
Cinema	0.4	0.4	0.5	0.5	0.6	0.6
	0.3%	0.3	0.3	0.2	0.3	0.2
TOTAL	138.7	167.8	185.6	200.7	249.3	270.4

Figure 9.1.   World advertising expenditure, by Medium Current US $ million and per cent, 1987–97 (Source: AA. *World Advertising Trends*, NTC Publications, 1999)

shopping malls and railway stations, the lids of takeaway meals, the cups of golf holes, bus and train tickets, balloons and blimps, and so on … almost endlessly. Much of the time, you yourself are an ad—your T-shirt, the carrier bag from your last shop, your trainers, even your watch proclaim brands and the type of person (hopefully an admirable role model) who uses them. If it moves, or even if it doesn't, you can advertise on it, and there is probably someone out there actively trying to sell it as the next big new medium. Except that everyone knows what *that* is: it's the Internet.

Within many media, too, there is an increasing proliferation of channels and possibilities. In the UK, we have just seen the launch of digital TV, which offers, depending on how you count, another 150 or so channels on top of the 30-odd that were the maximum most people could receive previously. Since 1987, some 400 new consumer magazine titles, bringing the total to some 2500, have been launched. Commercial radio, which is only 25 years old in the UK, has grown to over 200 stations, and it, too, is going digital, so that the number of possible channels may multiply fourfold or more. Cinema, which was pronounced dead some 20 years ago, sees the opening of new multiplexes almost weekly, and audiences and adspends are rising. The poster industry, though its sites are limited by planning regulations, has, instead, seen a series of creative changes and developments, and a whole new marketplace in superstore posters.

The same phenomena are occurring, albeit on different timescales, all over the world. For example, commercial TV is relatively new in Scandinavia. The development of satellite, cable and digital TV all show different patterns, even within Europe, where one would expect developments to be fairly similar. As we have seen, commercial radio is quite young in the UK, but it dates back to the twenties in the USA, and has long been a major medium in most of continental Europe. Outdoor advertising is very different, traditionally, from country to country, using different sizes and shapes of ads, and different reproduction techniques—including hand-painting—and in much of the South it is still largely non-existent outside the cities.

In addition, the development of satellite TV and advanced telecommunications have led to the parallel development of international—indeed global—media. TV stations like CNN and MTV literally cover the world, as do the various TV interests of Rupert Murdoch's NewsCorp. Newspapers and magazines, chiefly those appealing to an upmarket, business audience, are printed on several continents simultaneously—or, if that seems inappropriate, they are translated to new markets, with some shared, some local editorial, as has happened with some of the world's leading women's monthly magazines, Vogue, Cosmopolitan, Marie Claire, and so on. (Of course, Reader's Digest has been doing this for many years.) This globalization of the media is paralleled by the development of global media conglomerates—NewsCorp, Time-Warner, Disney, Bertelsmann, Kirsch, Hachette.

Faced by all this, the task of the media planner and the media buyer has become awesomely complex. In this chapter, we look at the sorts of decisions and choices that the planner has to make. The following chapters will examine the special characteristics of each medium, and how it is usually bought: this will mostly be UK-focused, but some major differences from other markets will be pointed out.

Media choices

Traditionally, media planners were faced by two types of choice: the *inter*-media choice, deciding which medium or combination of media to use; and the *intra*-media choice, deciding where and how to deploy the advertising within the chosen medium or media.

Increasingly, however, this is changing. In particular, inter-media decisions have become more difficult and more important. Media planners now have to be willing to recommend that the budget should be used across a range of media, working together to achieve benefits of synergy; or even to suggest that there are better, non-media-advertising ways of spending the money—perhaps through a programme sponsorship deal, a direct mail campaign (direct mail's relationship with media remains quite distant—see Chapter 12), or some other event. Again, intra-media choices have become more elaborate: we decide to use TV, but do we do it through standard spot advertising, or programme sponsorship, or 'infomercials' or DRTV (Chapter 10)? We use newspapers, but do we simply advertise in the conventional way, or use inserts, or advertorials? (Chapter 11). We use magazines, but do we want scented pages, or scratch-and-sniff? Or can we negotiate a sponsored feature? Or a wrap-round cover?

Where do we start?

The budget

Usually, we start with a budget. As we have seen in Chapter 3, this is not technically the best place to start, but in practice this is the usual reality. The budget automatically limits—or tends to limit—media thinking. You do not get very much mileage on TV for £50 000. (Nonetheless, a recent analysis of UK TV expenditures by size showed that three-fifths of all TV advertisers were spending less than £100 000 in the medium—see Figure 9.2.)

A very crude way of illustrating this is to look at how much the expenditure of a given sum of money could give you, making some fairly basic assumptions about commercial length, page sizes, and so on, in different media. The standard planning measures used in media are, simply, two:

☐ *Cover (or reach)*: the proportion of the target audience that an ad, or a campaign reaches, expressed as a percentage.

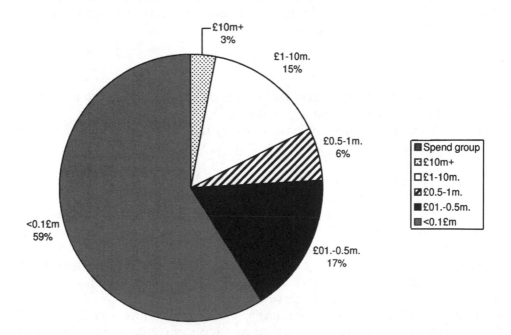

Figure 9.2. UK TV advertisers by size of spend (per cent), 1998 (Source: MMS)

□   *Frequency*: the number of times, on average, that anyone who is exposed to the campaign could see it. This is called OTS—'opportunities to see'.

An additional essential consideration is:

□   *The nature of the creative approach*: if the creative approach dictates TV, then TV is going to be the main medium (though cinema might be an alternative—and how about a version on the Web?)

Combining reach and frequency produces a measure of advertising weight that has a number of different acronyms. Because it started in TV, it is usually called TVRs (TV ratings) or, in the US, TRPs (TV rating points). From there, it was extended to other media, so we now talk of GRPs (gross rating points). One hundred GRPs means that the equivalent of 100 per cent of the target audience has been exposed to the ads once: 100 per cent cover ×1 OTS. In practice, no media work that way, so 100 GRPs will be made up of people who have seen the ad 1, 2, 3 or even more times, while some will not have seen it at all.

Opportunity to see is a long-established industry measure, which is actually as vague as it sounds—and differs in its precise definition according to the medium, since this is dictated by the standard research techniques used for the medium concerned. We will return to this in the individual media chapters: here it should suffice to say that a press OTS means that the ad appeared in a publication that was read by the individual (they need not ever have looked at the relevant page); a TV OTS means only that the individual was in the room with the TV on, tuned to the right channel (they may have been reading, arguing, eating, snogging); and so on.

If we look at what a significant, but not large, budget, say £500 000, would buy in the main media in the UK, the figures work out as shown in Figure 9.3 in terms of cover, OTS and an index (=GRPs) combining the two. Clearly, the same sum can buy widely different levels of both cover and frequency according to the medium used.

Medium	Size	GRPs	Cover (%)	OTS	Cost/000 (£)
Outdoor	48-sheet	625	45	13.9	1.7
Radio	30″	500	55	9.1	2.2
Newspapers	Page 38 × 6	335	70	4.8	3.2
Magazines	Page col.	250	50	5.1	4.3
Television	30″	150	60	2.5	7.2
Cinema	30″	40	25	1.6	27.1

Figure 9.3.   What you can get for £500 000 (estimates for UK–All adults-early 1999)(Source: Conquest)

Health Warning!! Because of the different characteristics of the media, and the different things that are actually meant by an OTS, Figure 9.3 is actually comparing apples with pears, with plums and, in the case of posters, parsnips. So all the table is, is a *very* rough illustration of the relative 'expensiveness' of different media.

What matters much more is how we use the different media to achieve our objectives for the advertising.

Setting media objectives

Media objectives are a subset of the advertising objectives. They are concerned with delivering the advertising messages to the designated target audience in the most effective and cost-efficient way. To do this, they have to take account of the competitive situation in the marketplace: it may be desirable to avoid the major competitor—or to outdo them in certain key media. They have, too, to deliver whatever the overall advertising objectives have laid down. To take a trivial example, if the objectives for a new product include a level of brand awareness of (say) 25 per cent , it makes little sense to produce a media plan that only reaches 30 per cent of the audience. There is no way that, in the short term, you will achieve awareness among more than 60 per cent of those seeing the advertising.

In practice, the basis of most media objectives can be translated into a combination of *cover* and *frequency*.

Cover vs. frequency

The key issue that the planner needs to address from the start is the question of whether to emphasize cover or frequency—and over what time scale. Most budgets will not allow the advertiser to advertise at a significant weight throughout the year, so that it becomes necessary to decide when, and when not, to advertise. It is then necessary to decide whether to use concentrated bursts of advertising ('flighting' in the USA) or whether to spread the expenditure out thinly over a longer period.

This has become a major area of debate in recent years. It used to be thought that it was necessary, in a reasonably short period, to reach the target consumer three times for an ad to be effective (so-called 'effective frequency'). It is now fairly widely believed that, other things being equal (which they usually are not) one exposure to an ad in a given period before the next purchase of a product category is enough. This derives from the work of John Philip Jones on single-source data, but reflects strategies that had been proposed much earlier by econometricians, purely on the basis of analysis of sales effectiveness of different schedules. The logical consequence of this is that media planners now tend to aim to spread their money thinly over a period, rather than concentrate into short intensive bursts. This is because, in most markets, only a few consumers are in the market for the product at any one time, and the best time to 'hit' a buyer is when he or she is just about to buy. This approach has been called 'recency' planning, because the idea is that as many as possible of the buyers in the market at any time will have seen an ad for your brand recently.

This means that it is more important, in theory, to try to achieve high cover of the target group than to reach them often. The problem, in practice, is that to achieve high cover requires a substantial volume of advertising, either in one medium or several: this means, inevitably, that people who are relatively heavy TV viewers (say) or generally heavy consumers of assorted media, will get many more OTS, while the light users—the last few to be reached—may only ever get one OTS.

Three further elements need to be considered: the life-stage of the brand, the 'response function' of the advertising and the behaviour of competition.

Brand life-stage

For a new brand, it is generally important to create awareness of the brand quickly, and this requires more exposure to the advertising than may be needed to remind people of an established and familiar brand. This means that it makes sense—usually—to launch with a relatively heavy campaign.

Response functions

'Response function' is a long-established term with a very loose definition. What it means is simply that the response to a campaign can be mapped on a graph. If a person or a group is exposed to a campaign, those who see more of it can be expected to show a larger response. The nature of the 'response' is unimportant, at least to this discussion: it could be measured, for example, in terms of brand awareness, advertising recall, direct response replies or even actual sales of the brand. The question that is important is the shape of the curve on the graph, beause this will influence how we deploy our advertising.

It used to be widely assumed that most, if not all, response curves were S-shaped (Figure 9.4). It required more than one exposure to the campaign for anything to happen, and the curve then rose rapidly with each successive exposure, until eventually diminishing returns set in. The recency theory rests on the more

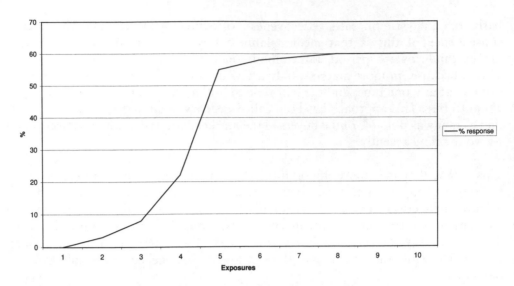

Figure 9.4.   An S-shaped response function

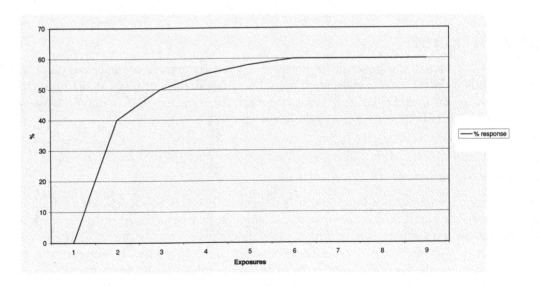

Figure 9.5.   A J-shaped response function

modern view that the normal response function is J-shaped, or convex (Figure 9.5): diminishing returns set in right from the start. The life-stage of the brand (or the campaign) may affect this: there is some evidence that at least some new brands' and campaigns' response functions are, in fact, S-shaped, while those of long-established brands are more likely to be convex.[1] The S-shape seems, however, to be both rare and short-lived.

Competition

As far as competition is concerned, it is clear that the 'share of voice' that a brand has in its market affects its share of market. This means that, even if we believe that one OTS per week, say, is sufficient, we will lose out if our main competitor is employing 3 OTS per week. In the same way, if we use bursts of advertising, our competitors' advertising bursts will tend to counteract our own. It is this that accounts for the relative stability of most established markets over the medium term (say a year or two).

Other considerations

Beyond the basic arithmetic of deploying the budget, there are a whole range of considerations that influence how a media plan is put together. Obviously, the shape of the market, both geographically and—especially—seasonally, is important. Normally, you will want to support peak sales periods, because this is a time at which it is likely to be easier to get extra sales, and it is also a time when competition will be especially active. At the same time, for some media, especially TV, the cost of advertising varies substantially across the year: so, other things being equal, it is going to be considerably more cost-effective to advertise when airtime is cheap. Similar considerations affect the areas where you should spend more or less money. In the UK, it is more expensive to advertise in London and the South-East, especially on TV, but it may also be the area where you generate most of your sales and profit.

Within individual media, there are a host of considerations of where and when the ads should best appear to appeal to your specific target audience, and an important overriding criterion is that in most media ads that appear in a particularly interesting editorial context are generally better noticed than those in less favoured spots.

There are differences, too, between ads that are basically image-building and those that are looking for a direct response of some kind. The dictates of cost-efficiency tend to mean that pure direct response ads have to be placed in less obviously favourable locations than image ads, because the favourable spots are too expensive.

---

[1] For a detailed, but old, study, see J. Simon and J. I. Arndt, 'The shape of the advertising response function', *JAR*, August 1980.

Then there is the whole question of how large a space, or how long a commercial, is needed to do the creative concept justice, and can it be afforded? This is examined in more detail in the chapters on the individual media.

Finally, there is a question—to which there is no satisfactory answer, though there are indications for one or two media. Is there a minimum spend below which there is no point in advertising? Either at all, or in a particular medium? The evidence suggests that there is not; it just depends what you need to achieve—and what you can afford.

The inter-media choice

Modern thinking about advertising suggests that it is outdated to think automatically in terms of *either* TV *or* newspapers *or* radio: it is more constructive to think of combinations. There is abundant evidence from campaigns using a combination of TV and magazines for fmcg products to show that a mixed campaign, taking perhaps 20 per cent of the budget out of TV and putting it into magazines, adds significantly to sales effects.[2] Similarly, research at 20-year intervals has confirmed that a radio commercial, using elements of a TV script, can successfully evoke detailed recall of the TV ad, a phenomenon known as 'visual transfer': because radio is basically a lot less expensive than TV, this allows for a fruitful combination of the two.

Nonetheless, even if we are going to think from the start about media synergy of this kind, we still need to look for a way of excluding some media, or of putting them in order of priority: and most budgets will not easily run to more than perhaps two different media, at most. What sort of criteria should we consider? Here, many considerations need to be at least borne in mind, even if they are not always all relevant to a particular case. In Box 9.1, I have set out a list of these, under a number of broad classifications, together with a view (which might be disputed) as to which of a range of media seem likely to score best on each of them. I do not claim that the list is complete—you may have fun trying to add to it—but it illustrates the fact that media is not all numbers: it needs judgement and analytical thought as well.

Box 9.1   Media choice: some considerations

Coverage
- ☐ Total cover achievable   Outdoor, TV
- ☐ Cover build-up   Outdoor, TV
- ☐ Selectivity   Magazines, ambient media

---

[2] See, e.g. A. Smith, 'More food for thought', *Admap*, February 1997, and references there.

Powerfulness
- Power — TV
- Immediacy — TV, radio, national dailies
- Intrusiveness — TV, radio
- Getting under the radar — Ambient media, radio
- Special features (sound, movement, demo) — TV, radio

Environment
- Editorial context — Magazines, ambient media
- Mood — Magazines, radio, TV
- Psychological distance — Radio, ambient (closest) TV (distant)
- Authority — Magazines, national papers
- Information — Magazines, newspapers

Adaptability
- Topicality — National dailies, radio
- Flexibility — Radio, ambient media
- Availability — Local papers, radio
- Continuity — Radio, national newspapers, Internet

Responsiveness
- Response — National newspapers, TV
- Interactivity — Internet, radio, (digital TV)

Financial
- Capital cost—time/space — (Highest) TV, outdoor (Lowest) radio, ambient media
- Capital cost—production — (Highest) cinema/TV, outdoor (Lowest) radio
- Cost per '000 — (Lowest) outdoor

There is, of course, one further consideration, which I have deliberately left out, because it should not influence the *initial* thinking about media: the preference of the creative people. They will, other things being equal, always want TV, and failing that outdoor or large colour spaces in the press. They *may* be right! But the media planner should aim to arrive at the best media solution for the brand—without, however, ignoring the creative possibilities.

How do we start to apply these criteria? There are a list of factors that are going to influence the way we decide on the media to use:

- The budget available.
- The target audience.
- The client's preference and past brand experience.
- The creative group's preference.
- The product category.
- Competitive activity.
- The likely reactions of the retail trade.
- The relative effectiveness of the media under consideration.

The budget

This has already been discussed. It will usually rule out at least some options—or, if you are lucky, be so large that you can consider anything.

The target audience

This can define the media choices—at least to an extent. If you want to advertise to teenage girls, you do not use *Woman's Weekly* (the oldest of the women's weekly magazines), or buy spots on *ITV Nightly News*. But then a broad housewife audience can be reached via TV, radio, newspapers, magazines, posters . . .

Past experience

Any client will have both personal preferences and the past experience of the company on which to build. Obviously, the implications of the latter depend on whether it has been judged successful or not. 'But we've never used TV (or radio or posters)' is not—necessarily—a good argument: but 'We tried posters and nothing happened' may be indicative. However, all such received wisdom should be questioned from time to time. If you can't change the media approach completely, you can always test in a small area.

Creative preference

Creative preferences are predictable (see above). But it's up to the media planner to be creative on his or her own account. Recent examples of this in the UK include:

- Strange shapes to make a point about the product: Mercedes A Class (see Box 7.1).
- Paste-on booklets on magazine ads: Fabergé.
- Running a 60-second cinema spot first in break followed by 10 sec spots scattered through the reel of ads: Levi's.
- Using posters on superstore sites of a particular store chain to support a promotion.

Product category

Many product categories find a natural advertising marketplace in particular media: the vast majority of computer hardware and software advertising, for example, is in specialized magazines, or now, on the Internet—though the bigger brands also use newspapers or TV to increase brand awareness. But should you follow the herd?

A few categories are excluded from certain media—TV in the UK has only accepted sanitary protection ads for a few years, and only recently allowed them before 9.00 p.m. Similarly, spirits were not advertised on TV for many years, under an industry agreement designed to head off anti-alcohol pressures, but have recently moved back on to TV again. Cigarettes, of course, are now being driven into a non-advertised limbo, in which the only possibility left is to advertise the Marlboro clothing range.

Marketplace considerations tend to dictate timings as well as media choice. With grocery shopping increasingly concentrated at weekends, superstores use the Thursday and Friday editions of newspapers for their advertising; travel ads concentrate into weekend papers, when people have leisure to plan, and so on.

Competitive activity

There are two schools of thought here. One says that you have to be in competition with your main adversaries in the media, as in the shops: because either 'We have to be seen to compete' or 'They must know what they are doing'. The other says that it makes sense to avoid head-on confrontation—especially with a bigger rival and seek instead to find a relevant section of the media where you can, as far as the product category is concerned, 'dominate' the medium.

(This concept of media domination is a popular one. Like most advertising jargon it is fairly inaccurate. You may manage to be the only widget advertiser on TV, but you are hardly able to dominate the medium, in the face of the other 2 650-odd (in the UK) TV advertisers out there. What you can do, sometimes, for tactical and PR reasons, is to take all the advertising space in a single issue of a newspaper or, even, magazine.)

The retail trade

Retailers used to be impressed by a brand being 'on TV'. These days, at least the larger chains are pretty blasé about this. It is possible, however, to use merchandising services provided by some media for test markets, and magazines such as *Vogue* and *Good Housekeeping* can do a job of point-of-sale support in departmental stores.

Relative effectiveness

This is the $64 000 question in media, and no one seems to be admitting to having any real answers. It is bad enough trying to arrive at a realistic basis for comparing costs as we have seen (page 131), cost per thousand is at best an extremely crude basis for comparing media. The problem is that the only way to answer the question would be to carry out a series of large-scale and costly experiments, and to judge the results econometrically—because no one is going to agree to assess media against each other by intermediate measures such as brand awareness per hundred GRPs. (Millward Brown have, in fact, come up with some very similar awareness index scores for TV and press media.)

As Box 9.1 suggests, different media are better—at least judgementally—for different things, so that precise comparisons are always going to be difficult.

As a very sweeping generalization, most people involved with advertising would agree that TV is the most powerful medium available, because it offers the combination of sound, vision and movement that can attract and hold us through more than one sense. From a practical media-based viewpoint, too, it can still build coverage more speedily and comprehensively than other medium (except perhaps outdoor)—always supposing that you have enough money for an adequate campaign.

By contrast, women's magazines, for example, provide an extremely attractive and well-regarded context for advertising; but coverage takes a long time to build, and you have to recognize that it may take several weeks even for a weekly magazine to be read by all the readers that research identifies, allowing for pass-on readership, and so on.

As usual, it becomes necessary to go back to the objectives. If you want to provide detailed information to potential customers, a 30-second TV campaign will not do the job.

One medium or several?

This is the crucial question, which the textbooks—and the training courses—tend not to answer. Not only do they not answer it, they rarely address it, which seems odd in a business that will talk about 'synergy' at the drop of a hat.

The 'classical' approach, with anything other than a very large budget, has been to concentrate on what is judged to be the most effective (or appropriate, which ought to be the same thing) medium. It has been widely accepted that you have to have some sort of minimum level of expenditure to mount a campaign in TV (especially), though no one has ever succeeded in defining what this minimum is, and the advent of multi-channel digital TV means that no one ever will.

More practically, we can think about the media in terms of impacts (or GRPs) that we need to achieve an effect. It used to be believed that you needed three (or more) OTS in a reasonably short period (say four weeks) for an effective campaign on TV; and that a rather higher figure was needed for press. Common sense suggests that only one exposure to an ad is unlikely to have any effect; but there is a growing body of evidence, from a variety of sources, to suggest the opposite, and the debate about effective frequency (page 132) supports this view.[3] What the proponents of so-called 'recency' media planning go on to say is:

1. You should aim for only one OTS in any one inter-purchase period for an established fmcg brand.
2. Since most brands are purchased infrequently, this could be quite a long period, for any one individual.
3. But people are making purchases all the time, so that *any* time is an inter-purchase period for most of the individuals who are exposed to an ad, and the ad will be shortly pre-purchase for some, at any time.
4. You should therefore aim to maximise coverage at one OTS over any short planning period.
5. For most brands, this actually means you plan on a monthly (or weekly) basis, but you usually cannot afford to advertise every month (or week) in the year.
6. However, if you do have enough money for this, you should reduce your planning time unit to three days, or even one day, or dayparts within a single day, rather than consciously aiming to increase OTS.

This 'model', which tends to be supported by econometricians, too, is focused on a single medium—TV—but the principles could equally apply to press: perhaps even more so, since it is evident from research that most people, if they actually get into a press ad, only need one exposure to it to get most of the message.

So, why should you use more than one medium?

The obvious answer to this is: when your main medium cannot do the whole job. Suppose, for example, you are a car manufacturer. You use TV to showcase your cars, and to create (hopefully) positive imagery and associations for the marque and the model. But you know consumers need more information than a pretty picture before making such an expensive decision, so you use press advertising to tell them more about the detail of engineering, safety features, design, pricing, etc.—and you give them a phone number or a web site to contact for even more information. You may, too, use the press to tell people about the amazing deal you are offering on the old model, available at the dealers just for this month, complete with a fantastic

---

[3] The key source is J.P. Jones, *When Ads Work*, Lexington Books, New York, 1995.

financial package (which will, with luck, lock people into the marque for life, because they can't figure out how to escape without losing money).

But this is not the only reason for using an extra, supporting medium. You can use it to make your money go further: a radio campaign (which will always cost less than TV) can build on the TV commercials, and even elicit visual imagery from the TV, through 'visual transfer' (page 80). More interestingly, there is evidence from marketplace experiments for fmcg brands that a mix of TV and magazine or TV and newspaper advertising can achieve greater sales than TV alone: it looks as if the press campaign adds an extra dimension, for some consumers, that the TV cannot.

Partly, this will come from improved coverage: the press campaign will reach people who are light or very light viewers of commercial TV. Partly, it may come from the press's ability to influence people who are so-called 'rejectors' of TV advertising (see page 165). Partly, the magazine ads may be adding an extra dimension of information, or atmosphere, or associations, that the TV is not. (And, remember, this discussion is ignoring all the other elements in the communication mix. These will need to be factored in.)

In the end, the decision on whether to use a single medium or a mixture must be based on a careful analysis of the tasks the ads have to perform and of the media habits of the target audience. But remember the magazine-plus-TV findings. Synergy does seem to happen, and you may be missing a trick if you do not use it.

The intra-medium decision

Deciding which spaces or spots to use for a brand within a given medium can be more securely based on available research—even though this, too, has its flaws and inadequacies. The choices involved come into three categories, basically:

- The choice of publication, or TV or radio channel, etc.
- The choice of position in the medium.
- The choice of size of space or length of spot.

Choice of individual medium

Until quite recently, in the UK at least, this was a choice that was far more complex in press media than in electronic media. TV and radio were essentially geographically distributed, so the choices were largely concerned with how much of the country could be covered within a budget, or where to put most weight to support strong sales or bolster weaknesses. Now, however, TV is beginning to fragment significantly, and the choice of channels is becoming both wider and potentially more difficult.

At the same time, the development of a variety of forms of sponsorship and similar deals, in all media, is beginning to influence the way in which media planning is done.

It is possible that TV channel choice will go the way of choice of press media—especially magazines, though the research available is somewhat different in character. Magazines are selected by applying data from readership research and known ratecard costs to specific target audiences. The analyst looks at two facets of the individual magazines' performance: their coverage of the target group; and the cost per thousand (ratecard cost of a page) against this group. For a typical analysis, you will get a table such as that shown in Figure 9.6. Standard analysis packages available from computer bureaux enable the planner to use the basic data to analyse the cross-readership of different publications, and build schedules that will achieve different levels of cover and frequency against the chosen audience.

The cost ranking is, of course, merely a well-ordered shopping list. There may be some 'banker' titles, delivering both high cover and low CPT (cost per thousand contacts), but deciding between closely similar scores will be a matter of judgement: a combination of the editorial appropriateness of one title rather than another; the buyer's ability to do an especially favourable deal; the willingness of the publication to provide specific guarantees of position and exclusivity; and so on. The planner has to balance, too, coverage—e.g. from *News of the World* in Figure 9.6—against precision (very high in Figure 9.6 for *Loaded, FHM, GQ* and *Empire*, all of which have quite low coverage).

For TV, or radio, the dimensions of choice are rather different. Not only do different channels offer different levels of cover, but they do so variably during the day. As will be seen in Chapter 10, this makes the planning of TV more complex to start with, before the extra dimensions of multi-channel fragmentation, which should, in theory, allow some quite precise targeting, are allowed to be considered.

For cinema, the make-up of the audience, in the UK at least, is already well skewed demographically. The media planner's task is to identify the best-pulling films, and to select the geographical locations required.

For outdoor, the situation is rather different, because the problem here is to select from the various offerings of different contractors, and fit this to a geographical template that meets the campaign's needs.

Publication	Readership (000)	Cover (%)	% 15–34	Index*	Unit cost (£/page)	CPT (£)
Daily Star	1 054	6.5	50	143	6 500	6.17
GQ	697	4.3	84	241	4 500	6.46
Empire	492	3.1	82	235	3 500	7.12
Loaded	1 081	6.7	93	266	8 000	7.40
News of the World	5 221	32.4	45	128	40 000	7.66
Q Magazine	652	4.0	78	224	5 000	7.67
Sunday Sport	604	3.7	68	194	5 000	8.28
The People	1 781	11.1	34	98	15 000	8.42
The Sun	4 432	27.5	44	126	38 000	8.57
FHM (For Him)	1 211	7.5	90	256	11 000	9.08
Rugby World	266	1.7	55	157	2 500	9.40
Arena	311	1.9	86	245	3 000	9.65
Sunday Mirror	2 581	16.0	36	103	25 000	9.69
The Mirror	1 980	12.3	31	90	25 000	12.63
Daily Record	651	4.0	35	99	8 500	13.05
Esquire	344	2.1	79	226	4 500	13.07
Total Sport	211	1.3	66	189	3 000	14.25
Mail on Sunday	1 925	11.9	31	88	28 000	14.55
Maxim	317	2.0	81	231	5 000	15.78
The Guardian	490	3.0	39	113	8 500	17.36
The Observer	441	2.7	36	104	8 500	19.29
Daily Mail	1 396	8.7	27	76	27 000	19.34
Ind. on Sunday	401	2.5	44	125	8 000	'19.93
The Sunday Times	1 493	9.3	39	111	30 000	20.09
Focus	145	0.9	59	168	3 000	20.75
Express on Sunday	793	4.9	26	74	17 000	21.44
The Times	649	4.0	33	94	14 000	21.58
The Express	657	4.1	24	68	15 000	22.84
The Independent	340	2.1	41	116	8 000	23.51
Sunday Telegraph	604	3.7	28	80	15 000	24.83
Daily Telegraph	563	3.5	21	60	19 500	34.64
Financial Times	269	1.7	40	114	35 000	130.24

* 35% (= proportion of all adults) = 100. Source: NRS 1997.

Figure 9.6.   A cost-ranking of selected press media based on adults aged 15–34 (35 per cent of adults) ranked in order of cost per '000 (Source: National Readership Survey, 1997)

Size and length

All media operate on the basis of certain 'standard' sizes, lengths or formats for advertisements, and the most popular are used as the basis for price setting—30 seconds for TV and radio, 60 seconds for cinema, and a single full page for press media. Posters are different—not least because sizes vary between countries, and the UK, at least, has four or five major formats.

The choice of size or length should clearly be dictated by creative considerations, to a large extent. Then it needs to be modified by what is affordable, which is nearly always shorter, or smaller, than the creatives would like.

Two points need to be made here—the detail will be addressed in the individual media chapters. First, there is usually an advantage to be had from going smaller or shorter, though the media price their offerings accordingly. There is not much difference in effectiveness between a full page in a broadsheet newspaper and a 38 cm × 5 columns ad (which takes up a large part of a page). There is not always much difference between a 30-second commercial and a 20-second one—though there is growing evidence to suggest that 10 seconds (in the UK) or 15 seconds (in the US) are less valuable than their costs would imply.

Position

Different positions in different media attract different audiences and different levels of attention to the surrounding editorial context. The evidence on this subject is sketchy and often conflicting, but there are clear indications that commercials in programmes that people enjoy are more favourably received, and achieve greater recall, than those in less well-liked programmes. Similarly, ads placed against 'good' editorial are better noticed and read than those opposite or among other ads or less 'good' editorial.

The media, of course, know this, and will charge accordingly. Press media tend to charge extra for 'fixing' the position of an ad, while TV stations both charge extra for strong spots and operate, in the UK at least, a system called pre-emption, by which another advertiser can buy out your good spot by offering more for it. In addition, TV stations usually aim to sell any advertiser a mix of good and poorer spots—which, indeed, is what most planners will aim to buy, or the overall cost per thousand will get too high.

Scheduling

As the media planner works through all this analysis, the basis of a schedule of media spaces and spots begins to emerge. At an early stage, in fact the planner will produce a very rough 'laydown': a chart showing blocks of expenditure spread over the campaign period (usually, but quite arbitrarily so, a year). This will be designed to fit the brand's requirements, in terms of brand or market seasonality, new product or variant launches, known competitive activity, media costs, and so on.

In addition to this, the planner will be taking into account the way in which media costs vary through the year: TV in the UK is cheaper in January and August than at other times; posters are cheaper in the winter, because they are visible for shorter periods (except for illuminated sites), and traffic, especially pedestrians, is normally lighter.

Importantly, too, he or she will be beginning to think about the shape of the campaign and the assumptions underlying it about how the advertising works. How long are the effects of the advertising expected to last? Should the campaign aim to be continuous, or should it consist of bursts?

Most advertising works over a period of time, because people remember it, and very rarely act on it immediately. However, the effects wear off: other advertising, or just life in general, gets in the way. At the same time, if a brand advertises successfully over a longish period, it achieves a build-up of effects that may continue for a long time—you can almost certainly remember ads from when you were a child: possibly, you are still buying the brand. Econometricians and model-builders call the accumulated build-up of advertising 'adstock', and talk about the half-life of a campaign. You can visualize the effect of a series of bursts of advertising in these terms as a series of loops (see Figure 9.7). The idea of thinking like this is that if you time the bursts right, you can create a build-up effect.[4]

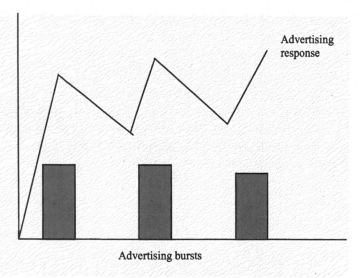

Figure 9.7.   Advertising decay: effects of a campaign

---

[4] For a detailed description of a very experienced practitioner's approach to analysing advertising with adstock modelling, see S. Broadbent, *Accountable Advertising*, NTC Publications, Henley-on-Thames, 1997.

Obviously, if you happen to have a brand that uses TV advertising, and is not especially seasonal, you could plan your bursts of advertising to run in January and then, among other months, August to take advantage of cheaper ad rates.

Set against this, however, is the argument of the 'recency' school, which suggests that it would be better in most cases to spread the advertising quite thinly over the year, rather than using bursts at all. While they will argue that this applies equally to all markets, the principle has only been demonstrated to work for fmcg products, though—for example—it is widely used by financial services advertisers. A common compromise between the two approaches is to use TV in more or less extended bursts, and fill in the gaps, as far as possible, with supporting media.

Evaluation

Once a campaign has been planned, bought and run, it should be evaluated. This has three distinct elements to it:

☐ Checking that the ads all appeared as and when scheduled.
☐ Checking that targets for coverage, frequency, etc. have been achieved.
☐ Checking that good value has been achieved.

(This is from the media point of view: what the advertiser, and the agency will want to know most is that the campaign objectives, in terms of sales, profits, etc., have been achieved.)

Checking the ads have appeared

Virtually all press media will provide voucher copies, to show that the ads have appeared. This is fine, except where you have run ads only in some regions; or perhaps where you have had a loose insert.

For TV and radio, BARB and RAJAR provide detailed data that show when every ad has run on every station, but the system is not as foolproof as the detailed information provided may suggest.

Cinema showing records are provided by the contractors themselves—perhaps the least reliable of the available forms of checking.

Poster campaigns are checked and monitored by the specialist poster buying agencies, but advertisers and their agencies are wise to make spot-checking tours to assess the quality and location of their sites.

Checking coverage and frequency

This is a (reasonably) mechanical process, using on-line data from BARB and the other research sources, to confirm what has been achieved. The two media for which this applies as a regular, short-term exercise are TV and cinema, since the radio and poster data are sufficiently infrequent to make the process academic except as part of the overall retrospective assessment of the campaign; and press planning and evaluation is all done against the six-monthly National Readership Survey.

Checking value

Again, the main 'objective' assessment that can be made is against ITV's Station Average Price (page 163), though this is not quite as simple as it looks, because it is necessary to take a variety of factors—especially the target audience—into account. Similarly, it is easy to say (and the buying agency always will!) that other media have been bought at a substantial discount to the ratecard: the issue here is whether this is as good as, or better than, the norm.

The only effective and objective way to assess this is through a *media auditor*. In the UK, these independent specialists are estimated to cover around 60 per cent of TV expenditure, and to work for the majority of the top 100 advertisers.

Summary

- There is a very wide choice of media available to the advertiser. These choices can be divided into *inter*-media and *intra*-media.
- Media selection usually starts, in practice, with a budget: the choices have to be affordable—and capable of performing the tasks set for the advertising.
- These objectives, for media, are set in terms of cover and frequency. Modern thinking tends to emphasize cover over frequency, in the short-term, plus continuity, which leads to frequency.
- Different media deliver different types of environment for advertising, and deliver different relationships with the audience. It helps to define your criteria before trying to make a choice.
- Modern thinking suggests that multimedia campaigns are likely to be more effective than single-medium concentration.
- Within individual media, choices are largely dictated by the flexibilities inherent in the structure of the media offer. TV offers choices of region, daypart, programme, commercial length, for example.
- Once implemented, media campaigns require evaluation: checking for the value of the negotiation, the quality of the planning; checking that the ads have actually appeared as scheduled; and checking that the schedule has delivered the planned contacts with the target audience.

Questions to consider

1. You want to ensure that your ad is seen by as many people as possible—you are running the National Lottery or a crucial government health campaign. What medium—or which media—would you consider using? Why?
2. You have a product that, ideally, needs to be demonstrated to consumers. What media would you consider using, and what factors might influence your decision?
3. Your brand has its peak sales at Christmas, but media costs at this season are mostly exceptionally high. How might you be able to keep your cost per thousand down?
4. What factors might influence your choice of space size for a press campaign, between full pages or page-dominant sizes and smaller spaces?

10 Television

Why should people pay to go out and see bad films when they can stay at home and see bad TV for nothing?

Sam Goldwyn

Commercial television has chalked up over 50 years' history, and has penetrated almost every corner of the globe. In the last few years, with the introduction of satellite broadcasting and the more recent development of digital signals, which allow many more channels to use the same bandwidth, the structure and character of TV have been changing very rapidly. This has been happening all over the world, on slightly different time scales from country to country, while the different start-points, defined by the industry's structure and regulation, lead to varied patterns of development, in terms of penetration, share of total adspend and the way in which commercials are exposed. In general, however, TV's share of total media spending by advertisers has been rising, consistently, worldwide, for many years.

At the same time, especially in Europe, there exist alongside the commercial stations non-commercial public broadcasting channels, of which Britain's BBC is the best known. (Some 'public'—state-owned—stations in Europe carry ads, unlike the BBC.) Where non-commercial channels are strong, they have the effect of reducing the audience and the potential for commercial channels—and this creates constant debate. If, it is said, the BBC took advertising, the cost of TV advertising in the UK would come down. The fallacy here is that, should this happen, while the cost per thousand of TV advertising would come down, it is reasonably certain that the big advertisers who make the most noise about this issue would advertise more, thus neutralizing any gain that they expected to make.

Commercial TV in Britain

While British TV is unique in some of its features, it represents the sort of hybrid pattern that the market in most countries has come to show. It is therefore worth describing it in a little detail, as an illustration of a dynamic TV marketplace and the problems it poses for advertisers and their agencies. Other countries will have different but not dissimilar situations. Of UK households, 99 per cent can receive commercial TV, and 60 per cent have two or more sets. Over 80 per cent (high by European standards) have a video recorder—even if many people still do not know how to programme it. British consumers are among the world's heaviest TV

150

viewers, watching on average 3.5 hours a day—virtually a whole day per week—though this figure has been falling slowly but steadily in recent years. The big problem for the commercial sector is that the BBC manages to hold on to over 40 per cent of TV viewing.

The possibility of the BBC taking advertising has been discussed for years, but this still appears far off.

Terrestrial TV

The UK has three commercial terrestrial channels, ITV1, Channel 4 and Channel 5, that compete with two BBC channels. ITV1 consists of 13 regional stations which are now marketed to the consumer mainly as a single brand, though the individual stations have a legal obligation to provide a proportion of local programming. For the advertiser, however, time on ITV1 is sold by just three sales houses, each representing several stations, plus a separate one for the breakfast-time service, GMTV. Channel 4 sells airtime either nationally or divided into six 'macro' regions, but is a single company. Channel 5, on air since 1997, covers only some 70 per cent of the country, and sells on a 'national' basis.

Satellite TV

Satellite TV is provided essentially by one contractor, BSkyB ('Sky'), though Sky's programming, together with that from some other satellite broadcasters, is available through cable contractors (see below). Sky offers its subscribers a wide range of programme packages, which includes all the 'free-to-air' BBC and ITV channels plus a range of channels that are either Sky programming or programmes from other programme houses such as Flextech (becoming a major source of material for all stations—including the BBC), CNN, MTV, etc.

Cable TV

Cable TV, like satellite, is relatively new in Britain, and the two combined had only reached 29 per cent of households by autumn 1998, in contrast to over 90 per cent in some Continental European countries (see Figure 10.1). Cable in the UK was set up on the basis of a large number of local franchises each covering potentially, on average, somewhere between 100 000 and 200 000 homes, though the largest franchises could reach nearly half a million, and some small ones less than 20 000.

While there were originally a large number of cable contractors, the expense of laying cable, the relative inadequacies of cable marketing to the consumer and the resulting slow growth and high rates of 'churn' (people giving up their subscriptions) have led to rationalization of the industry by merger and takeover, until there

	% cable	% satellite	Total
Netherlands	4.0	94.3	98.3
Belgium	2.5	93.1	95.6
Switzerland	13.3	78.7	92.0
Germany	33.7	53.4	87.0
Austria	34.6	33.0	67.6
Denmark	40.3	26.6	66.9
Sweden	18.2	46.3	64.6
Hungary	22.1	39.6	61.7
Norway	18.6	41.8	60.5
Ireland	9.6	45.2	55.7
Poland	17.6	30.1	47.7
Finland	8.3	38.3	46.1
United Kingdom	18.2	9.3	27.5
France	11.6	9.6	21.2
Spain	9.6	3.3	13.0
Italy	3.8	0.0	3.8

Figure 10.1.   Cable and satelllite penetration in selection European countries per cent (end 1997)(Source: AA. *The European Advertising and Media Yearbook 1998*, NTC Publications)

are now only two or three operators of any size. Nonetheless, cable penetration has been growing faster than satellite recently.

Cable offers the potential, at least, of a far more extensive and flexible service through digital TV, but so far (mid-1999) the technology to exploit the more interesting forms of interaction with consumers—the 'return channel'—is not in place. Cable programming consists primarily of the same mix as Sky's, in a variety of packages, though there are some programmers selling only to cable and not on satellite.

Cable and satellite households are considerably more promiscuous in their viewing habits than those with terrestrial TV only—hardly surprisingly. The combined BBC and ITV channels account for only around 60 per cent of their viewing. Nonetheless, Flextech's research has shown that cable households normally limit their viewing to a repertoire of at most a dozen channels, and concentrate on far fewer than this.

Digital

Digital TV offers superior sound, sharper vision, the possibility of compressing far more channels into the same amount of bandwidth as analogue TV, and a wide range of interactive viewing and trading options. Already introduced in several

European countries, digital made its UK commercial debut in October 1998 when Sky launched Sky Digital, promising up to 200 channels—including over 40 music channels and pay-per-view film channels. This was closely followed by the ground-based OnDigital, offering a considerably simpler range of packages, and autumn 1999 sees the launch of NTL's and Telewest's cable service, which should—in theory—be able to offer a far higher level of interactivity than the broadcast services. The BBC also transmits digitally, and is available through the other platforms. ITV launched its digital service, ITV2, at the end of 1998, and—at least initially—ITV2 was not available on Sky Digital.

At the time of writing, it is far too early to predict the rate of take-up of digital services, not least because the supply of set-top converter boxes has been limited, both in volume and by problems over the compatibility of different systems. The British government aims to pull the plug on analogue TV sometime before 2010, in order to sell the freed-up frequencies. This is, of course, a political decision of some delicacy, because it may involve having either to offend a substantial minority of the population, or to offer them heavily subsidized conversion. Given that satellite and cable, combined, are in fewer than 30 per cent of households after 10 years, the prospects are—at least—uncertain.

From the point of view of advertiser and TV buyer, the growth of digital creates a plethora of opportunities, and a mass of problems. In theory, at least, digital will offer a wide range of focused, specialist channels, which will enable buyers to buy specific target audiences, much as is the case in the consumer magazine market. At the same time, if this actually becomes possible, it will mean that the ability of TV to provide a broad, large audience will have disappeared, removing TV's most potent advantage. Buyers' ability to achieve coverage without excessive frequency, and the need to buy an enormous number of spots, will have gone for ever.

From the consumer's viewpoint, of course, finding your way around 200+ channels is potentially a nightmare. The TV companies have provided an elegant solution with the Electronic Programme Guide, an on-screen system for identifying the programmes you wish to view. On the evidence so far, EPGs are very user-friendly, but lend themselves to manipulation by their owners, in favour of the owner's programming. They are, also, a massive threat to the big-circulation programme magazines (page 179)

How TV is bought and sold

The available products

Historically, TV advertising in the UK has been entirely spot TV: short ads, combined into 'breaks' in transmission of a programme, or between programmes.

Legislation has restricted the number of minutes permitted in any one hour, and the average hourly minutage over a day to 7 minutes, and in fact the TV companies have tended to restrict the available time a little more than this. Breaks *within* programmes do not usually exceed 2 minutes, and there are usually no more than three within an hour-long programme. The breaks *between* programmes are liable to be longer, but they are also combined with the stations' own 'trails' for coming programmes. In other countries, practices vary. In the US, commercial breaks tend to be much more frequent, and a considerably higher proportion of peak-time programming is taken up with ads. In some Continental European countries, it is the practice to have ads only between programmes, and you may have a block of as many as 15 or 20 commercials together.

More recently in the UK, programme sponsorship has been permitted, and is becoming quite widespread. A classic example is Cadbury's sponsorship of the long-running leading soap opera, *Coronation Street*. This involvement of advertisers is likely to extend into programme production—much as Procter & Gamble invented the soap opera in the 1930s on radio—as the plethora of channels available on digital TV look for affordable programme content. Already, advertisers are initiating programmes—the *Pepsi Chart Show*, for example.

An interesting innovation—still technically an ad—was the production of a brief 'entertainment' spot called *Miller Time* by Miller beer, which ran on Channel 4 in the late evening, supported by advertising in other media.

Television spots are sold in units of 10 seconds, with the 30-second spot the 'standard' around which planning and pricing revolves. Prices for spots are not pro rata to length, because it is judged that shorter spots are relatively more desirable (or perhaps effective) in relation to their length (see Figure 10.2). A 20-second spot costs 80 per cent of the 30-second rate. Spots longer than 30 seconds are not subject to the same differentials. The longest 'standard' spots on UK TV are 90 seconds, but it is possible to negotiate longer spots for special purposes—a quite common

Length of spot	Index of actual length	Cost index
10″	33	50
20″	67	80
30″	100	100
40″	133	133
50″	166	166
60″	200	200

Figure 10.2. Cost ratio of different lengths of commercial-UK: 30 sec = 100 (Source: BBJ Media)

Breakfast	▨▨▨	1.5
Daytime	▨▨▨▨▨▨▨▨▨▨▨	6.5
Early peak (5.30--8p.m.)	▨▨▨▨▨▨▨▨▨▨	5.8
Late peak (8--11p.m.)	▨▨▨▨▨▨▨▨▨▨▨▨▨▨	8.8
Late night	▨▨▨▨▨▨	2.5

Figure 10.3.   Average viewing levels by Daypart, UK: Millions of households (Source: BARB)

practice is to run a long message primarily targeted at a company's own staff in the small hours of the morning, and get them to video it.

An exception to all this is the so-called 'infomercial', which can run for up to half an hour, and is common on US shopping channels on cable. These have not yet become widespread in the UK, but the cable shopping channel QVC is one available platform for them.

The TV time is conventionally divided up into standard 'dayparts' (see Figure 10.3) which are reasonably self-explanatory, and which provide a framework for pricing and for planning campaigns. Some dayparts have very clear audience profiles: breakfast TV, especially at weekends, is largely child viewing time; most of the daytime audience consists of non-working housewives and the retired (more of the latter in the afternoon); early evening is 'mother-and-children' time; and the audience becomes more broad-based at peak time, but business people can usually not be easily reached until late peak (this explained the popularity for many advertisers of ITV1's—now no longer transmitted—*News at Ten)*. Late night attracts a varied and peculiar mix of the drunk, the insomniac and the followers of strange cult programmes.

The TV stations' aim in life is to maximize revenue, so they try to sell as much time as possible, throughout the day, for as high a price as possible. They achieve this through two main devices. For popular spots, they conduct, in effect, an auction: the ratecard, which can be and is quite heavily discounted, is a starting point for negotiation; but all spots can be 'pre-empted'. This means that even if you have booked a spot, carefully chosen because your brand fits with the expected audience profile, some other advertiser can offer the contractor a higher price and take the spot. For less popular spots, the contractors will encourage a buyer to take a 'package' of spots which may involve a mix of dayparts and days of the week. Indeed, the stations offer deals to advertisers that guarantee a certain level of coverage, as GHIs—Guaranteed Home Impressions. There are, also, other special deals available—for genuinely local advertisers, for test markets, and so on.

Quite apart from specific deals that an advertiser may do when buying a specific spot or group of spots, the contractors offer advertisers discounts for exceeding certain levels of spend, or, frequently, conditional on a certain amount of the total network spend going on a particular station ('share deals').

How TV is planned

A TV campaign is put together by a TV planner, who is usually, these days, a specialist. Their task is to find the most cost-effective way of meeting the campaign objectives, in a marketplace that is a mixture of the fixed and the dynamic. It is 'fixed', in the sense that consumers' viewing behaviour follows broadly predictable patterns. People tend to view the same programmes, or to view at the same times, more or less consistently. They have, and report in surveys such as *TGI* (see page 64), programmes that they really like to watch ('appointments to view'). This information is the planner's bread and butter. It makes it possible to select the points in the day's or the week's viewing schedules when the defined target audience are significantly more likely to be watching a commercial station. The market is fairly fixed, too, in terms of cost. At any one time, the planner will have available a reasonably good idea of the cost per rating point of reaching a given audience: 100 30-second TVRs on ITV1 will cost, on average, some £350 000. In the UK at least, this will vary over the course of the year, by about 10–15 per cent either way, and all large media buying agencies develop their own forward estimates of this average cost.

The marketplace is also dynamic, in that programme schedules change; people switch channels, with the aid of the remote control; they record programmes on their VCRs (and sometimes remember to view them); even fixed programme slots carry material that may be more or less attractive to viewers, or to a different sort of viewer—feature films are an obvious example. So a planner has to work with the aid of both history, in terms of the available research, and foresight, in terms of knowledge of the up-coming schedules and estimates of how they may affect viewing. The same applies, too, to costs: TV buying is a marketplace, and the ultimate price is fixed by demand. Certain programmes, or certain events, will be priced highly. For an example, see Box 10.1.

Box 10.1   The TV market in action

An interesting example of TV cost fluctuation catching planners off-guard occurred around the June 1998 football World Cup. The UK's TV planners assumed that TV time during the finals would be very expensive, and that female audiences would be relatively low; so they pulled a lot of female-oriented advertising (in particular) back into April and May. The cost of time in April and May rose sharply, and that in June fell—well below what the TV stations had been expecting. What's more, female audiences for the football were far higher than anticipated.

Station average prices (= CPT)
1997-1998: All TV stations
Index on annual average = 100

	1997	1998
Jan	77	82
Feb	81	92
Mar	100	86
Apr	107	110
May	129	124
Jun	107	91
Jul	93	84
Aug	83	84
Sep	118	112
Oct	115	120
Nov	107	112
Dec	82	79

Source: A.C.Nielsen–MEAL

The costs reflected the fact that TV spending, which usually drops off in July–August to its summer trough, fell sharply, by around 20 per cent, in June, apart from two spikes in activity when England played Romania and Argentina.

The planner must take a whole series of decisions before the plan can be finalised, and these need to be made with due reference to the target audience, the competition and the dynamics of the market in which the brand competes.

Key issues that will need sorting out include:

☐   *Definition of the target audience*   The planner has to translate the creative target audience (pages 64–7) into an audience against which the campaign can be bought, which will be defined by the demographics of age, sex, class, region, because that is how TV audience research (below, page 164) is reported, and time is sold. The aim of the planner will be to identify channels, dayparts and programmes that do relatively well—'convert' well—against the defined target. ('Conversion' is media jargon: if the all-adult viewership of a programme is—say—5 per cent, a 'rating' of 5, and our target of 16–34 adults scores a rating of 7, then 7 indexed on 5 is 140. 140 is the 'conversion' of the programme for 16-34 adults.) You should always recognize, however, that at present TV is a broad-brush, mass medium: it is very difficult to be highly selective. This will gradually change with the arrival of digital TV.

Delivers 55% cover
Average OTS 1.82

1+ OTS	/////////////////////////////////	55%
2+OTS	/////////////////////////	30%
3+OTS	///////////	15%
4+ OTS	////	5%

Figure 10.4.   Typical OTS distribution for 100TVRs (Source: BBJ Media)

☐ *Desired levels of reach and frequency*   How much of the target audience can be reached economically? Is this enough? And how often, over what period, do they need to be reached, on average? As we have seen (page 132) there is an increasingly accepted theory that there is no need for a consumer to see more than one ad for a brand in the (fairly) short term. However, the simple arithmetic of achieving a high level of overall cover dictates that at least some of the target audience will see a number of ads: you need something like 500 GRPs to reach 80 per cent of most UK audiences, and this means that the *average* number of OTS per person reached will be six (500/80 = 6.2). Since some will only see one ad, others will be seeing perhaps a dozen or more (see Figure 10.4).

☐ *Minimum levels of support*   US practice and experience suggest that less than 50 GRPs per week is too little to have any effect. It is, however, unclear whether this simply reflects the lack of sensitivity of the available research. UK experience certainly supports the *feasibility*, for established fmcg brands at least, of running at no more than 80–100 GRPs per week over an extended period.

☐ *Burst vs. drip*   The whole 'recency' argument (pages 131–2) revolves around this question, and favours a 'drip' approach—keeping the advertising as continuous as possible, but at quite a low level. There is no doubt, however, that for a new product, or a brand where there is a need to achieve a substantial increase in consumer awareness, it is desirable to use bursts, at least initially, in order to get over the initial barrier of consumer ignorance. Bursts may also make sense, in relation to competitive activity, or an extremely seasonal market. The adstock approach to analysing the effects of ad spending (page 146) also tends to suggest that—so long as the advertising has a carry-over effect—bursts may be a perfectly good alternative in many markets. It seems to me that slavish adherence to recency theory is unnecessarily limiting.

☐ *Seasonality*   The shape of the market's and the brand's sales is likely to affect the schedule. As a general rule, it makes sense to support strengths in sales— your advertising is directed against a larger audience of people willing to

Region/station	£/000
London	11.07
Central	6.32
Granada	5.24
North	4.09
Scottish TV	4.76
Grampian	3.51
HTV	4.93
Meridian	8.48
Anglia	7.43
Westcountry	4.96
Border	2.46
Ulster	4.10
National ITV1	6.41
National Channel 4	6.37
National Channel 5	4.92
National GMTV	5.30
National Satellite	3.83

Figure 10.5.   UK television costs adult cost per '000, by ITV region and national, £, 30 sec equivalent, 1997 (Source: Young and Rubicam)

consider buying when there is a seasonal peak It may be a desirable objective, though, to extend the 'shoulders' of the peak, by starting a little earlier, and continuing after the market has started to fall back.

☐   *Choice of channels*   Part of the intra-media choice. Here, the planner has to consider the objectives in terms of cover and audience selectivity. In the UK, it is virtually impossible to reach 80–90 per cent of a broad target without using ITV1; but other audiences can be reached perfectly adequately by using Channel 4, Channel 5 or satellite (or combinations of these) and at what is usually a lower cost per thousand.

☐   *Choice of stations:*   The other side of intra-media choice. In the UK, this is usually a matter of regionality, rather than competition. The only effective competition within a region on ITV1 is between the weekday Carlton station in London and the weekend LWT. The problem the planner does face, though, is that CPTs vary widely between regions and channels. (see Figure 10.5). This means that it is necessary to consider how the weight of advertising should be distributed in relation to brand sales: do we support strong areas or aim to build up weak ones? And to consider the relative costs: should we allocate our money on a cash basis or on a GRP basis? If we aim to equalize GRPs across all regions ('equal impacts'), for example, London and Meridian will get grossly inflated shares of the budget, relative to population. If we aim to equalize spend pro rata to population, the level of GRPs in London and Meridian will be sharply lower than elsewhere.

☐ *Dayparts*   Choice of dayparts is largely dictated by the target audience. However, there is plenty of scope for choice against most targets, between, say, early and late peak or early evening or late night. Again, peak is significantly more expensive.

☐ *Programmes*   Detailed rating information is available for all ITV programmes from BARB (see below). This enables the planner to make quite precise analyses of where the target audience is most likely to view, and this can be supplemented by viewing preference data from *TGI*. The trick is then to arrive at a mix of programmes and programme genres that delivers the desired coverage and frequency against the target group at an acceptable price— because simply buying the top five programmes will inevitably be a very expensive way of doing it. Also, regardless of what the target audience views, it is desirable to fit the advertising, if possible, into an appropriate context. While it is simple to put a brand of trainers into *Football Italia* or *The Big Match*, the choice of programme for a detergent or a small car may be less obvious.

☐ *Spot lengths*   A typical TV commercial is 30 seconds long. Many campaigns, however, aim to blend 30 seconds with 20 seconds or 10 seconds, or occasionally longer ads. It is inevitably tempting to use shorter spots, because they are cheaper, and can increase frequency—though the GRP calculations ought, as is normally done, to be converted back into 30-second equivalents, since this is the industry's currency. Most campaigns using a mix of 30 seconds and 20 seconds or 10 seconds (15 seconds in the US) will be planned and bought in ratios between 60:40 and 40:60. It is fairly rare for the proportion of short spots to be much higher than this—not least because of the growing suspicion, increasingly borne out by modelling, that 15 seconds and 10 seconds are not very effective, and certainly not as effective as their price ratio to 30 seconds would imply. One creative use of a combination of 30 seconds and 10 seconds, which is increasingly popular, is to 'top-and-tail' a break—run (usually) the 30-second first in the break, and a 10 second reminder at the end.

☐ *Place in break*   Research from a number of markets (some of it reported in Franzen)[1] shows that the first ad in a break, and the last, are more likely to be recalled (at least) than those in the middle. TV stations usually charge extra for allowing an advertiser to fix a spot as first in the break, but this may be worth it, especially where breaks are longer.

☐ *Other media and marketing activity*   Obviously, if other media are being used for advertising alongside TV, the TV campaign should mesh appropriately with these. This may involve using TV simultaneously, to add weight and increase synergy, or using the other media to fill gaps between TV.

---

[1] G. Franzen, Advertising Effectiveness, NTC, Henley-on-Thames, 1994.

Taking all these factors into account, the planner starts by mapping out a rough laydown of the TV schedule, and then , after discussion with the TV buyer, the rest of the account group and the client, puts the detailed flesh on it. This will look quite detailed (see Figure 10.6), but will, in fact, be primarily a *brief* to the buyer. Certainly, some spots or packages will have been pre-negotiated by the buyer, as the client has approved a particular recommendation, but most of the schedule will have to be bought after it has been planned and agreed by the client. As an advertiser, you need to recognize that the number of spots on the chart is not any indication of advertising weight: if you run 700 spots each with a rating of 0.1, you get no more—probably less, in fact—than if you run 10 spots each rating 7. There is nothing special about large numbers of spots.

Increasingly, TV planners are able to use so-called 'Optimizers': computer programmes that will analyse a proposed schedule against set parameters to deliver the most cost-effective combination of coverage and frequency. Like all such programmes, these are only as good as the assumptions that are fed into them and—in particular—they take no account of the varying quality of different ads, or of different programmes.

Thinking beyond spots

Spot TV accounts at present for over 90 per cent of expenditure on TV advertising in Britain, with less than £50 million going into sponsorship on ITV, but perhaps 5–10 per cent of Sky's revenue coming from this source. This is undoubtedly going to change dramatically in the future, as sponsorship opportunities become more widely available, and advertiser programme initiatives more feasible. At present, it is probably fair to say that both experience and understanding of TV sponsorship in the UK are very limited, and neither advertisers nor agencies are very sure how best to use or to evaluate sponsorships.

In the same way, managing the interaction between TV and other media is a surprisingly underdeveloped art. There are some obvious considerations—using images or sounds from TV to reprise the campaign in other media, for example. But the whole area is one that is ripe for further experiment and research. The growth of digital, too, will gradually facilitate the use of far more interactive versions of TV selling, either directly or through cross-links to the Internet, for example.

Future TV planning will have to loosen the ties of established practice, and open out to more channels, more formats, and new kinds of interaction, both with other media and within TV itself.

Lansdown Conquest Media Schedule

Lansdown Conquest Media

Client :   **xxxxxx**

Product :   **video release**
Plan 1 - Spot Advertising

Date :   **#######**
Status :   Proposal 1
Release Date :   3/22/99

Television	Length	Cost £	A16-34 GRPs	Cover	Freq	B10-15 GRPs	Cover	Freq
ITV	10"	139 900	40			26		
Channel 4	10"	58 300	25			21		
Channel 5	10"	33 250	14			9		
Nickleodeon	10"	10 500	5			8		
Sky 1	10"	29 500	15			13		
Sky Sports	10"	19 700	10			10		
Sci Fi Channel	10"	5 200	3			2		
MTV	10"	6 100	3			3		
Cartoon Network	10"	5 200	3			4		
		307 650	118	52%	2.3	96	46%	2.1

Coverage of key audiences:

16-34 Adults		Boys 10-15	
TVRs	135	TVRs	111
Reach	55%	Reach	50%
OTS	2.5	OTS	2.2

8-Mar	15-Mar	22-Mar	29-Mar	5-Apr	12-Apr

Figure 10.6.   A short-term TV schedule (Source: Lansdown Conquest)

How TV is bought

A TV buyer is usually not the person who planned the campaign. The buyer will be given a detailed buying brief by the planner and the client, which will specify the target audience, the length of spot (or combination of lengths), targets in terms of GRPs and, usually, coverage and frequency as well, specific programmes or types of programmes that are to be especially aimed for, and so on. The campaign laydown will specify the type of campaign to be bought, its desired duration and the budget available. Normally, the buyer's aim will be either to maximize GRPs within the budget or to achieve the targeted GRPs (etc.) at the lowest possible cost within the budget, thus creating savings for the client. Assuming, however, that the planner has done a good job, there will be little leeway for saving money.

The benchmark used by buyers to assess their performance is Station Average Price—the 30-second CPT for the station, calculated on a monthly basis. This is a factor of the station's revenue during the month, the amount of airtime sold and the audiences delivered. It varies significantly from month to month. SAPs become available only 8–10 days after the end of the month: a buyer uses predictions of SAP for the coming months as a target against which to negotiate, and the actual SAPs, retrospectively, both to demonstrate the effectiveness of buying and negotiation and, more importantly, to earn pre-agreed discounts from the TV stations. A media consultancy, Billett and Co, has published estimates for the *average* discount achieved against SAP on ITV1 in 1998 as 17 per cent, with far higher figures for Channel 4.

There is a substantial debate within the industry as to whether SAPs are a sensible trading currency, but no one has yet managed to produce an acceptable alternative, given the way the UK market operates at present.

In the UK, plans are frequently put together and bought about three months before the campaign is due to start: the TV companies operate an eight-week cancellation period—after eight weeks before the advertising is due to run, you have to pay a penalty for cancelling. In other countries, it is often the practice to book an entire year's advertising, or at least the majority of the campaign, in advance. (In the UK, you may sometimes be able to get a better deal by doing this, but you need to be very sure of your plans, and it removes the possibility of playing the market on any scale in the short term.)

Just as the TV contractor will be hoping to maximize revenue per spot, so the buyer's job is to buy as cheaply as possible, while fulfilling the brief. Buyers will have their own tricks—disguising the precise criteria against which the campaign is bought is an obvious one—and will aim to play one contractor off against another. As the options available increase, this becomes more readily feasible, and the seller's task more difficult.

TV audience research

The whole structure of TV planning, selling and buying is founded on audience research, which provides the currency—ratings against specific audiences—that the industry relies on.

In most of the world, TV audience research is currently done by 'people meters'—individual handsets linked with boxes that sit on the TV set and are programmed to record who is in the room and what programmes are being watched—or viewed on the VCR via time-shift. In the UK at least, this involves a large (4500), nationally representative sample of households maintained for BARB (Broadcast Advertising Research Board) by two major market research companies, RSMB and TNSofres. BARB is a joint venture of the ITC, BBC, advertisers and agencies. BARB records viewing behaviour for every minute of the TV day—but cannot tell the researcher what the people in front of the TV set are actually up to. Various pieces of research have shown that this could be anything—use your imagination!

The problems that face BARB and its equivalents elsewhere in the world are becoming very large. A proliferation of channels, most of them probably with very small audiences, will want to be measured, so as to enter on to planners' candidate lists. The problem is that most will have audiences too small to be trackable by a sample the size of BARB's (which is larger than the US Nielsen panel), while the design of the people meters will have to be substantially modified to cope with the number of channels. Around the world, there are a variety of experiments in progress, trying to produce new, better measuring technology to deal with the new scenario. It remains to be seen which of two or three main kinds of competing technology wins through.

Whatever happens, there will remain a big problem for smaller channels: BARB cannot be relied on to cope with programmes gaining less than a 0.5 per cent household share—and Nielsen in the US is even less sensitive, as well as providing less minute-by-minute detail. It is likely that the mainstream service will have to be supplemented by other techniques—perhaps on the lines of the diary-type research used by RAJAR for radio audience research in the UK (see below, page 199). It remains to be seen whether this will be done by BARB itself, or whether BARB will act as some sort of methodological screening house for tailored research carried out by individual channels.

BARB, of course, is a head-counting mechanism that already provides more data than planners can easily handle, with limited accuracy even for existing small channels, before the introduction of digital TV. Planners need, however, more than this. As the TV audience fragments, and as targeting attempts to become more precise across the whole world of marketing communications, people are looking for ways to add qualitative judgements to the numbers. What sort of programmes

Simply watching TV	38
Talking	23
Eating	20
Reading	19
Telephoning	12
Doing handicrafts	10
Sleeping	9
Ironing	4
Playing with children	4
Attend to pets	3
Doing homework	2
Do odd jobs	2
Other	7

Figure 10.7. Activities while watching TV: Germany, 1992 per cent of adults (Source: BAT Freizeitforschungsinstitut, 1992, in G. Franzen, *Advertising Effectiveness*, NTC)

do our target audience actually *like* to view, so that we can find them among a plethora of channels? Are they, or will they become, loyal to particular channels? What sort of programmes do they really *enjoy*, so that we can place our ads in a context where they may be watched with extra attention (as research suggests they will be)? How can we relate the way people use the media to the way they shop, in terms of time of day, day of week, mood and focus of interest?

While there are some published sources of data that provide a start to answering these questions and others like them, much of the most valuable work is being done on a proprietary basis by the big media agencies. Typical projects look at the relationship between programme genres and the recall or other effects of the advertising run in them, the levels of attention to different programmes or at different times during the day and the effect of this on advertising recall, and so on. (One of the problems about much of this research is that it tends to be based on sophisticated measures of media exposure and media use, but rather limited measures of advertising effects.)

For example, attention to the programme is something that clearly matters. Research in several countries shows that, in general, people are quite likely to be doing something else while watching TV—eating, household chores, reading, talking. Figure 10.7 shows some findings from German research. Recall of ads from the centre break is on average at least a third higher among people who are giving the TV their full attention than among those giving it less than average attention.

One final aspect of TV audience research is the whole question of advertising avoidance. A survey done for *Campaign* in August 1998 found over 50 per cent of

UK adults saying that they actively avoided TV commercials, by changing channel or by doing something else during breaks. Earlier work, by a variety of researchers,[2] had identified a substantial minority—some 25–30 per cent of adults—who could be described as TV 'ad rejectors', and this has been refined in work by Carat that shows that ad rejection tends to vary both by medium and by product category. There is ample evidence of people using their remote control to 'zap' commercials, or fast-forwarding through commercial breaks on programmes they have recorded on video.

Once again, this calls attention to the definition in the BARB research of a TV OTS: presence in the room with the set turned on. It all goes to emphasize the need to understand the target audience, and its relationship with the medium, the channel or station and the programmes in which you seek to advertise.

TV commercial production

This book is not going to tell you how to physically produce ads, but there are some general points that have to be considered about production for each of the main media. For TV, you need to recognize that a commercial can be an expensive investment in its own right, and that the costs do not stop once the film is in the can. The range of costs for a 30-second commercial can run from a few thousand pounds up to £500 000 and well beyond. In 1998, a typical commercial produced in the UK would be likely to cost £150–200 000.

The costs of production include fees to a specialist production house, the director, actors and specialist assistants like make-up artists, home economists, animal trainers, etc.; set building, locations; music, and 'post-production' (the work of editing, grading the picture, addition of special effects, titling, computer manipulation, etc.). Once the film is complete, enough copies have to be made for all the stations that are going to play it out, and there are industry-negotiated payments to performers (actors, musicians, etc.) to be made every time the film is aired. Equity, the UK actors' trade union, and the IPA have regular disputes about the scale of repeat fees, leading to various forms of industrial action—the latest of these ran through 1998.

Production costs have tended to rise as a proportion of the total cost of TV advertising (see Figure 10.8), in spite of serious attempts by the industry to restrain them. Arguably, this growth reflects the desire by agencies and advertisers to maximize the effectiveness of their advertising by putting money into the creative product. The difficulty faced by most clients is to judge whether a cost is justifiable or not. Major advertisers have sought to find ways of controlling production costs,

---

[2] J. Samuels and R. Silman, 'Who are the TV rejectors?' *Admap*, April 1997, and references.

Year	Production as % of spend
1985	13.7
1986	14.0
1987	13.3
1988	13.1
1989	13.0
1990	13.8
1991	14.3
1992	14.7
1993	14.8
1994	15.0
1995	14.8
1996	15.0
1997	15.0

Figure 10.8. TV production costs as a percentage of TV adspend UK 1985–97 (Source: AA, *Advertising Statistics Yearbook 1998*, NTC Publications)

in some cases by insisting on all their commercials being produced by a single production house. This is not entirely satisfactory, especially from the viewpoint of the agency creative people, since the agency view is that it is the director who makes the main difference to the production qualities of a commercial, and directors are— in the UK at least—generally tied to specific production houses. A joint AFVPA/IPA/ ISBA report[3] lays down some practical guidelines for controlling production costs.

A TV commercial will start off as an idea—a scenario perhaps with a few words of script. This is then worked up into a script (Figure 10.9), which may be converted into a storyboard—a combination of script and illustrations or, occasionally, photographs—for presentation to the client. The storyboard may also be used for research purposes, to see whether consumers understand and respond to the idea. It may, too, be converted into an animatic (page 115) for research purposes. Once agency and client are happy with the script, the whole process of casting actors, selecting director and producer, finding locations or building sets, finding or commissioning music, etc., gets under way, and then the film is shot. Shooting sounds romantic, but is actually pretty boring for spectators, especially if it's done in a studio somewhere in a grimy suburb; and those location shoots in the Bahamas are depressingly rare. Within all this, too, the script and the final film have to be cleared by the BACC (page 237), to ensure that it meets the demands of the Code of Practice. Without this clearance, it cannot be shown.

---

[3] *Producing Advertising Commercials*, AFVPA/IPA/ISBA Working Party, 1996.

LANSDOWN CONQUEST   4 FLITCROFT STREET, LONDON WC2H 8DJ.

TELEPHONE: +44-171 240 4949   FACSIMILE: +44-171 240 9094   ISDN: +44-171 379 3303

BACC TEAM NUMBER: 5
BACC EXECUTIVE: KATE WHITE
AGENCY CONTACT: JOANNE CRESSER/EILEEN QUIRKE
PRODUCT: NIKON F5
TITLE: WALK
DURATION: 30"
CLOCK NO: LAU/NIDA132/030

We open looking down Cleethorpes promenade at an old woman, smiling. Cut to close up of the lady.

MVO: YOU'RE WATCHING A MODERN DAY MIRACLE.....

Cut to the lady sat on a bench next to the pier. Cut to the lady walking past a fish and chip shop" large manikin on the street, cut to the lady next to a fibreglass rhino in a fairground, cut to the lady next to a miniature steam train. Cut to her shuffling past the camera on the promenade: we turn to keep looking at her: this leaves us facing a mirror. For the first time we see our reflection....shooting with a Nikon F5.

MVO: BECAUSE THIS FILM WAS SHOT ON A CAMERA THAT ONLY TAKES STILLS.

We see Alastair Thain (photographer) zoom in on the reflection and we are left with a close-up of the Nikon F5, taking its own mirrored packshot.

MVO: THE NIKON F5. TECHNICALLY THE QUICKEST CAMERA IN THE WORLD.

SUPER: IN AUTOFOCUS MODE

Cut to the old lady walking away from the camera along the promenade.

Figure 10.9.   Post-production script for TV commercial (Source: Lansdown Conquest)

The whole process, including all the post-production work, is likely to take anything up to three months, though it can be done much faster, if the will and the need are there, and real polish is not essential.

Summary

□ TV is a dynamic medium, world-wide, which is now changing rapidly under the impact of new technology.
□ The industry's structure varies quite widely by country, as do buying practices and the nature of commercial breaks.
□ Most countries have in place more or less sophisticated continuous research, which enables buyers to analyse their prospective and bought schedules in

considerable detail, and proprietary 'optimisers' enable the planners to fine-tune coverage, frequency and cost.
□ In the future, spot TV may become less central to TV advertising, as sponsorship and advertiser-originated programming grow in importance to fill all those new digital channels.

Some questions to consider

□ Your agency tells you that the available budget will not buy you a year-long, national campaign at more than 80 TVRs for 26 weeks' advertising. What considerations do you expect them to take into account in proposing a TV schedule for your brand? Very broadly, what sort of alternative schedules would you expect them to put forward?
□ You are the advertising sales manager of a small channel available on digital TV. How would you go about convincing an advertiser or agency of your value to their schedule?
□ Your media auditor tells you that your agency has achieved a discount of 15 per cent against SAP. What does this tell you, and is it good or bad?

11 The press

I make it a rule never to look into a newspaper

Sheridan, *The Critic*

Modern advertising began in the press, and there is still more money spent in press media, worldwide, than on TV. You know the press: it is all over the newsagent's shop or the kiosk—newspapers, magazines, in different shapes and sizes, in black and white or colour, on different types of paper, and with a breath-taking range of content.

In essence, the press can be divided into two main groupings: newspapers on the one hand and magazines on the other. They have different characteristics and a wide variety of subgroups in each category. The detailed structure of both categories varies from country to country, and this chapter will mainly be concerned with the UK. The principles of using the press for advertising, however, are broadly similar worldwide: the main factors that differ between countries are language and literacy, though in much of the South the availability of both materials and modern machinery is a constraint on quality.

Newspapers

The UK has a plethora of newspaper titles, but is characterized by the strength of its national daily and Sunday papers: this strength is not unique, but there are few other countries with the same strength in depth in national papers, especially on Sundays. Indeed, in some continental European countries, the only truly national newspapers are specialized sports papers, like *Corriere dello Sport* in Italy, or *L'Equipe* in France. Other developed markets (such as France) tend to have city, regional or provincial newspapers as their main print news medium. This means that the UK has three of the top four newspaper circulations in Europe, after Germany's *Bild*. In addition, it has a wide range of local newspapers, both daily (usually evenings) and weekly. The latter include a substantial number of free papers, financed solely by advertising. The national papers dominate the newspaper display advertising market, but regionals have an enormous classified advertising business—which is increasingly vulnerable to the Internet.

The UK national papers divide into three 'tiers': the 'quality' papers, which are broadsheets (60 cm × 38 cm), such as *The Times, Telegraph* and *Guardian*; and

	1988	1989	1990	1991	1992	1993	1994	1995	1996	1997	1998
Daily Mirror	3120	3146	3106	2919	2815	2631	2495	2525	2443	2353	2236
Daily Record	770	773	778	761	755	751	751	748	723	691	673
Daily Star	991	902	916	858	803	768	743	744	757	727	591
Sun	4183	4095	3896	3679	3566	3640	4078	4053	4016	3834	3617
Total popular	9064	8916	8696	8217	7939	7790	8067	8070	7939	7605	7117
Daily Express	1658	1582	1574	1542	1525	1460	1338	1271	1220	1215	1157
Daily Mail	1776	1737	1689	1702	1713	1743	1774	1832	2974	2196	2217
Today	478	589	560	475	520	548	597	499	—	—	—
Total mid-market	3912	3908	3823	3719	3758	3751	3709	3602	3294	3411	3374
Daily Telegraph	1134	1108	1081	1066	1040	1021	1042	1060	1065	1111	1054
Financial Times (UK only)	206	202	195	183	177	173	170	171	171	172	176
Guardian	454	435	427	421	415	407	401	397	397	406	375
Independent	381	408	412	383	372	335	281	294	272	259	222
Times	444	435	426	396	385	390	544	658	738	770	760
Total quality	2619	2588	2541	2449	2389	2326	2438	2580	2643	2718	2587
TOTAL	15595	15412	15060	14385	14086	13867	14214	14252	13876	13734	13078

Figure 11.1. UK daily newspaper circulations, 1988–98, in thousands (Source: ABC)

two tabloid (38 cm × 30 cm) groups: the 'mid-market' *Mail* and *Express*; and the 'popular' *Sun, Mirror,* etc. The one exception to this tidy classification is the popular broadsheet Sunday, the *News of the World.* Total national newspaper circulations[1] are falling, but within this the qualities, which only account for some 20 per cent of the combined circulation, are growing. The only tabloid showing consistent growth is the *Daily Mail.* Circulations range from under 200 000, for the specialist *Financial Times,* to over 4 million for the *News of the World* and 3.6 million for the *Sun* (see Figure 11.1).

All the national dailies now offer advertisers full colour, as well as the traditional spot colour (one colour only), but this is less readily available for the Sundays, where most colour advertising goes into the various magazine supplements that have proliferated in recent years.

The quality newspapers, in particular, have split themselves into an increasing number of parts in recent years, in an attempt both to tempt advertisers and to cater to specific target audiences. This process is most extreme on Sunday, where the *Sunday Times,* though nowhere near as weighty as its New York equivalent, comes

---

[1] Circulations of most significant print media in the UK are measured by the Audit Bureau of Circulations (ABC), which also now audits web sites and mailing lists.

Type	No of titles	Circulation ('000s)
Mornings	17	1 073
Evenings	72	4 343
Sundays	9	2 263
Paid-for weeklies	464	6 027
Free weeklies	610	27 800

Figure 11.2.   UK regional newspapers combined circulation, by type, 1997. (Source: AA, *Advertising Statistics Yearbook 1998*, NTC Publications)

in no less than nine sections. In recent years, the Saturday editions of the national dailies have begun to acquire some of the features of the Sundays, and this has probably contributed to the decline of the Sundays' circulations.

Regional newspapers

The UK has over a thousand regional papers, the vast majority weeklies, though the largest paid-for circulations—up to 200 000, in some instances—are achieved by the major evening papers. The weeklies divide into two categories—paid-for papers and free papers. In many cases, these compete against each other, both for readers and advertising moneys. Unsurprisingly, because the free papers are delivered free to all households within their circulation area, these have significantly larger circulations than their paid-for competitors. The largest, the Manchester *Metro News*, has a circulation approaching 450 000, compared with the *Manchester Evening News* (paid-for) figure of some 180 000. The disparity is illustrated by the total combined circulations of the regional papers (see Figure 11.2).

The regional press is dominated by about a dozen publishing groups, which have emerged from a process of consolidation that has been in progress for many years, and is still continuing. Scotland, is a special case, with a plethora of 'national' papers competing, successfully, with the English-based nationals.

Newspaper readership research

Newspaper readership is tracked by the *National Readership Survey*, carried out by IPSOS-RSL for NRS Ltd. The NRS is a long-established survey that covers both newspapers and magazines, and provides a measure of 'average issue readership' among adults aged 15+. Apart from the national newspapers, it collects data for reading 'any' regional paper, across the main categories. Research into regional papers is carried out by JICREG for the Newspaper Society. NRS data provide detailed demographic breakdowns of the readers of each paper, together with some information about their reading interests and ownership of selected durable products. The data can be used to cross-analyse the readerships of any combination of papers. Duplicated readership is quite significant, since the *average* reader reads 1.3 national newspapers—but only 57 per cent of adults in the UK reads a daily national newspaper at all.

On the other hand, loyalty to newspapers is quite high, with most readers of most papers reading them more or less regularly, and a substantial proportion having a regular delivery from their newsagent. Nonetheless, aggressive promotional pro-grammes, primarily by the Murdoch (NewsCorp) titles, *The Times* and the *Sun*, have introduced some volatility into the market. At the same time, the *Daily Mail* has successfully captured a substantial part of the natural constituency of the ailing *Daily Express* , and also gained readers from the *Daily Mirror*, the more intelligent of the three downmarket tabloids.

From the reader research point of view, newspaper research is rather limited. The NRS takes only the broadest view of newspaper sections: It collects data on readers of the main colour supplements, but has so far made no attempt to cover the various sections that both dailies and Sundays have spawned. The only public research into these has come from an initiative that the newspaper proprietors have so far refused to support, the *Quality of Readership Survey* (QRS) (see page 181).

In addition to the industry readership surveys, newspaper readership can be related to a wide range of products and brands through the *TGI*, and the major consumer panel researchers (see page 119) collect data on newspapers and magazines as part of the demographic data on panel households. This has been used to provide single-source data (page 65), combining readership and brand purchasing behaviour.

There is surprisingly little published research on how people actually read news-papers and how they relate to the advertising in them. It is clearly an observable fact that people do not read papers from front to back, nor from cover to cover; and although reading and noting surveys (in which readers are taken through a recent issue of a paper or magazine and asked which pages—including the ads—they looked at and read) are out of fashion, we know that different parts of papers are ignored by varying proportions of their readership. It is generally assumed by advertisers and their agencies that an ad has a better chance of being seen if it is early in the paper, and on a right-hand page. Research by J. Walter Thompson, summarized below (page 174) sheds some light on this.

How newspaper space is sold

Newspaper space in the UK is sold by the column centimetre (ccm), though for larger spaces the space size may be described as a whole, half or quarter page. In

	1994	1995	1996	1997	1998
Popular/mid-market Dailies	25.1	29.2	30.8	33.8	36.1
Quality Dailies	33.9	41.3	43.2	44.4	45.8
Popular/mid-market Sundays	38.1	42.0	42.1	43.8	46.4
Quality Sundays	50.6	58.8	59.5	65.1	66.4

Figure 11.3.   Colour advertising in national newspapers percentage of ad pages in colour, 1994–98, by type of paper (Source: MMS)

some countries, space is normally described purely in terms of cm², which can be disconcerting to Britons, and, even more, to Americans, who still deal in column inches. The papers publish quite detailed ratecards, which are summarized in a useful monthly publication, *BRAD* (*British Rate & Data*).[2] The ratecard, as for TV, is a basis for negotiation, but, since press space is theoretically very flexible—a paper can quite easily be expanded or contracted in size, within limits—there is nothing very like the TV pre-emption system. Instead, the ratecard carries premium rates for specific positions in the paper, additional charges for fixing a position, and so on. An advertiser can earn discounts for exceeding a certain volume of advertising in a given title, and may negotiate (at a price) various forms of exclusivity for the advertising: the first retail ad in the paper; all ads to be next to editorial matter; all ads to be solus on the page; for example. Similarly, where a proprietor owns several papers, the advertiser may do a deal that covers space in all of them—perhaps with a guarantee that the advertiser will not use a competing publication.

An added variable for newspapers is the use of colour. In the past, the most that papers could offer was spot colour—a single colour that could be used to lift an ad and make it stand out. For some years now, though, full colour has been available on all the nationals and quite a selection of regionals, and a substantial proportion of national advertising is now in colour (see Figure 11.3).

As with TV, there is good evidence that response to ads varies with the size of the ad, and spaces are priced accordingly. Research in the 1950s established a simple mathematical relationship between ad size and response, and recent work by various media agencies has confirmed that the rules still hold. An ambitious project by J. Walter Thompson extended the simple size measurement to include colour and position in the paper. A summary of their findings is included in Box 11.1.

---

[2] *British Rate & Data*, Maclean Hunter, London, monthly.

> ### Box 11.1   *Newspaper reading and advertisements*
>
> Research by JWT among national newspaper readers produced a range of specific conclusions about reading habits and ad noting:
>
> □ Ad noting is higher, the better read the page is: an increase in page traffic from 10 per cent to 20 per cent (= ×2) increases ad noting by ×2.8—a 1.4 : 1 ratio.
> □ Ad noting increases with size of ad, but diminishing returns set in around the 50 ccm point for broadsheets and 40 ccm for tabloids: a 25 × 4 ad is the most cost-effective.
> □ Colour helps, especially, smaller ads: the effect peaks at 300 ccm, where a colour ad gets 50 per cent more noting than a mono ad. After this, the gap falls, sharply, and mono ads are as good over about 430 ccm.
> □ This means that in broadsheets, a colour ad is as effective as a mono ad two sizes bigger—i.e. a 33 × 5 is as good as a mono page, while in tabloids the difference is one size—a 25 × 4 is as good as a page (38 × 6).
> □ In tabloids, left-hand pages are as good as right-hand, but in broadsheets right-hand pages do better.
> □ There are clear advantages in being in the front third of the paper.
>
> Source: Daniele Cardillo and James Walker, 'Does size matter'? *Admap*, January 1998

Newspaper space is often bought at fairly short notice, because a lot of the advertising carried in papers is related to promotions or other tactical marketing activity, or dictated by topicality. It also shows very different patterns by day of the week. A recent analysis of national newspaper advertising by day of week showed that Saturday is far and away the most important day for the dailies, accounting for 40 per cent of dailies' ad revenue, but that Sunday alone takes a third of all national newspaper advertising, and is no less than 40 per cent bigger as a marketplace than Saturday (see Figure 11.4).

The same analysis showed that different product categories spend their money very differently over the week, with retailers, cars and mail order concentrating towards the weekend, but government advertising, for example, is heavily weighted to the beginning of the week, which is likely to provide a cheaper buy.

Newspapers as an advertising market

National newspapers' business is predominantly in display advertising, which accounts for 75 per cent of total ad revenue and 65 per cent of advertising pages and is broadly based. No less than seven broad categories of goods and services account for over 5 per cent of expenditure, with none taking more than 15 per cent. By contrast, the regional papers are a massive classified advertising market, and

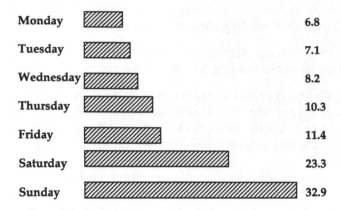

Monday	6.8
Tuesday	7.1
Wednesday	8.2
Thursday	10.3
Friday	11.4
Saturday	23.3
Sunday	32.9

Figure 11.4.   UK newspaper adspend by day of week, per cent, 1998 (Source: MMS)

Category	National	Regional
Retail	415	221
Financial	409	31
Motors	329	296
Business-to-business	269	62
Travel/holidays	265	40
Mail order	228	–
Office auto/telecoms	216	22
Publishing	72	22
Entertainment	58	44
Industrial	55	328
Household furnishings		19
Total (all categories)	2817	1180

Figure 11.5.   UK newspaper advertising, by broad category, top ten, 1997, £ million (Source: A. C. Nielsen-MEAL)

three categories of advertiser—retail, motoring and household equipment—account for over 50 per cent of the total spend (see Figure 11.5).

Magazines

Magazines are the richest and most diverse advertising media, in terms of their sheer variety and scope. The UK is a particularly rich market for magazine publishing, with over 2500 consumer magazine titles recorded by *BRAD*, and well over 5000 business and professional publications. Because of the currency of the English

	France	Germany	Italy	Netherlands	UK
Cosmopolitan	245	386	na	108	461
Elle	339	212	139	59	213
Marie Claire	514	143	189	91	416
Nat. Geographie	46	na	50	56	437
Readers Digest	773	1193	294	350	1446
Vogue	102	na	84	na	202
The Economist	21	na	12	10	119

Figure 11.6.   Circulations of selected magazines in selected European countries, 1997
(Source: Media and Marketing Europe/Mindshare)

language internationally, at least some of these magazines have substantial overseas circulations, and some UK trade and technical publications are the recognized global authorities in their field.

On the consumer side, too, a number of magazines have in recent years been internationalized, whether from the UK or elsewhere—titles like *Vogue, Cosmopolitan, Bella, Prima, Best, Hello*! have joined long-established travellers such as *Reader's Digest* and *National Geographic*. News magazines such as *Time, Newsweek* and *The Economist* have long had extensive worldwide circulation, and—at least for advertising purposes—reflected this in regional editions (see Figure 11.6).

For the advertiser, the beauty of magazines is their specificity. They are read by specific and usually clearly defined audiences—defined by age, sex and/or common interests and enthusiasms. They cover, editorially, specific subjects—which may be modern dance, or sexual relationships, home economics or vintage motorcycles—and so represent a specific marketplace for brand owners catering for these interests. They often have a unique style or mood which reflects the character and expectations of their readers: in the relatively new UK men's magazine sector, the mood, and to an extent the content of, say, *Loaded* is very different from that of *FHM*.

What this means, of course, is that it becomes possible for the advertiser to use magazines to talk to people who are genuinely interested, in some way, in a precise set of topics, which should, with luck, include the advertised brand. It will not always succeed in this, because even the precision that magazines appear to offer can cover a range of involvement from the fanatical and positively nerdy to a quite casual interest. To take car magazines as an example, their readership splits into two main groups: real enthusiasts, who live and breathe cars, and people who are just coming into the market for a new car and use the magazine as a research tool.

For most car marques, most of the time, it is the latter group who are the real focus of interest.

Magazine editors will tell you that they have an extraordinarily close relationship with their readers: this is often true. Magazines are stored, collected, read and reread. They are mined for information, and trusted as sources of advice. Their letter columns are often vigorous, controversial and well-informed. They are, at their best, the precursors of the Internet chat site, but with, always, a degree of editorial control—which lends them a genuine authority that is missing from the Internet. This, of course, has led inevitably to the migration of magazines to the Internet: both as a way of extending their coverage and of providing a more informal channel of communication than the traditionally paternalistic editor–reader dialogue.

At the same time, there is a degree of enthusiasm among some magazine proprietors for a closer relationship with television. So-called 'masthead' TV—the creation of a close relationship and shared editorial stance and some content between a magazine and a TV programme—has been prohibited, until very recently, on UK commercial TV, though permitted elsewhere in the world. As a result, UK masthead TV has been pioneered—very effectively—by the non-commercial BBC, which has built highly successful magazines around programmes such as *Top Gear*, *Gardeners' World*, *Good Food* and *Clothes Show*. There seems every likelihood that this kind of relationship, but starting from the magazine rather than the programme, will grow far more common with the spread of digital TV, with its rampant appetite for programme content.

A final form of migration of magazines from their traditional independence is the burgeoning market for so-called 'customer magazines': magazines created, usually by one of a few specialist publishers, for (usually) service marketers who use them as an element in customer loyalty programmes. Probably the first of these were the airlines' in-flight magazines, such as BA's *High Life*, but they are now commonplace among retailers, financial institutions, car manufacturers (*Ford* magazine is far the largest car magazine, in circulation terms), charities, and so on.

The enthusiasm with which magazines are read is paralleled by their breadth of reach: they are often borrowed or passed on, so that each magazine may have a large number of readers (it varies widely by title and category). Part of this, of course, is the dentists' waiting room readership, but many magazines are shared a great deal more systematically than this. As a result, while weekly magazines tend to accumulate no more than three or four readers per copy, which is only slightly more than the figure for national newspapers, monthlies may get as many as 10–15 readers each. Of course, this takes time to accumulate, which makes it important in planning magazine advertising to recognize that the effects are likely to be more spread out than those of a TV or even newspaper campaign. It may take six months or more for a monthly magazine to achieve 90 per cent of its eventual cumulative readership. (Readership of monthly magazines may be inflated in research.)

Magazine categories

In the UK, at least, magazines are conventionally divided, both for research and for media planning, into a number of categories. The main split is by publishing frequency, with weeklies being treated very differently from monthlies (or other longer intervals). Within weeklies, there are three major categories: women's weeklies, TV and radio programme magazines, and current affairs titles. In addition, there are a variety of special interest weeklies, for example *Angling Times*, *Amateur Gardening*, *Autocar*, *NME (New Musical Express)*, *Shoot!*, and so on. Most special interest titles, though, are monthly, and the monthlies include major categories of fashion, household, men's magazines, sports publications, motors, general magazines (such as *Reader's Digest)*, and general women's magazines like *Cosmopolitan*, *Company*, *She*, etc. Included in this last group is a variety of titles that are more or less age-specific, especially for teenagers, such as *Just Seventeen*, *19*, and the fortnightly group of *More!*, *Big!*, *Mizz* and *Shout*.

All of these groups can be found elsewhere around the world, though not always in quite such density. The media world is always almost as ready as the advertising business to rip off a good idea, though it is not always easy to make the necessary translation, and often the originator does it first, as happened in the UK with *Hello!*, imported by the Spanish publishers of *¡Hola!* and subsequently imitated by *OK!*. There is no British equivalent of the US *Sports Illustrated* (or, indeed, of *L'Equipe*), just as there is no real parallel anywhere for the UK comic magazine, *Viz*. In the same way, Britain has no equivalents to weekly illustrated news magazines like *L'Express*, *Nouvel Observateur* or *Le Point*.

The biggest circulations are those of the TV programme magazines, a category with three titles selling over a million copies plus the huge give-away *Sky TV Guide*—but highly vulnerable to the development of Electronic Programme Guides (EPGs) which are a key element in the offerings of the digital TV operators (see page 153). The other category that sees a number of very large circulations is the customer magazines, where the *AA Magazine* has an even larger distribution than the *Sky TV Guide*—just over 4 million—and several retailers' titles reach one million or more. Of the 'content' magazines, *Reader's Digest*, selling 1.3 million copies, is far and away the largest. Only about half a dozen other titles, a group that includes three women's weeklies, top the 600 000 mark (see Figure 11.7).

Business magazines are usually categorized by subject-matter, which is either industry-specific, like *Caterer & Hotelkeeper*, *Accountancy Age* and *Drapers Record*; or discipline-based, like *Human Resources*, *Marketing* or *The Engineer*.

Active purchase	Circ.	Non-active purchase	Circ.
What's on TV	1765	AA Magazine	4085
Radio Times	1400	Sky TV Guide	3404
Reader's Digest	1303	Safeway Magazine	1997
Take a Break	1274	Cable Guide	1850
TV Times	850	Somerfield Magazine	1177
FHM	751	Debehams	1110
TV Quick	741	Omagazine—consumer	864
Woman	711	Jazzy Books	800
Woman's Own	654	Ford Magazine	667
Bella	611	VM–Vauxhall Magazine	627
Woman;s Weekly	595	Homebase Living	599
That's Life	540	The Legion	557
Hello!	511	You & Yours	511
Prima	510	Saga Magazine	498
Best	501	National Geographic	366
Chat	497	The Renault Magazine	350
Cosmopolitan	476	Motoring & Leisure	329
Candis	459	The Caravan Club Magazine	291
Loaded	457	Diamond Free Ads	289
Sugar	452		

Figure II.7.   Major UK magazine circulations—1998, '000s (Source: ABC)

Business titles vary between weekly and monthly publication, and cover or subscription prices can differ widely. A substantial proportion are actually or effectively free, while others may cost up to £250 per year. The free magazines are often 'controlled circulation': every recipient has to provide details of their employment once a year, so that the publication can be sure that its audience is as defined.

Business titles mostly have relatively small circulations, with none, apart from *The Economist*, which is something of a hybrid, exceeding 150 000. Most of the largest titles are, in fact, at least partly consumer publications—computer titles with an across-boundaries appeal.

Magazine research

Research into magazine readership and reading habits is not everywhere as well developed as it should, ideally, be—though this is an area where the UK seems to be well ahead of the US. A limited range of the larger magazines is covered by the NRS, which looks at over 150 titles, and many of these are also listed in *TGI*. This provides the basis for top-line magazine planning, especially with the aid of appropriate cross-analyses. Beyond this, the most important piece of research, which was sponsored by a range of interested parties, but excluded the Newspaper Publishers Association, who seemed reluctant to be involved in non-NRS reader research that aimed to look at readership of newspaper sections, is the *Quality of Readership Survey (QRS)*, first published in spring 1998.

This survey looked at some 240 consumer magazines and the national newspapers, with the aim of establishing in greater detail than hitherto what people actually read, and how intensely they do so. A brief overview of the findings is given in Box 8.2. Apart from the light that the survey throws on the readership of newspaper sections, the element that the publishers like to emphasize is the PEX (page exposure) measure. PEX, based on an earlier measure called MPX (multiple page exposure), shows that magazine readers often reread, or at least reopen, their magazines, so that an ad may be seen several times by the same reader in the same magazine. What this means, it is argued, is that the number of exposures to a magazine campaign, which has typically been measured as one OTS per reader, is considerably higher than the old OTS measure suggested. Thus, magazine CPTs ought to be considerably lower than conventionally estimated, so making magazines far more competitive.

Box 8.2   *QRS: A top-line overview*

The QRS follows NRS techniques for measuring overall readership, and correlates closely with that survey. In addition to readership (which includes data for all the main newspaper sections and supplements), it also measures: length of time spent reading frequency of reading frequency of looking at the average page and overall attitudes to the publication.

- Newspaper supplement/section reading data show that, if reading the paper is taken as 100, individual sections may score as low as around 30. Notably, sport sections score 45–55, across a range of papers. In general, the older (colour supplement) sections score best.
- People spend, on average, nearly an hour reading a magazine. This covers a range from virtually 75 minutes (for science and gardening titles) down to 35 for football publications. Sunday newspapers get 56 minutes, dailies only 39, and sections and supplements average 25 minutes.
- PEX measures show that younger people, men and ABC1s spend more time with their magazines than others. Interestingly, newspaper supplements and sections get more attention from older readers and women.
- By magazine category, PEX scores range from a high of 6.99 for bridal magazines down to 1.3 for in-flight magazines and 'selling' magazines like *Exchange & Mart* and *Auto Trader*. Every magazine category does better than newspaper sections/supplements, which score 1.2.
- PEX scores can be used to weight conventional OTS calculations, and to provide a measure of frequency that is closer to TV OTS.

Against this, however, it could be argued that the way in which people use press ads is different from the way they use TV. On TV, the commercials are intrusive, and unless you are using the ad break to make tea or are quick with the remote, you watch the ads. In the press, you can simply carry on reading the editorial or turn the page. If you decide to look at—or even study—an ad, one exposure is usually sufficient to take out its message. What's more, you know what it says, so there's no need to read it again. The only benefit, in most cases, from PEX then becomes the reinforcement of the memory through whatever recognition you give the ad. This is a controversial area. There is some old (1960s) US research that suggests that some effects of an ad are about 10–15 per cent higher when it has been seen twice than when it has been seen only once, but there are technical problems in comparing the two types of research.

An extensive analysis of available research—some of it going back many years—has been assembled by the Periodical Publishers Association (PPA), under the title *How Magazine Advertising Works*.[3] This dates from before *QRS*, though it discusses the original MPX research. The publication covers: readers' relationships with magazines, the effects and effectiveness of magazine advertising and sales and sales-related evidence both for solus magazine campaigns and for magazines working together with TV.

Key points that are made in this analysis include:

- The role of magazines may vary from primarily information (TV guides) to almost pure entertainment (erotic publications): people have a rich variety of ways of relating to magazines.
- Readers generally have a close relationship with their magazines—and a relatively weak one with newspapers' colour supplements. (This leads to newspaper supplements achieving a PEX score of 1.2, against 2.4 for the magazines).
- Most readers have a repertoire of magazines, catering for different needs, moods and interests.
- Because of the close relationship between readers and their magazines, brands that can plug into this involvement have an evident opportunity to communicate and build their brand values in a favourable and sympathetic environment.
- This can be achieved with quite precise targeting and minimal wastage.
- The differences between magazines and their editorial environments and character means that creative material should, ideally, be tailored to the individual title—and the quite rapid wear-out of individual ads means that a

---

[3] Guy Consterdine, *How Magazine Advertising Works II*, PPA, London, 1997.

campaign should consist of several different creative treatments if it is to maximize its effect.

- Various magazine-specific research projects, especially IPC Magazines' 1994 AdTrack[4] study, show that magazine advertising can result in measurable increases in ad awareness, on a par—at least—with TV on a gain per GRP basis, and at lower cost; and have demonstrated significant increases in sales.
- More specifically, there is a growing series of studies that examine the relationship between TV and magazine advertising in mixed-media campaigns. These studies strongly suggest that a magazine element in a campaign can significantly enhance the effectiveness of the campaign (see Box 8.3). This appears to happen for at least two reasons: first, magazines are able to reach light viewers of TV, who would otherwise be underexposed to the campaign; and, secondly, the magazine message can amplify or explain points that the TV commercial is too short to get across effectively.

Box 8.3   Kenco Coffee: A mixed-media success

In 1996, IPC Magazines published the results of a test mounted by Kraft Jacobs Suchard to evaluate the effect of shifting 25 per cent of their TV budget for Kenco coffee into magazines.

The resulting schedule increased both ABC1 housewife coverage (marginally) and frequency (from 13.2 OTS to 17.7).

The results, from both Neilsen store audits and from AGB panel data, showed the brand's market share in the test areas (35 per cent of the country) performing significantly better (retail share was 28.5 per cent higher), and ad awareness on the Millward Brown tracking study was also above the TV-only area throughout the test.

Source: Alan Smith, 'More Food for Thought', *Admap*, February 1997.

Beyond this fairly general research, individual magazines have traditionally carried out their own reader research. In much of the trade and technical press, this may be the only useful source of data, because there are few, if any, industry-wide reader surveys (in the UK, Banner's annual study of the computer magazine market is one well-established exception). Reader surveys need to be viewed with care and, indeed, suspicion. They have a tendency to be postal surveys or in-magazine surveys, and in both cases they are therefore vulnerable to an enormous potential bias: respondents will consist solely of those who are prepared to take the time to reply and will inevitably be a small minority of the readership. There is no way of

---

[4] IPC Magazines, *Ad Track 94*, IPC Magazines, London, 1995.

telling how far they may represent a valid sample of readers or how the non-repliers may have differed from the repliers.

The one partial exception to this is the data collected by 'controlled circulation' magazines: these titles have, annually, to ask all their readers to complete a fairly basic form to remain on the circulation list. From this, the magazine can describe its readers reasonably accurately, in terms of the types of company they work for, their job titles, and so on.

A second exception is the syndicated survey, covering a group of magazines in the same market sector. The construction industry magazines, for example, have had available quite comprehensive surveys of this kind from time to time.

Buying magazine space

Magazine advertising is sold primarily on the basis of pages and subdivisions of a page, rather than the ccm basis of newspaper space. Magazine advertisers tend to be sensitive to position in the magazine, whether their ad is on a left- or right-hand page, and the editorial material which it faces. As a result, magazine ratecards place premium prices on the covers, inside and out, early pages and right-hand pages. My personal candidate for the most over-priced space is the inside back cover, though there is some research evidence to suggest that it is slightly better than one might fear.

Most magazine advertising is in colour—to the extent that using black and white could be a clever creative strategy, except that the available research evidence— mainly from American research by Roper Starch—shows that noting scores for colour are markedly higher (but then, so are the prices). A colour page is some 25 per cent more likely to be noticed by a reader than a b/w page—but colour page prices in magazines are anything from 15—50 per cent more expensive, as the Figure 11.8 shows.

Apart from colour and b/w, the magazine advertiser has the option to 'bleed' the ad on the page—to do without any white margin around the ad. This is, in fact, pretty standard practice in the UK, but the Roper Starch research quoted above suggests that bleed may be 10–15 per cent more effective. (It does, naturally, carry a 10 per cent premium for most magazines: these guys know their stuff.)

Beyond the fairly obvious use of pages, or double-page spreads (DPS), there are a variety of other possibilities in magazines. It is possible, for a price, to negotiate a branded wrap-round cover; or a fold-out cover ad; or any number of consecutive pages; or a scratch-and-sniff or tear-off fragrance strip; or a variety of loose inserts,

Publication	Circulation 000s	*B/W vs. Colour*		
		Page b/w (£)	*Page colour (£)*	*b/w as % of colour*
AA Magazine	4 084	n/a	26 000	n/a
Reader's Digest	1 303	18 000	24 500	73.5
TV Times	799	n/a	18 500	n/a
FHM	751	n/a	12 000	n/a
Woman	667	15 400	21 950	70.2
Hello!	510	n/a	14 250	n/a
Prima	501	9 591	15 986	60.0
Best	498	9 800	16 225	60.4
Cosmopolitan	476	n/a	13 560	n/a
Loaded	457	5 600	9 390	59.6
Sugar	452	6 905	9 490	72.8
Sainsbury's Magazine	411	*n/a*	9 800	*n/a*
Good Housekeeping	400	n/a	14 350	n/a
BBC Good Food	304	12 170 (fm*)	11 064	(110)
Smash Hits	295	7 780	13 300	58.5
Computeractive	219	n/a	5 513	n/a
Vogue	202	n/a	14 300	n/a
BBC Top Gear	181	4 100	7 400	55.4

* facing matter—a premium priced space

Notes: 1. Many magazines' abbreviated ratecards, as quoted by BRAD, do not give b/w prices, but b/w space is available by negotiation—sometimes at very little discount to colour.

2. The relationship between a cost and circulation varies significantly. This is partly due to the variation in readers per copy, but also reflects the 'desirability' of the reader profile.

Figure 11.8.   Page costs of selected magazines b/w versus colour (Sources: ABC, BRAD)

which could be limited to particular areas of the country; and so on. Magazines are quite flexible—the only real limit is your imagination (but the editor is entitled to dig his or her toes in if you try to go too far).

Press planning

Planning a press schedule, whether on its own or in conjunction with other media, involves a series of choices that can be greatly aided by computer analyses that are readily available from the main specialist bureaux, and have been enhanced in various proprietary ways by leading media agencies. As usual, the key variables are coverage and frequency, and the data from NRS and other sources make it possible to calculate the cross-coverage effects when a range of media are selected. For an indication of newspaper readership duplication, see Figure 11.9.[5] The planner has to set parameters for cover, frequency, time scale and CPT and can then select titles according to the relevant criteria for the campaign. Usually, these will include the definition of a specific target audience, which has to be translated into demographics for most cost comparisons and for cover and frequency analysis. However, they may well be supplemented by criteria for editorial style, mood and context, and perhaps by a variety of softer, more psychological descriptions of the audience derived from *TGI* or proprietary survey data.

The planning process can start from a cost ranking of titles (see page 143) against relevant demographics, and this is the conventional start-point for most planners. But it is perfectly possible to set other criteria: taking a set of titles as a 'must-have' list, and then building the schedule around these, using additional titles to improve cover, for example.

Other considerations that then need to be taken into account are the frequency of insertions within a given title, the position within the publication, the day of week to advertise (in a daily paper), when in the year to advertise, in relation to market and brand seasonality, and so on. Where these various considerations are not rated as important, it will always be cheaper to buy space on a 'run of week (ROW)' or 'run of paper (ROP)', basis for example, allowing the publisher to put the ad in as and when it is convenient. Indeed, for some products it may make sense to arrange for the publisher to offer space on a distress-purchase basis—if it needs an ad to make up a page, you keep copy with the publication to be used when the price (from your point of view) is right.

One final—and important—consideration is to take note of the way in which a magazine schedule, in particular, builds coverage only slowly (page 178, above). Because each issue may need several readers to reach its full readership, this takes time. It is also important to remember that many magazines may have a cover date of, say, October, yet appear on the streets early in September: you need to be sure to check publication dates. A typical short-term press schedule is shown in Figure 11.10.

Press production

Finally, a few words about the highly technical subject of production. Production methods are changing rapidly, and it is now possible—in theory—to create an ad on a computer and send it down an ISDN line to a publication's production department, without any hard copy ever being produced. You will need, of

---

[5] Note: the pattern of duplication of readership—and also of TV programme viewing—can be shown to follow the pattern indicated by Ehrenberg's Dirichlet model (see p. 48).

Readers of \ who also read: %	Sun	D. Mirror	D. Star	D. Express	D. Mail	D. Telegraph	Times	Guardian	Independent	FT
Sun	–	25	11	4	9	2	2	2	1	1
D. Mirror	30	–	11	7	10	4	3	2	2	1
D. Star	55	40	–	7	11	4	3	2	2	1
D. Express	16	17	5	–	15	7	6	3	2	2
D. Mail	17	13	4	8	–	8	6	3	2	3
D. Telegraph	9	8	3	7	15	–	12	6	4	7
Times	12	10	3	8	17	17	–	9	8	10
Guardian	12	10	3	5	13	12	15	–	11	6
Independent	12	14	3	8	17	16	21	19	–	11
F. Times	13	14	3	9	22	28	31	12	12	–

Figure 11.9.   Daily newspaper readership duplication 6-day average issue readership (Source: National Readership Survey, January–December, 1997)

PRESS SCHEDULE

Client: XXXXX
Product: Savings

Date: 23/3/98
Plan No: 2
Status: Booked

Medium	Size	Rate	No	Position	Mar 2	Mar 9	Mar 16	Mar 23	Mar 30	Apr 6	Apr 13	Apr 20	Apr 27
Mail on Sunday	Page	15 500	4	Financial		15		29		12		26	
Times	37 × 6	6 547	3	FH*				23			13		27
Evening Standard	Page	5 005	4	FH			18		30	7		20	
Daily Mail	25 × 4	7 104	4	FH			18		1	8		20	
Daily Express	25 × 4	2844	2	FH				25			14		
Daily Telegraph	25 × 4	4 439	1	FH							15		

TOTAL COST   £140 204

* FH = 'Front half' (of the newspaper)

Figure 11.10.   A short-term press schedule

course, to scan any necessary illustration or photograph into the computer, but then it's up to the machine.

In practice, most serious ads are produced in a more elaborate way. In particular, colour pictures require a great deal of nursing by production experts to ensure that they appear as intended. Copy and pictures will normally be produced separately, and will need to be married together in an appropriate form for the publication concerned, and technically different processes may be required, depending on the type of pictures being used: line drawings are much simpler to handle than 'half-tones' (pictures with shading, such as ordinary photographs).

Most agencies will put their work through one or more chosen studios, and this has led in the past to agencies profiteering on this part of their business. As a result, many larger clients these days insist on having all their studio work centralized in a studio of their choice, with whom they have negotiated rates for all but the most unusual jobs. One obstacle to this remains the practice of some large newspaper groups insisting that all work is made ready for their presses by designated 'gatekeeper' studios, which tend to be relatively expensive.

Summary

- The press divides, effectively into two sectors, newspapers and magazines, which are rather different in character, and offer different benefits to the advertiser. Both sectors vary somewhat by country.
- Britain is characterized by strong national newspapers, both daily and Sunday, which offer advertisers a spectrum of quality and style. These are underpinned by a very extensive range of regional and local papers. National papers are used by national advertisers, while the regionals are especially important to the retail trades.
- Press space offers an increasingly varied and flexible choice to the advertiser, and choice can be made on size, position, colour and editorial context.
- While larger sizes can be shown to have greater effects, effects are proportional to size in a way that makes smaller sizes more cost-effective: the planner has to balance impact against economy.
- The growing and large range of magazine titles provides an opportunity to target, quite precisely, audiences with a vast range of special interests.

Questions to consider

1. Take a pair of daily newspapers—a broadsheet and a tabloid—and go through

each, noting the ads that appear. What do the two lists suggest to you about the readers of each paper?

2. In the same papers, can you identify which ads have been bought in a specific, fixed position in the paper? How can you tell, and why do you think each was fixed where it is?

3. Can you identify any ads that are especially unusual in their shape, position, etc.? What does this tell you about the advertiser and their strategy?

4. Take two magazines in the same category (women's lifestyle monthlies or teenage, for example). How would you expect an ad for the same product to differ between the two titles, on the basis of the editorial style and character? If you can find ads for the same brand in both, do they in fact differ? If so, how? If not, which magazine does the ad seem more appropriate for? Why?

5. You are the manufacturer of a brand of expensive fountain pen. Draw up a preliminary list of up to a dozen (only) titles in which to advertise. Why have you selected these? What criteria have you used? How might these affect your final choice?

12   Secondary media

I think that I shall never see/ a billboard lovely as a tree

Ogden Nash

In this chapter, I want to look quite briefly at the other main media that are used for advertising—outdoor, radio and cinema—together with the motley collection of tiny media collectively known as 'ambient media'. The next chapter will cover response media—direct marketing and the Internet.

Outdoor advertising

Arguably, outdoor advertising is the oldest form of advertising. Certainly, it existed in Pompeii, and probably in ancient Egypt and even Babylonia. The fact that Belshazzar's feast was interrupted by a bit of interior graffiti suggests that the idea of writing messages on walls was nothing unusual. What are most inscriptions, but public service ads?

Outdoor advertising is probably the least homogeneous medium, in international terms, with local laws, practices and ad sizes varying widely. There are growing trends, however, towards the internationalization and harmonization of at least some practices, with the international development of companies such as the French JC Decaux and the UK's More Group, which was acquired in early 1998 by the US media group Clear Channel Communications.

Outdoor is a very diverse business: its products range from neon signs on rooftops in city centres through billboards of various sizes to bus shelters, cross-track ads on railway and underground stations, bus sides, taxis, and so on. In the UK, the conventional poster business—far the largest part of the total—has seen substantial changes in recent years, with a reduction in the overall number of sites going in parallel with shifts in the nature and make-up of the available sites and in the technology that supports them.

The most interesting thing about posters, in the modern media world where fragmentation is increasingly the characteristic of all forms of media, is that they now represent the one medium available that is genuinely mass market in character—if you choose to use it that way. As such, posters can be used to create widespread awareness for a brand, on a national basis, in the way that used to be easy on TV but has become increasingly difficult. Conversely, of course, posters can be extremely flexible and local in character: a retail store might have just one poster site directing people to it, or you can buy sites to target people who use a single underground line or bus route.

Using posters

Posters in the UK, at least, are mostly bought in 'packages' put together by the big poster contractors, and these tend to be structured by size. While Continental European posters are normally described in square metres, the UK talks of 'sheets', with sizes going up from 4-sheet (5 ft (52.5 cm) high × 3 ft 4 in (101.5 cm) wide) through 6-, 12-, 16-, 32-, 48- and 64-sheet to 96-sheet (approx. 12 m wide by 3 m. high) (see Figure 12.1). A large advertiser may buy a national campaign of 96-sheets plus 48-sheets; or a supporting campaign for another medium, consisting of 6-sheets. Over and above the 96-sheets, there are a limited range of 'supersites', typified by those on London's Cromwell Road, by Earl's Court, which are used for specially constructed, often 3-D ads.

Normally, posters are booked for 2-week periods, and nowadays most poster campaigns are booked *ad hoc*. Up to about 10 years ago, the big tobacco and drink companies used to have semi-permanent poster holdings, booked on a 'TC'—till countermanded—basis, but these holdings have now been effectively liquidated, and the market is a lot more flexible.

Traditionally, posters have mostly been used as a 'support' medium, to extend a TV campaign or to add weight and visibility to a press campaign. Relatively recently, however, a variety of advertisers have managed to use poster campaigns as a means of generating PR and publicity. The classic case is that of Wonderbra, where some £200 000 of media expenditure is claimed to have created the equivalent of £10 million-worth of press coverage, if the total column centimetres of comment are translated into ratecard ad costs. In the same way, the French Connection fashion retail chain's 'fcuk' campaign has undoubtedly paid off handsomely in notoriety, aided by ASA bans. More functionally, too, a number of smaller fmcg brands, such as Hula Hoops, with its Harry Enfield-derived 'Oi No' campaign have managed to make very positive use of Adshels (bus shelters). (See Box 12.1.)

Box 12.1   Hula Hoops

Hula Hoops is a long-established leader in the UK snack market, which had been losing ground among teenagers–the key market. Consumer research showed that the shape was key to the brand, and led the agency to a campaign strategy based on the 'defence of the shape'.

While the campaign used a variety of media, the most visible format was Adshels, where the brand made consistent—but extremely varied—use of a catch phrase of comedian Harry Enfield: 'Oi ... No!' This was used whenever any suggestion was made of a Hula Hoop that was not hula-hoop shaped, with promotional ideas centred on square and twisted shapes, and the topical use of celebrities.

The brand launched a Hoop Party Manifesto for the 1997 general election, and the campaign became part of the language, as well as attracting frequent references in the media.

Poster contractors have worked hard to develop the technical side of the medium. Larger sites frequently now have three ads revolving on them; more sites of all sizes are illuminated; it has become possible, at a price, to add sound to some bus shelter sites (Disney's *1001 Dalmations* had Adshels that barked) and most recently 3-D ads for the new Peugeot 206 were used; and so on. Similarly, work has been done on developing new packages of sites: for example, illuminated sites within grocery superstore precincts—the so-called 'point-of-sale 6-sheet market.'

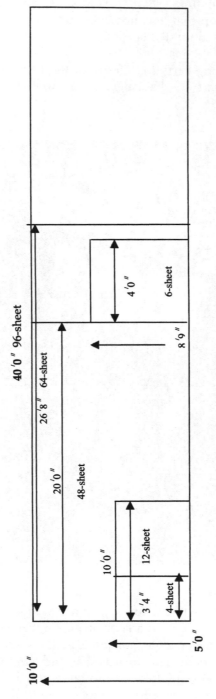

Figure 12.1. Main UK poster sizes (measurement in feet and inches)

Poster research

The industry has also tried hard to enable buyers to rate sites more scientifically. A first attempt at rating every site in the country by its traffic potential under the acronym OSCAR has been succeeded by an altogether more sophisticated research tool, POSTAR. POSTAR covers some 100 000 roadside sites which have each been evaluated for traffic flow and pedestrian traffic and by scientific measures of visibility. The data can be analysed by a variety of demographic groups, for every ITV region, and details are available for every site of the proximity of multiple retailers and other geographical features. The data are updated on an ongoing rolling basis. From POSTAR, it is possible to estimate the OTS for any site in the country, with a far greater degree of accuracy—and credibility—than before. Similar systems are being developed in France and Germany, but elsewhere the medium is less well researched.

Other outdoor opportunities

In addition to outdoor posters, the UK has a thriving transport advertising business, now owned by the US firm TDI, which has been able to increase expenditure dramatically on advertising in the London Underground system, with the aid of improved quality and a tailored research programme, TRAC. It is worth mentioning, too, the existence of a thriving informal fly-posting 'industry', which is mostly used by music companies, but also, from time to time, by other advertisers hoping to connect with the elusive and ad-suspicious youth market.

Finally, there are taxi ads, marketed in the UK by Taxi Media Ltd, and bus ads, marketed, like the Underground, through TDI. Both media offer the possibility of making distinctly creative use of the whole vehicle, as well as the more conventional ad panels.

Poster buying

Buying posters in the UK—and some other countries—is complicated by the fact that it is usually done through a specialist poster buying agency, which works alongside the main media agency. These companies provide specialized knowledge of the market together with checking services. The major problem for advertisers is getting the right posters in the right places at the right time. Although advertisers prefer buying line by line, because this means that all their posters will be on sites they have actually chosen, the contractors prefer to sell packages, if possible, because this reduces 'voidage'—sites with no current poster—which tends to increase as contractors reduce the package percentage in their holding. For the advertiser, the question is how to balance the convenience and relative economy of the package against the certain fact that the one genuinely duff site in the package will inevitably be on the CEO's route to work. This, of course, ensures endless inquests into the inefficiency and incompetence of the marketing department, the ad agency, the poster contractor and anyone else in the line of fire.

Poster advertising is a dynamic sector in which the opportunities for creativity are considerable. The problem, as always, is to achieve impact and branding, because there is little room for words—except on Underground cross-tracks. Then there is the production cost, which is relatively high, and the need to ensure that sites are checked, both to be certain that the ads are actually posted and to watch over quality of posting, damage and graffiti, etc.

The cinema

Cinema advertising is the oldest audio-visual medium, but has long been in the doldrums since the introduction of television. In the last 10–15 years, however, cinema in the UK has seen a dramatic revival, with the introduction of multiplexes and the restructing of old cinemas to increase the number of screens and film choice. Between 1987 and 1998, the number of screens doubled, and admissions rose from 75 million to 150 million which is still less than three visits per year per person. Multiplexes now account for virtually half of all screens.

In practice, the cinema audience is much more interesting than this makes it sound. While 75 per cent of the population ever go to the cinema, regular cinema-goers represent a young, relatively well-off group of the kind that advertisers find it difficult to reach cost-effectively through TV. The typical cinema audience is 60 per cent aged between 18 and 34, and 68 per cent ABC1. More than a third of 25–34-year-olds go to the cinema at least once a month, compared with only 10 per cent of over-35s.

Cinema research

Cinema-going is covered, in broad terms, by both the *NRS* and *TGI*, and admission statistics, in considerable detail, are available from the Cinema Advertising Association (CAA), which also sponsors the regular *CAVIAR* (Cinema and Video Audence Research) surveys, covering cinema and video viewing of films, which provide quite detailed information about the size and make-up of the audience for individual films.

The data from *CAVIAR* can be used to predict reasonably precisely the profile of the audience for most types of film, from the older, upmarket profile of, say, *Life is Beautiful* to the younger, more downmarket *Payback*.

The data also make it possible to distinguish between the mainstream cinemas and the so-called 'Art Houses', which account for only some 4 per cent of screens and reach a much more upmarket and older audience than the mainstream.

Long-term trends in cinema-going show that the audience is, in fact, broadening: although only 10 per cent of over-35s go once a month, this has risen tenfold over the last 15 years.

Planning and buying cinema time

Cinema advertising in the UK is sold by two organizations: Carlton and Pearl & Dean. Carlton covers some 70 per cent of screens. As with posters, the cinema media prefer to sell packages, but it is perfectly possible to buy individual cinemas, if you are prepared to do the necessary analysis.

The simplest way to buy cinemas is to buy a weekly Audience Guarantee Plan: taking the two contractors together, this guarantees a fixed CPT and an audience of 2.6 million per week. It is possible to buy this regionally, by ITV region, but you have to buy all the screens in the region.

Cinema is normally bought one week at a time, because this best captures the standard visiting behaviour of cinema-goers, and reflects the way in which cinemas schedule their films. To run advertising continuously leads to excessive wastage and duplication of audiences.

While the standard buying module for cinema is 30 seconds, most major advertisers tend to use 60-second commercials, and some are even longer. The reason for this is the perception that the audience has come to expect to be entertained by cinema ads, and it is easier to do this in an extended filmlet, rather than the tightly-constructed confines of a typical 30-sec TV commercial. TV commercials do not, as a result, translate terribly well to the cinema, and most big users of cinema advertising make films specially for the medium often at very considerable cost: the Smirnoff vodka campaign is a good example (see Plate 6).

The Smirnoff example points up the fact that the cinema has been a very important medium for products that cannot, or do not, use TV. Cinema was the last audio-visual refuge of cigarette advertising before it was banned, and the spirits advertisers for years had a voluntary agreement not to use TV, which only came to an end in 1997. As a result, drinks (including soft drinks) is far the largest single category of cinema advertiser.

Radio

The largest of these media groups, both in the UK and worldwide, in spend terms, is radio, though it nowhere exceeds around 10 per cent of spending, and in the former has just reached 5 per cent. Although Radio Luxembourg provided commercial radio coverage of the UK for many years, and pirate radio ships flourished in the

1960s and early 1970s, UK-based commercial radio only started in 1974. This, of course, is in marked contrast to experience elsewhere, where advertising on radio may date back to the 1920s.

By now, UK commercial radio has over 200 stations, a mix between AM and FM broadcasting, and four national channels as well as the plethora of local services. All of these have to compete for listeners with the public service, the BBC's five national channels and their numerous local stations. Between them, the BBC services take just under half of the total radio audience. The next development is digital radio, for which the first commercial licence was awarded in late 1998, and which offers the prospect of a substantial increase in the choice available to listeners, as the technology becomes more widespread.

Radio, therefore, has come to represent a thriving, crowded and complex market-place, which offers advertisers a wide range of possibilities. Indeed, in metropolitan areas like London and Manchester, the choice has become very wide: London has no less than 19 commercial channels.

Radio as an advertising medium

Radio is unique among ad media, in that the majority of listening is done when the audience is actually doing something else—driving, cooking, ironing, reading, working. This means that it needs either to create an intrusive noise to get noticed or, somehow, to creep in 'under the radar'. In spite of this apparently secondary role in people's lives, radio is a very friendly medium, very close to people. The Radio Advertising Bureau (www.rab.co.uk), which has done much to market radio as a medium in the UK, visualises it as shown in Figure 12.2—closer to the listener than other media, and on a more human scale.

It is easy to believe that, with a proliferation of stations available, people will develop massive listening repertoires. This does not seem to happen: people are actually very loyal to individual channels, and often to individual broadcasters or time slots. A study by the RAB, based on data from RAJAR, the industry's standard research service, shows that listening repertoires (stations listened to per week) have remained remarkably stable over the last five years, and that even in London the number of stations listened to is only 10 per cent above the national average, which hovers around 2.5 (only).

Radio has a different pattern of usage to TV, as it tends to dominate the early part of the day, especially pre-breakfast, breakfast and the journey to work ('drive time'), though it also has a slight relative 'blip' between 4 and 5 p.m. (drive time, again). What this means is that radio ads can easily be very close to a shopping expedition, in a way that TV commercials rarely are.

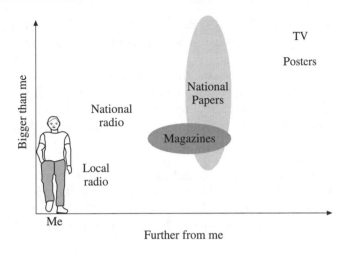

Figure 12.2. Media relationship (Source: RAB)

Radio is, too, extremely local: some stations' catchment areas are as small as 100 000 people, and the content of their broadcasts is tailored closely to the area. This can enable even a multiple retail chain to appear part of the community—so long as their advertising is tailored to the station.

The fragmented nature of radio makes it a natural market for advertiser-originated material to appear as part of the broadcast content. While not strictly advertising—more a form of publicity—this kind of activity will certainly become more common with digital radio. As it is, a variety of major advertisers, from Gordons Gin to Orange, have produced material or programme ideas that have gained free airtime, or provided the basis for a programme which carried significant paid-for material.

Radio audience research

The main on-going audience research into radio is provided by RAJAR (Radio Joint Audience Research Limited), a body jointly funded by commercial radio and the BBC. RAJAR collects data by asking some 3 000 people per week to fill in a listening diary for one week. Respondents tick the times and stations they are listening to every quarter of an hour, except for half-hour slots between midnight and 6 a.m. In addition they indicate whether they were listening at home, in a car or somewhere else. (While in-home listening accounts for the majority of radio listening, out-of-home takes the main share in mid-morning and also around 7–8 p.m.).

RAJAR publishes quarterly reports, with every report covering national stations and the largest local ones (those with transmission areas with population over four million). Smaller areas are reported on either six-monthly or yearly.

In addition to radio, RAJAR collects data on other media for comparison, and also provides geodemographic information to aid geographic planning.

Beyond RAJAR's mainstream work, the RAB publish their own special analyses of RAJAR data, and also carry out a variety of *ad hoc* research projects. From all of this, the RAB is able to provide a wide range of information and advice about using radio, some of which is summarized in an annual *Radio Advertising Handbook*.

Examples of other radio research include work done by Initiative Media in Holland, (replicating studies by Radio Luxembourg in the 1970s) which shows that a radio ad that uses sound elements from a TV commercial evokes visual memories of the TV ad—a phenomenon known as 'visual transfer'.

Buying radio time

The 200-odd radio stations' airtime is sold by a relatively small number of sales houses, which simplifies the evident problems facing the buyer. Buyers can buy on a station-by-station basis, or it is possible to buy 'network' packages, ranging from the NNR (National Network Radio) frequency packages, which allow advertisers to buy airtime guaranteeing a given frequency against a defined target group, to the NNR Sports Package, available on all dedicated sports programmes between 2 p.m. and 5 p.m. on Saturdays, and the IRN Newslink, which offers solus spots in the peak morning news bulletin on 165 stations.

Buyers will often buy station packages, by the week, which provide a fixed number of spots across the week and across the day, but it is more common to identify the target consumers' listening habits, and aim to buy at the time or times they are most likely to be listening. Thus, to be obvious, businessmen are frequently targeted in morning or evening drive time, and teenagers in particularly high-rating music shows, like the Network Chart Show, sponsored by Pepsi since 1993, which gets over 2.5 million listeners per week.

Radio can provide very considerable frequency of advertising, in comparison with TV, though the cost of advertising nationally is now substantial. A typical radio campaign might, over a month, reach a housewife 16 times, against no more than 7 for a TV equivalent. This means that, if the 'recency' arguments (page 133) mean anything, radio has a far better chance of reaching a housewife close to a shopping occasion than TV has.

It is therefore not surprising that the heaviest users of radio, by far, are retailers, followed by car dealers (retail again), newspaper and magazine publishers and entertainment.

For the advertisers, radio has the great advantages of flexibility and speed and simplicity of production. It is perfectly possible to plan, produce and air an ad in—literally—hours, though this requires a fast-track clearance by the Radio Advertising Clearance Centre (page 234). Distribution of ads to the stations can be handled centrally, through one of two organizations, Satellite Media Services and Independent Media Distribution, that use sophisticated technology to distribute the commercials.

Ambient media

'Ambient' media—media you meet in your ambiance, or possibly mobile media—are another attempt to reach an audience by getting under the radar. There are a vast range of possibilities, some of which lie in a grey area between advertising and promotion, and the total expenditure involved in them is still pretty trivial, but there is no doubt that they are growing in importance and in variety.

Probably the most sensible way to think about them is in terms of the locations in which they are encountered. Unsurprisingly, these tend to be close to a variety of points of sale: retail outlets, leisure and sports facilities, travel installations and vehicles, offices and factories. If you want to advertise beer, you may well advertise it on a beer mat—or in any one of several possible locations in the toilets of pubs, bars, clubs and the like. Or, perhaps, on the tee signs and in the cup of the 18th hole on the local golf course.

The range and ingenuity of ambient media marketers is considerable. Not only can you advertise on the lids of takeaway meal dishes, or on milk bottles, or even on eggs: you can place messages on the nozzles of petrol pumps at filing stations, on bus tickets or even on a weekly wage packet. There is nothing remotely new about advertising on postmarks, but it's still a thriving market. London's sex business has lived for years on fly-posted postcards in telephone boxes—so now BT are trying to market 'Phonesites' as a medium in their own right, to get rid of all those exotic-sounding ladies (and lads).

Every 10 or 15 years, someone gets national publicity for using the cows beside a major motorway or railway mainline as mobile posters. Probably, riches do not lie in this area. But whoever dreamed up the idea of using cinema and theatre foyers as distribution points for slightly strange advertising postcards at least earned the price of the paper.

And, of course, most of us are walking billboards. No, not sandwich men, though some have probably filled this role as students to earn a little towards paying off the loan, but as wearers of designer labels and carriers of carrier bags blazoned with fashionable (or not-so-fashionable) logos.

A guesstimate by the Concord outdoor consultancy puts total spending on these and similar ad 'media', always including the Goodyear blimp, at some £60 million—substantially more than spending on 'webvertising' in the UK has yet achieved, but no more than 1 per cent of total media advertising.

Summary

- While TV and press dominate the media scene in most countries, there are substantial and lively markets in secondary media.
- Posters, where markets differ widely in character between countries, offer a highly visible and flexible means for achieving wide coverage and a high level of brand awareness—but with some restriction in creative terms.
- Cinema is, in the UK at least, a niche medium, with a very clear audience profile, that can be made even more precise by careful film selection.
- Radio is a very personal medium for most listeners, and psychologically close to its audience. It is fragmented and complex, but this makes it accessible to small advertisers and it can be used on a very local basis.
- Beyond these three, there is an almost endless range of so-called 'ambient' media, that are constantly being added to and reinvented. They are particularly good for reaching hard-to-contact youth audiences, and for achieving currency for a brand without appearing to be too overtly commercial.

Suggestions for further study

1. Access the RAB web site, and explore the research data provided. What does this material *not* tell you about radio that you would like to know? Where might you find this material?
2. Next time you go to the cinema, be sure to catch the commercials. Watch the audience reaction to each ad. What conclusions can you draw from this about (a) which ads are most appropriate for a cinema audience and (b) what the audience is expecting from ads? Do you think the 'successful' ones, in these terms, will sell a lot of product to this audience?
3. Take a tour of your town or area of the city. How many poster sites did you pass in, say, a 15-minutes' journey? What sizes were they? How visible were they? Were they illuminated? What advertisers were using them? With this data, and any other observations you may have made, what does this tell you about the neighbourhood in which you live, and the people who shop there? How do you think each advertiser is expecting the ads to work?
4. Next time you are out for an evening, keep your eyes open for ambient media use. Who is doing it? Who are they apparently targeting? Are some advertisers using several techniques, or do they all use just one only? Are these advertisers also using major media, as far as you know? If not, what does this tell you about their strategy?

13 Response and interactive advertising

O ay, letters—I had letters—I am persecuted with letters ...

Congreve, *The Way of the World*

The one-to-one agenda

Direct response advertising has long been a core element within advertising as a whole, and many serious theories about advertising in the 1920s and 1930s were based on direct response: Claude Hopkins, who wrote *Scientific Advertising* in 1924, derived his thinking from selling by mail order to the rural mid-West.

In the 1990s, the growing power of computer databases has provided the technological infrastructure to enable advertisers to approach direct marketing with potentially far greater precision. At the same time, thinking about customer relationships, and the value to a business of its existing customers, has led to the development of a whole industry of 'relationship marketing' (or the new acronym CRM—customer relationship management—see www.crm-forum.com). This movement is predicated on the Pareto principle: that approximately 80 per cent of your business (or profits, or whatever) will be generated by 20 per cent of your customers. Calculations originally by Bain & Co., widely bandied about by the marketing press, suggest that it costs 5 to 10 times as much to get a new customer as to keep one, and that businesses should therefore concentrate (all? most?) efforts on the retention of their (best) customers.

The way to do this is through another buzz-word, 'one-to-one' marketing. Which is where direct response, direct mail, the Internet and the interactive opportunities of digital TV come together. The key to success in customer retention lies in developing and maintaining a dialogue with the customer, and tailoring this dialogue, through the knowledge that is gathered into the data warehouse, to create, as far as possible, a genuinely one-to-one relationship with each individual.

This is fine, and has obvious relevance to a wide variety of product fields and, especially, service businesses. Where I part company is with the evangelism of the direct marketers, who clearly and sincerely believe that the principles can be applied—literally—to fmcg brands, too. Hence, there was frenzied excitement in direct marketing circles when Heinz announced that they would take a large part of their considerable UK TV budget and devote it to a direct marketing project (see page 80). This they did, and developed a database of some four million homes, to which they mailed a customer 'magazine', consisting largely of more or less tailored promotional offers. After some two years, they stopped—and the conventional advertising commentators gloated, while the direct marketers bit their lips and muttered about Heinz retaining and continuing to use the database. It seems to me fairly clear that having a dialogue with a can of baked beans or a bottle of ketchup wasn't a bundle of fun, and the absence of the brand's conventional style of advertising was leading to a gradual erosion of carefully nurtured brand values.

Be that as it may, direct response and direct marketing, both through media advertising and the mail, the telephone and the Internet, is a massive growth sector of the advertising business, and worth a book on its own. The UK Direct Marketing Association (DMA) produces an annual 'Census' of direct marketing activity, which claims a total expenditure on all forms and aspects of direct marketing in 1997 of over £7 billion, compared with total advertising expenditure of some £12 billion. (Direct mail, in fact, ranks third in terms of total expenditure, behind press and TV.) The related IDM has produced a three-volume *Guide to Direct Marketing*,[1] which provides a wide range of advice and information on all aspects of the business. This chapter can only sketch in some of the broader elements, starting with direct response advertising in conventional media, and going on to look briefly at the mail, telemarketing and the Internet and webvertising.

In the context of integrated communications, direct marketing can be simply part of a programme, combining with brand-building advertising and PR. Or it can take over the whole, or virtually the whole, communications programme, as the business becomes more established. It is important to remember, however, that marketing is a 'leaky bucket' business: however hard you try, you will lose some customers, over time, and need to replace them—and, too, you will need to gain new customers if your business is to maintain dynamic growth.

Some principles

Direct marketing has what Drayton Bird[2] has called 'three Graces'—the ability to isolate the individual customer; continuity, or potential continuity, of contact; and the ability to test.

As Hopkins identified in the 1920s, direct response lends itself to testing. The chief difference between direct and general media advertising lies in this. It is possible to test everything about a campaign, because you measure the results by what you get back—initially in the form of orders or enquiries, and then in their conversion into cash. You can test, for example:

[1] Bryan Halsey (ed.), *Direct Marketing Guide*, Institute of Direct Marketing, Teddington, 1998.
[2] Commonsense Direct Marketing, 3rd edn, Kogan Page, London, 1993.

- The offer, including any promotions or incentives.
- The ad copy, and details of it—including colour, size, typeface, and, for mail programmes, things like the address format, the shape, size and colour of envelopes, envelope messages, the number of pieces in the mailer, and so on.
- The nature of the response mechanism—a coupon (how large?), a telephone number (free? local rate?), a URL?, all of these?
- The choice of media (both 'inter' and 'intra').
- Positions in the media.
- Frequency of insertion—overall and in individual media.
- The target audience and subgroups of it, be they geographic, demographic, psychographic or whatever.

Interestingly, little of this is ever pre-tested, by conventional advertising research techniques, though there are signs that more pre-testing happens these days, as the big non-specialist ad agencies become more involved with direct response work.

Techniques of creating direct response material are somewhat different from those for brand advertising. Because the ad (or letter) has to make the sale, it has to provide the target audience with enough information to buy, even though any mail order business has to guarantee to accept a return if the customer is not satisfied, or allow a cooling-off period for a service sale, especially of a financial product. This means that DR copy tends to be long—indeed, some experts will argue that the longer it is, the better—and full of detail. Ads are large sizes, TV commercials are 60 or 90 seconds (or, on the dedicated shopping channels on cable, such as QVC, half-hour 'infomercials'). Letters—if they are well enough written, can run to three or four pages, and the conventional wisdom is that the CEO's preferred 'one side of A4' is too short to be effective.

A final point to note, which puts the claims about direct marketing into perspective. Response rates are generally quite low, especially to new lists or in the media. The average claimed response to consumer mailings in the UK has crept up to just over 7 per cent, though rates for individual mailings to existing customers by successful and experienced companies are claimed to run as high as 30–40 per cent. Press ads may achieve no more than 0.3–0.5 per cent (calculated on circulation), though they can go as high as even 5 per cent; and DRTV (direct response TV), where data are limited, may reach 3 per cent on occasions. As DMIS data show, response rates vary quite significantly according to the type of response offered (see Figure 13.1). Response varies, too, by type of industry (see Figure 13.2).

Direct response advertising

According to the DMA, which has, of course, an axe to grind, over 70 per cent of UK TV commercials now carry a response device, of some kind, and 90 per cent of

Post, phone and fax	9%
Visit to shop	8%
Post and phone	5%
Post	5%
Phone	4%
Fax	3%

Note – no Internet data

Figure 13.1. Response rates by type of response offered—1997 (Source: Precision Marketing/DMIS Response Rate Survey 1997)

Food/drink/fmcg	10%
Consumer services	9%
Retail	7%
Other consumer goods	6%
Automotive	5%
Entertainment/leisure	5%
Mail order	4%
Consumer magazines	3%
Travel	3%
Charity	3%
Books	3%
Insurance	2%
Investments	1%
Other financial	1%

Figure 13.2. Response to mailings by industry type. Percentage of adults replying to mailings in last year (Source: Direct Mail Trends Survey 1997, DMIS)

press ads do so. However, only about 15 per cent of TV expenditure can legitimately be described as DRTV, and of this a significant proportion is also trying to build brand image.

In press, the DMA claims 53 per cent of adspend is direct response, and this rises to over 65 per cent on Sundays. The main press users of direct response are financial services, travel and mail order shopping. The traditional response method of the coupon is becoming gradually obsolescent: almost twice as many ads carry a phone number as an address or coupon, and e-mail addresses (or Web URLs) are already up to 20 per cent. Of the main media, the fastest growth in direct response is in TV, where expenditure has nearly trebled over the last five years. In addition to straight direct response advertising in papers and magazines, a substantial business has developed in loose inserts—the bits that fall out on your feet when you open a magazine in the underground. These have the virtue of flexibility, in that they can be fairly tightly targeted geographically.

Increasingly, direct response advertisers use ads almost purely for *recruitment* of new customers, and then maintain contact with them by letter or telephone. Even where substantial volumes of business are done 'off the page', this is only the start of a relationship, at least for the more sophisticated operators.

Media selection can be, and is, done on the basis of systematic testing, though experience can be valuable: among national newspapers, for example, it has long been the case that, other things being equal, the *Daily Mail* will pull better, and more cost-effectively, than its close rival the *Daily Express*, and outpull most other papers. Newspapers will normally work faster, and generate more responses, than magazines—even though the latter offer more precise targeting and less wastage. As ever, the media equations require balancing of costs, volumes, timing and the value of the responses obtained: in the last resort, what matters to the direct response advertiser is making a sale—an enquiry that remains unconverted is not good enough.

From direct response operations, it is possible to cross-check the analyses of conventional advertisers' research into the effectiveness of different sizes and positions of ads. The square root relationship between size and effect (page 173) is common to both disciplines, which encourages the thought that the less direct measures of effect have at least something relevant to tell us about what our advertising can achieve.

Direct mail

If you are an AB executive living in a leafy suburb in the South-East of England, your mail box will be well filled with direct mail—or, as journalists delight in calling it, 'junk mail'. If the companies concerned are doing their job, much of this should not be junk—it should be at least potentially useful and, even, valuable to you. But you may receive two or three mailings per day (the AB weekly average is just below six, and rising, and geography intensifies the effect), and this means that you become, rapidly, very selective about what you bother to take notice of.

This puts the onus on users of direct mail to be diligent in building up and maintaining their mailing lists, highly selective about what they decide to mail and sure that they offer real value to the target reader. No one likes to receive mail addressed to 'Dear Deceased', especially if it's offering life assurance.

Mailing lists come from two sources: from customers who have—one way or another—got into contact with the firm and from bought-in lists. Increasingly, companies are building databases of customers, which can become comprehensive and extremely well-informed banks of information about individuals. This provides the basis for the company to decide what to offer to a particular customer, how to do it and when to do so. For example, if you know someone's date of birth, it *may* be appropriate to send them a birthday card or a birthday present—though this could be regarded as an appalling intrusion! Once you start building a database, you have, by law, to register with the Data Protection Registrar and observe very precise rules about how you collect and use the data you have (see Chapter 15).

Apart from your own customers, lists can be purchased from a variety of sources, collectively described as 'list brokers', which may include other commercial organizations (and you can rent your list to others, so long as you have obtained permission to do so when you collected respondent's details). In theory, at least, you can buy lists of people or companies against very detailed specifications, in terms of their demographics, their interests and at least some of their buying behaviour. A major source of these lists has become the proprietors of the so-called 'shopper surveys', mailed surveys that have by now collected data from about three-quarters of the country's households. The two main operators, Claritas and Experian, can both provide lists of people against a company's specification and take the company's database and 'profile' their customers against their own database. This can provide the company with new insights into their customers and into the strengths and weaknesses of their customer portfolio.

The quality of commercially available lists is quite variable, and there are moves to provide an equivalent of the newspaper and magazine ABC (page 171) checks on them. In any case, if you buy in a list, you will need to cross-check it against your own ('de-dupe', or 'merge-purge'), to avoid addressing long-established and loyal customers as if they have never even heard of you, and then compounding the sin by sending them not one but two letters.

Mailings offer their own opportunities for testing and experiment. There are several different styles of mailing, ranging from the straight letter to multi-piece extravaganzas that require you to take bits off one page and stick them into another. Mailers may be three-dimensional, or pop-up, or musical, or scented. They come in plain envelopes, or coloured ones; in standard shapes, or jumbo-size; with or without messages on the envelope. They include tear-off offers—'bang-tails'—attached to the reply envelope's flap. They are mailed from the Netherlands or the US, so they come with unfamiliar stamps. They include exhortations to reply now, or miss the opportunity of a lifetime. You name it, someone's probably done it. What's more, someone has also set out to measure the results, and who am I to argue that my name, misspelled, lasered on to every third line of copy is or is not more effective than something that is less obviously trying altogether too hard? The numbers give the answer. All that's wrong is the targeting ...

Once you have attracted a customer, of course, your direct mail need not always be selling anything—at least not too openly. If you have an established customer relationship (something that the customer is, of course, the best judge of) you may be providing information, thanking him or her for their business, or whatever. You should not, of course, miss the opportunity to use a contact to try to sell, but it can be done discreetly, through an offer of information on a new product, or an invitation to ask about some new topic.

Box 13.1   *Marks & Spencer Financial Services: a mail-based business*

Marks & Spencer are a leading UK store chain, with an affluent shopper profile skewed towards the older age groups. The stores have a massive reputation for quality, and the company is a regular feature among the UK's best-respected companies (though their late 1998 performance saw this halo slip a bit). M&S have never accepted third-party credit cards, but in the mid-1980s they decided to launch their own store credit card—which they misleadingly called their charge card—as a necessary service to customers who were increasingly likely to have general credit cards.

The card was launched purely through point-of-sale material, and has never been advertised. Over the years, it has accumulated over four million holders, with a credit-scored profile similar to M&S shoppers in general—an ideal market for a general financial service marketer. M&S early adopted a policy of careful control of the use made of the customer database they acquired: all contacts through the mail should be of some recognizable value to the customer, and the frequency of offers should be carefully limited. Customers were mailed with news about the stores and the merchandise, and—over time—offered a range of products, from the simple extension of card insurances to more diverse lines such as unit trusts, pensions and loans. Although M&S have advertised their loans, pensions and unit trusts from time to time, the vast bulk of their business has been created by mail, mostly through 'statement stuffers' (material inserted into the monthly account statements), but occasionally through solus mailings.

The resulting business now contributes a substantial share of M&S's profits even in a good year.

Finally, of course, you do not have to use the mail: it may be as effective to distribute your message door to door. You can then target geodemographically, and delivery is surprisingly cheap—if slightly unreliable. It's the mail equivalent of the targeted newspaper or magazine insert.

As the Marks and Spencer example (Box 13.1) shows, it is important to have a 'contact strategy' for mailings. This can be both general ('No customer to receive more than x mailings per month/year/etc.') or specific. Because the database enables you to track very precisely how a customer is behaving, you can select specific customers or groups of customers who offer the greatest potential, and concentrate on them. Key guides to selecting these best prospects are the three key words *recency*, *frequency* and *value*. In other words, your best prospects for making another sale are those who have bought recently from you, those who already buy relatively frequently, and those who have spent a lot of money. It's hardly rocket science, but it works.

Telemarketing

Telemarketing in the UK consumer market is predominantly 'inbound'—handling responses to ads, customer queries and complaints, and so on. There is considerable resistance among consumers to 'cold calling'—or, in the jargon, 'unsolicited outbound telemarketing'. The telephone is, however, a vital link in the direct marketing chain, since so much of the market is now geared to this form of contact. This means, in turn, that there is an enormous onus on marketing management to ensure that the call centre operators are able to 'live the brand', as represented in all those positioning statements and the advertisements.

Interactive media

Direct response is, of course, interactive. But doing it electronically, via Teletext, a TV screen or the computer, has hi-jacked the name. Teletext, by now, is becoming outdated, and is not very flexibly interactive, but it has acquired, in the UK at least, a substantial role in one or two markets, notably travel.

The exciting new frontier, however, is interactive digital TV and the Internet, which are rapidly converging, and causing headaches for marketers and advertising agencies alike. At present, there are few, if any valid, business models of how to manage these channels in consumer markets, although 'e-commerce' has become a reality for some business purposes, and there are IT marketers, such as Dell computers, who do most of their business in this way.

The problems are quite complex, and rather different according to the mechanism used. It is not quite as simple as it might appear to apply orthodox direct marketing principles to the new environment.

One of the most successful web sales operators

The Internet

Internet advertising in the UK has so far been insignificant, although it is known to be growing rapidly and is forecast to reach a quite substantial size over the next five years or so—though no prediction I have seen takes it above the current scale of radio advertising ($+/-5$ per cent of UK adspend). In the US, expenditures are already approaching $500 million.

To advertise interactively on the net, you have, first, to establish a web site, to which your ads can be linked. This may cost around £50 000, on average, as of early 1999. You then have to buy space—'banner' ads, page sponsorships, etc.—on suitable sites that can provide you with traffic that may click on your link and visit your site. You then have to provide the visitors to your site with enough excitement, stimulation, information and motivation for them to place an order—and you need to give them the reassurance that you can be relied on to deliver and that the transaction is secure enough to avoid their credit card being hijacked by Chechen mafia hackers.

This means that your site has to be well designed—not just pretty, but functional, too. There is nothing a web surfer hates more than hanging around while an elaborate set of graphics slowly loads itself on to the screen. Also, if your site is good, popular, and attracts a lot of traffic, you have to be prepared to alter it—or at least parts of it—quite frequently, so that regular users' interest remains stimulated. The same applies to web ads, too. The life of a single creative for a banner is reputedly no more than a week or so, in most cases. The great thing, though, is that you can get systems that will measure the response to both the ads and the individual pages of your site, so that you can tell which ones are getting a good response and when it is starting to wear out.

In the UK, the marketplace in which you can do this is as yet severely underdeveloped, and the measurement tools quite primitive. Only around 100 sites have, as yet, achieved ABC certificates, and the basis of charging for ad space is still not firmly established. A study of the 'New Media' section of *BRAD* reveals considerable uncertainty, if not positive obfuscation, about charges, though there is the beginning of a move to charge by either exposures ('page traffic') or clickthroughs, on a CPT basis. For example, the Excite Network, which has one of the leading web gateways, charges from £30–65 per thousand, with a minimum buy of 50 000 impressions (£1500), offering a range of options from 'general rotation' to individual keywords.

Interactive TV

The ways in which advertisers are going to use interactive TV are still at a very early stage of development in the UK. The scenarios that have been sketched out in the media appear essentially unrealistic—as has been pointed out, TV is a 'slump-and-watch' medium, while a PC is 'sit-up-and-act'; yet most thinking about interactive TV has assumed it will work just like the Internet. Similarly, all the reported experiments with interactive TV, from the US as well as the UK, seem to have been quite disappointing for the operators.

For many advertisers, the key to interactive TV is likely to be the channels' need for programme content. Even if advertisers or their agencies do not actually create programmes (and the signs are that some, like Japan's giant Dentsu agency, will do so), programme sponsorship will become far more widespread than at present.

Failing this, advertisers are going to have to develop credible and compelling ways of luring the potatoes off their couches enough to interact with an ad—a process that may well run over beyond a commercial break and into the programme which is what the viewer actually wants to be involved with. While the technology may be available to enable viewers to interrogate the clothes the star of their favourite soap is wearing when they appear on-screen, this seems to have little to do with enjoying the programme.

Summary

- Direct marketing, of all kinds, is a dynamic part of marketing communications.
- Direct techniques offer the ability to target precisely and limit wastage—though even then response rates may be quite modest.
- In modern marketing jargon, direct marketing is the key to building and maintaining profitable customer relationships.
- Direct marketing lends itself to testing and experiment, and, correspondingly, to precise evaluation.
- It has permeated all advertising media, but its most potent weapons are 'non-media'—the mail and the Internet.
- Like all marketing communications, direct marketing has to be planned strategically, and may work better when integrated with other types of activity.

Some questions to consider

- Direct marketing is clearly more appropriate to some types of product than others. Suggest some products for which it might be particularly right, and the reasons for this.
- Direct marketing is particularly concerned with making sales. Can it contribute to (or damage) brand values and reputation? How could it do this?
- A marketing strategy that relies solely on direct marketing may be unable to maintain a company's customer franchise. Why should this be so? And what should the company do about it?

14 Planning the campaign

The clever combatant looks to the effect of combined energy

Sun Zi, *The Art of War*

Most advertising campaigns are planned over a year. This is simply because most companies' operations are usually planned on this time-scale. What is more, because major public companies, especially those quoted on US stock exchanges, report quarterly, many companies also look at their financial results—including those from the advertising—on a quarterly basis. The fact remains that although the half-life of a burst of advertising is unlikely, as we have seen, (page 146) to exceed three or four months, we will usually hope that our activities have an effect beyond the confines of a year. This is, in essence, what the whole concept of brand building, and its measurement by brand evaluation or brand equity, is all about.

What this means is that we have to approach a brand's communication programme by looking at it over the whole of the planning period, *and* with an eye to the future beyond that. It will not be very satisfactory to blast off all our money in the first two months of the year, and then watch helplessly as the brand gradually declines and we have no money to do anything about it. We have to think about the shape of an *annual* programme, and about how our various activities—of which advertising is only one—can be effectively knitted into a powerful whole. We need to integrate the relatively expensive advertising activity with other, usually less costly, forms of communication, so as to provide continuity of messages to our target audience. And we are also going to have to be able to convince our CEO and CFO that the whole project is earning its keep.

Obviously, the thinking that goes into planning the campaign is likely to be rather different for different sizes of brand and budget. If you have £10 or £15 million to spend, you can be reasonably confident of providing a high degree of continuity of message through the year, if you judge that to be appropriate. If you only have £250 000, or less, the problem is altogether different.

A big budget campaign

Usually, if you have a large budget, you have competitors who are equally well endowed. You have to work hard to compete. Nonetheless, you have a wide range of options. You can be selective about when and where you spend your money; you can address particular subgroups of your target audience in different or unusual ways; and you can afford to put sophisticated evaluation research in place. The big questions are strategic (and apply equally to any scale of budget). The issues that you need to address, long before you get down to the detail of the planning of any particular medium, are questions such as these:

- What are the precise, detailed objectives of our communications programme, in order of priority? (Page 63)
- What are the roles of the various forms of communications in reaching our objectives? (Pages 61–2)
- What proportion of the budget should be devoted to each objective?
- And which method(s) are best for achieving the objectives concerned?
- Does seasonality matter in our market? If so, do we support strong seasons, or are we aiming to extend into weaker periods?
- Does geography matter? Should we support stronger or weaker areas differentially?
- How far do we aim to respond—aggressively or defensively—to anticipated action by each of our leading competitors?
- Can we see ways of leveraging the effects of specific campaigns or activities with the aid of other kinds of communication?

Out of the answers to these questions—which will have informed the entire strategy for the brand in ways discussed in earlier chapters, based on the way consumers buy in our market and the factors that are known to influence them—it becomes possible to start to plan the campaign.

What, in practice, are the key decisions?

These fall into five main areas:

- Should we use bursts of activity or aim at continuity of message through the year?
- How should we balance and combine different types of activity?
- How should we balance and combine different media?
- What do we expect the competition to be doing, and how will our plans counter this? Do we need to allocate resources to counter unexpected threats?
- How are we proposing to evaluate the campaign?

In addition, the manager planning the campaign will have to take due note of the lead times involved both in booking the advertising time or space and in producing the ads to fill it. At the same time, too, the whole plan needs to be closely co-ordinated with other functions within the organization—especially sales (the goods have to be in the right shops at the right time, or the training programme for the telesales operation put in place); production (who will need to know what they have to produce, when, and where it needs to be sent to); and finance (who will want to manage cash flows, quite apart from hoping to have your budgets justified in advance).

Bursts vs. continuity

Traditionally, large advertisers used to divide their spending into substantial bursts of heavyweight advertising, spread through the year, with gaps between, which might be filled by sales promotion. Where there was a seasonal variation in market sales, the advertising tended to be deployed to support the strong sales periods, except where a brand leader hoped to extend the seasonal peak, or even to try to build sales in the trough periods.

The new theory of recency planning (page 133) suggests that this is likely to be inefficient. In most, if not all cases, it will be better to spread the advertising more or less evenly through the year, so as to maximize the number of weeks in which there is at least a minimum of advertising—no more than perhaps 70–80 TVRs (or equivalent) per week.

Recency planning, however, allows little or no weight to longer term effects of advertising, and there is still a good case to be made, especially for a new campaign, for running at least the start of the campaign at a considerably higher weight, in order to create an initial 'bank' of awareness and understanding of the campaign message. Regardless of the message of single-source data about the effect on sales of a single exposure to the advertising, there is no doubt that any brand-building effects in the minds of consumers are going to be enhanced by repetition of exposure: this is how memory is strengthened.

Forms of communication

Media advertising is, in capital terms, relatively expensive. PR practitioners will argue—without very adequate tools to prove it—that PR can be vastly more cost-effective, in terms of its ability to deliver media coverage of the brand, in an editorial context that actually provides an authoritative third-party endorsement for the brand.[1] The problem, of course, is to guarantee that the PR story actually appears in the media, and that it does so in the form the brand owner would like. Undoubtedly, though, PR can work with the advertising—and, indeed, sometimes feed off it, as happened with Wonderbra and, more controversially, fcuk and, from time to time, Benetton.

Similarly, sales promotion—which can be quite economical to use, except when it involves price reductions, which are always highly expensive—can work to bridge

---

[1] See, for example, J. Speed, 'More Bang for your PR buck', *Admap*, January 1999.

gaps in the ad schedule, or to enhance the message of the ads. For example, there is a specialist agency, IIG, which develops promotional programmes that are designed to get people to watch ads in order to participate in quiz games; and another, Fast Marketing, which uses a technique of combining door-to-door sampling with advertising to generate product trial, both with very positive results.

Sponsorships—of various kinds—provide a means of keeping the brand name in front of the public, while giving the company opportunities for entertaining customers and for creating linked promotions and even advertising campaigns.

And then there's always the company web site—if you know how to manage it properly—though for most brands the potential coverage of the target audience is, and will remain for some time, rather limited.

Finally, if you have the right sort of brand—and this probably means anything other than an fmcg brand—you are likely to have, or be developing, a customer or potential customer database, which can be used for direct marketing. As the old P&G example (page 7) makes clear, mailing, with any frequency and on any scale, is not cheap: but there may well be ways in which you can usefully maintain contact with this tightly targeted audience, at times when you are not advertising (or when you are).

Different media

The increased fragmentation of the media means that it is no longer possible to reach huge audiences through a limited number of TV spots. We know, too, that there are substantial groups of 'rejecters' of some or all advertising, but who may be more susceptible to press or radio or outdoor ads than to TV (see page 165).

Further, there is growing evidence, from the work of the magazine publishers (page 183), that a combination of TV and magazines is likely to be more effective than TV alone; and the same appears to be true of TV and radio in combination. Similarly, we know that people use the ads in different media in rather different ways, taking from TV the more emotional brand values, or simply a desire to know more, but using press ads, or direct mail or leaflets, to gather more detailed information.

The chances are that any campaign will be aiming to achieve a combination of brand awareness, brand understanding and knowledge, and the development of more or less emotional brand values. The balance between the media used should depend on the priorities between these types of objectives. A typical example is the way in which car manufacturers generally use TV, or perhaps posters, to create awareness and a desire for a model; but use press ads (plus direct mail and point-of-sale material) to provide more detailed information about the car's specification and features, and to set up the basis of a deal.

Thinking about the competition

In any established market, the leading contenders have a very good idea of how their competitors behave, and one of the tasks of marketing management is to maintain intelligence about their competitors' activities. Specifically in advertising, it is easy enough to get hold of competitive ads in any of the main media; to monitor competitors' expenditure, through MMS or A.C. Nielsen-MEAL; and to check on their mailing activity through Market Movements. (These are all UK research services, but they have their parallels in many developed advertising markets: the Register Group provide a pan-European advertisement search service, covering TV and press media, for example.)

From an analysis of their past behaviour, a knowledge of their planned product introductions, and any other information you can get hold of, you usually have a reasonable idea of what the opposition are likely to throw at you. The only problem then is one of lead times. You may have too little time between learning of some major new activity to make the best of countering it. (It is easiest to watch the process at work in the newspaper field, where a major serialization of a new book by one paper may provoke a vigorous spoiling action by its nearest competitor—whose efforts always look a bit crude because they have not had the time to do a better job.)

In fast-changing markets such as mobile phones or computers, or even parts of the financial service market, it may be necessary to plan the detail of campaigns on only a three- or six-month cycle, and be prepared to replan at quite short notice.

Evaluation

You will need to work out in advance how you intend to measure your results: the bigger the budget, the more it is coming under scrutiny—and the more you can, in theory, afford to go about the job of assessment properly.

This means that you have to set up the right measurements (Chapter 8), and budget for them, from the start. A £10 million budget should include a total research allowance of around 5 per cent—to cover creative development research as well as evaluation—and at least 2 per cent, or more likely 3 per cent, will go to evaluation. For smaller budgets, these ratios should, ideally, be higher.

Putting the plan together

How does all this come together? A typical example of a large budget would be a car brand—a single model from one of the leaders in the market, or possibly a minor marque with several models. Let us look at a hypothetical small-medium car, like a VW Golf, with a total marketing communications budget of £17–18 million.

The ingredients that the plan has to deal could be quite complex (See Box 14.1).

Box 14.1   Car brand (fictional): campaign 'ingredients.

Market factors
□ Seasonality (UK peak in August, when new licence plate letter introduced–changed in 1999 to March and September).
□ Own model established, but upgrade variant available autumn.
□ Leading competitor: new model replaces tired equivalent: launch due October.
□ Market buyer split moving from heavily male towards female—forecast 60 per cent male for this segment this year.
□ Fleet (company car) buyers around 30 per cent of segment.
□ Over-supply will mean continuing pressure on prices.

Campaign ingredients
□ Media: TV, press, specialist press, possible outdoor, radio (nb: new commercials needed—should be available end March).
□ PR: general and specialist, including sponsorship, etc.
□ Direct mail—company has comprehensive, centralized database of owners, but the dealerships 'own' the customers.
□ Point of sale: brochures, interactive kiosks, display material, branded merchandise, gifts, etc.
□ Dealer advertising: co-operative programme (financed 50 : 50 with dealers).
□ Used-car advertising.
□ Finance deal/credit facilities.

Using this set of information, we can map out the basis of a campaign plan, as in (Figure 14.1). This plan blends together a variety of elements to meet a range of requirements implicit in the information in Box 14.1:

□   The need to build interest in the car in advance of the peak sales period—recognizing that decisions to purchase cars have quite a long gestation (usually a minimum of three months, and frequently longer).

□   The need to appeal to both men and women, and to fleet managers (plus the people they buy for).

	Jan	Feb	Mar	Apr	May	Jun	Jul	Aug	Sep	Oct	Nov	Dec	GRPs	£000
Media														
TV		▨	▨					▨	▨	▨			2550	8 500
750TVRs / 1800TVRs														
Press:														
Newspapers (Theme campaign)		▨	▨	▨	▨	▨	▨	▨					1100	1 500
Magazines												▨		300
Dealer support				▨			▨				▨			850
Used cars				▨			▨							500
Finance			▨	▨				▨						350
Outdoor			▨		▨			▨					1250	1 000
PR														
(General)			▨	▨	▨	▨	▨	▨	▨	▨	▨	▨		350
Launch up-grade									▨					150
Direct mail (inc. production)			▨	▨	▨	▨	▨	▨	▨	▨	▨	▨		1 250
Sponsorship (events)					▨	▨			▨					250
Web site			▨	▨	▨	▨	▨	▨	▨	▨	▨	▨		150
Theme advertising GRPs													4900	
Production Costs														1 850
TOTAL COST														£17 000

Figure 14.1. Campaign lay-down for car model

- The recognition that different media have a part to play—including the value of PR, which, however, works best for new car models or variants.
- The need both to launch the new variant in the autumn and to fight as best the brand can against the new competitive launch.
- The fact that a new variant will make some cars in the showrooms out of date, so a dealer-based promotion to help clear these stocks is desirable.
- The need to make sure that the dealers are clear about what is expected of them.

Even with a substantial budget behind it, there are places where support for our fictional car looks a bit thin. What can you do about a small budget—say £250 000?

Small budgets

£250 000 is actually *not* a small budget, in statistical terms. The majority of the brands recorded by Nielsen-MEAL or MMS spend less than £200 000. Nonetheless, this is a scale of budget where the constraints of resources dictate a rather different approach, and it is the sort of budget where many of the leading ad agencies are reluctant to become involved, and start muttering about 'minimum fees'.

The constraints are clear:

- The budget will not buy you effective mass coverage—let alone frequency against a large audience.
- It will be difficult to spread it over the year at an effective level.
- It effectively precludes the use of the most powerful medium, TV—even if you use TV in a very tightly limited way (on selected cable channels, for example), the cost of producing any but the crudest commercial will take far too large a share of the budget to make it practical. (It is quite possible to produce a TV commercial, of a very simple sort, for around £10 000: but this will look as cheap as it is, and experience in the UK at least shows that people are usually very dismissive of this kind of advertising. It will do nothing for the brand, in terms of reputation and image, though it may generate some sales. One other solution, available to some brands, is to use a campaign from another country: in this way, you split the production costs with perhaps richer markets—but you meet problems of adaptation and translation.)

There are some proven solutions to the problems a small budget raises. Mostly these revolve around targeting: the more precisely you can identify your target audience, the easier it is to find one or more media that reach it effectively. The other key dimension, of course, is size: ads do not have to be full pages, or even quarter pages. They can be a lot smaller than that. The only problem is that, as we have seen (page 174), smaller sizes get smaller results, even though they are proportionately better than large sizes. Finally, there are ways of amplifying the effect of the advertising. Wonderbra achieved a massive sales success by spending less than £250 000 on posters, because the campaign generated immense PR coverage (crudely, and certainly inaccurately, estimated as being equivalent to £10 million-worth of media ads). Unfortunately, there is no way you can guarantee to achieve anything like this, and most attempts merely end up being banned after complaints to the ASA (Chapter 15).

Another problem that affects the small budget is that it is likely that the resources available to do anything else will be limited, too. This will often be a matter of people as much as of money: a brand with a small budget cannot justify the amount of time it may really need to do a proper job for it—either on the part of the brand owner or of the agency.

Targeting

Most brands—even large ones—sell to a small proportion of the population. Which means, of course, that any broad-based ad campaign inevitably carries a lot of wastage. As a result, targeting has become an important feature of everyone's media planning. Smaller brands, with smaller budgets, have even smaller user groups. The problem then becomes one of identifying very precisely who these groups are, so as to find media that can target them accurately. This is likely to be easier for a specialized product—a camera, or a computer—than for a food product.

With small brands, targeting has to be both tighter and in some ways more arbitrary than for larger brands. Where a large brand can realistically, if slightly wastefully, target a quite broad demographic group—women aged 25–40 in white-collar jobs, for example—this is too broad for a small budget. Ideally, you want to be able to define them by specific habits or specific media: you may be able to do a good job if you decide to target only readers of the *Daily Telegraph Magazine*, or *Company,* or *Practical Photographer*. In the same way, you could, in UK media terms, decide to target shoppers at Sainsburys (who you could then advertise to exclusively through superstore poster sites and *Sainsburys Magazine*); or British Airways passengers (who could be reached through posters at Heathrow and other airports, ads in *High Life,* and banner ads on the BA web site, and soon on the in-flight video system).

Another route is to exploit geography. This is fine, if your product is distributed only in part of the country or is far stronger in some areas than others. You can then use local press, local radio, localized poster campaigns, and so on, supported by region-specific PR, promotions, door drops or whatever. Or, it may be that a geodemographic analysis of your brand on *TGI* (which can be obtained reasonably cheaply) might show that it is bought far more by the inhabitants of certain ACORN or MOSAIC or Superprofiles areas than others. This provides the basis for either a programme of mailings and door drops or a media analysis designed to find newspapers or magazines with a good match to your profile. The most local media are regional papers, posters (which could be specific to a single bus route or a single town) and radio. Radio, in the big cities, can be used to target both area and lifestyle on specific stations, and because of the different ways in which the audience is made up over the day you can aim to reach businessmen, office workers, housewives, and so on.

Within the next 10 years, but not yet, you will almost certainly be able to use geodemographic knowledge to deliver messages by e-mail or by cable or digital TV on a tightly targeted basis.

Size

Size, according to the new (1998) Renault Clio launch ads, does matter. It certainly matters to the smaller budget. Do you blow the budget on full-colour, whole pages in your chosen publication(s) or do you box clever and aim for far greater frequency by taking a half or quarter page—or even small ads? (The same applies in other media: you can use 10-second TV commercials, if you have a campaign available, or 6-sheet posters.)

Partly, this depends on your market. Some product categories develop 'market-places' within the media: there's a plastic surgery market at the back of *Cosmopolitan* for example, and travel marts in several of the upmarket weekend newspaper supplements. It may be that you actually do better for a small budget by advertising here with quite a small ad than by wandering into unknown, solus territory, where you might strike gold, but could just shrivel up in the wilderness before any customers come upon you. The low-risk strategy is to go where the crowds are.

Where there is no such marketplace, it is less easy to rely on small sizes. A useful strategy is to create your own marketplace: use a small ad, but arrange with the publication to have it appear always in the identical place: this will cost you more, unless you are a good haggler, but it means that you will begin to build familiarity with the publication's readers. Look at the crosswords in the broadsheet news-papers: they all, most of the time, have regular advertisers using small adjacent spaces, or sometimes sponsoring the puzzle. Similarly, there is a space in the middle of *The Times* share prices that is regularly used by two or three advertisers.

'Amplification'

It is very tempting to think that you can enhance the effectiveness of your advertising by making it part of the news, in its own right. It happens, though very rarely. I've already mentioned Wonderbra—twice—in this chapter, because it

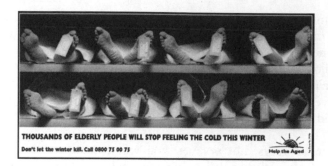

THOUSANDS OF ELDERLY PEOPLE WILL STOP FEELING THE COLD THIS WINTER
Don't let the winter kill. Call 0800 75 00 75
Help the Aged

Controversial ads' effects can be amplified by controversy

is not only a very good example, but one that won an IPA Effectiveness Award. It is also one of very few small budget campaigns to have successfully done this without breaching the Code of Practice (Chapter 15). Historically, the most successful use of this kind of tactic has been by charities, who have, and sometimes use, the opportunity to shock the public (or those most shockable cynics, the media) by using horrific or painful images in their ads. This can be enhanced by recruiting stars and supermodels, as has been done by the anti-fur campaign Lynx. Most recently, Help The Aged succeeded in causing a fuss with an ad depicting a row of elderly feet as if on trolleys in a morgue. This so offended the editor of the *Daily Telegraph* that he not only refused to run the ad but wrote a wonderfully pompous letter to *Marketing* magazine defending his decision.

Whatever you do, a small budget will always have to concentrate on: one media category; a limited range of options within the chosen media; a few periods during the year. In most cases, it is probably best to organize the advertising in bursts, since this can create a greater impression of importance for the brand. On the other hand, if you are in a response business, you will do better to spread the campaign through the year, as far as possible. Recency planning is generally a luxury for the rich, and so are the more complex forms of integrated communications (though business-to-business advertisers seem to manage pretty well).

Small budgets in practice

Possible solutions to the problems posed by smaller budgets can be illustrated by two examples. The first is a financial product. Here, the brand is just one of many products marketed by a leading institution, so it may benefit from other parts of the company's substantial ad budget; but the product has to compete within its own market, and attract customers off the page—to telephone the company for more information and, perhaps, to buy over the phone.

The resulting programming has six characteristics:

☐ It uses small press spaces—nothing more than a broadsheet 25 × 4 cols, plus very selected magazine inserts.
☐ It uses a very narrow selection of media (which have been proven by experiment to work for this brand in this market).
☐ It aims as far as possible to spread the advertising over the year (in this, it is helped by the observation that too frequent ads in any one publication lead to reduced response, so that a 3–4 week interval is regarded as obligatory).
☐ The advertising is supported, as far as possible, by PR in the specialist press and the publications used.
☐ There is a small-scale supporting effort using statement stuffers to selected customers of the company's regular-contact products (current accounts, credit cards, for example).

Based on these elements, a typical plan would look like that shown in Figure 14.2.

The second example is a food product, which is part of a range of products marketed by a major multinational company. The brand is a traditional speciality, with a small but loyal, ageing usership. The company wishes to develop a new market for the brand, and has identified mothers of young children as a key target, since the vitamins and other nutrients in the product provide an antidote to the day-to-day drain on energy imposed by looking after infants.

This has been translated into a two-pronged advertising strategy: to talk direct to the mothers, through both ads and PR in the mother-and-baby press; and to encourage the mother's mothers to talk to their daughters about the product, through selective ads and PR in women's magazines that appeal to an older age group—the current users. In addition, the brand will receive PR coverage in the grocery trade press.

Because of the need to get noticed, this campaign uses two bursts of advertising, rather than the extended pattern of the previous one. The resulting campaign laydown is shown in Figure 14.3.

Summary

☐ Planning the whole campaign, especially when it is an integrated operation involving a mix of activities, is quite complex. The key to it is to retain an overall perspective, and a focus on the agreed objectives.
☐ While large campaigns present greater potential complexity, and the opportunity for radical and creative thinking, smaller budgets are equally challenging, because they demand the identification of ways to extend and amplify the money available.

Activity	Format	Jan	Feb	Mar	Apr	May	Jun	Jul	Aug	Sep	Oct	Nov	Dec	Cost £
Media														
Daily Mail	20x3	x	x	x	x	x	x			x	x	x		35,500
D Telegraph	25x4		x	x	x	x	x	x		x	x	x		39,000
Mail on Sunday	25x4		x	x	x	x	x			x		x		20,500
Inserts														
Reader's Digest	(650K)			x						x				35,000
Radio Times	(700K)				x						x			25,000
PR		▨▨▨▨▨▨▨▨▨▨▨▨▨												50,000
Direct Mail (share of general programme)		▨▨▨▨▨▨▨▨▨▨▨▨▨												25,000
Production														20,000
TOTAL COST														**£250,000**

Figure 14.2.   Campaign lay-down for financial product budget £250 000

Activity	Format	Jan	Feb	Mar	Apr	May	Jun	Jul	Aug	Sep	Oct	Nov	Dec	Cost
Media														
YOU mag.	Page*				x						x	x		
Parents	Page					x					x	x		
Mother&Baby	Page					x					x	x		
Top Sante	Page*					x					x			
Woman	Page					x					xx			
Woman's Own	Page					x					x			£160,000
PR					▨	▨				▨	▨	▨		£ 75,000
Production														£ 25,000
TOTAL COST														£250,000

* Advertorial

Figure 14.3. Specialist food product campaign lay-down budget: £250 000

□ In both cases, the major problem is to find ways of stretching the money across the year at a rate that will be competitively powerful.

Question for analysis

□ As the marketing director of a major charity, with a seven-figure communications budget, your main marketing effort has been put into direct mail for the last two years. Research tells you that your charity is less top-of-mind than it was among givers in general, while the rate of response from known givers is tending to slip. Your returns are also highly sensitive to natural disasters in the third world, which generate both a massive demand for your services and a substantial increase in donations. What factors should you take into account in planning your communications activity for the next year? How will you aim to balance, for example, mailings, advertising and PR?

Plate 1 A clean, efficient ad for a discount retailer. Heavy use of spot colour creates effective stand-out in the newspaper

Plate 2 A long-running global campaign (see page 244), which works in several media. Emotion and information effectively integrated

Plate 3   Recipes are a food advertising stand-by, this one creates an image too

Photo: Seamus Ryan

Plate 4   Making the recipe part of editorial endorsement adds power to an otherwise ordinary ad (the recipe was bound-in beside the ad)

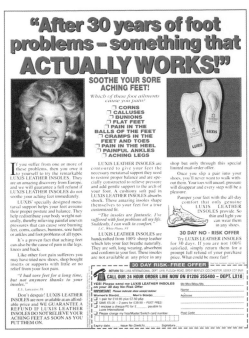

Plate 5 A very typical direct response ad: long copy, lots of reasons for purchase, easy to respond to—by phone or post

Plate 6 Smirnoff's 'through the bottle' campaign exploited the cinema medium to the full

Plate 7 Direct comparative ads are a potent weapon to challenge brand leaders

Plate 8 Carpets are dull, so Brintons turned them into fashion. An established campaign enables a variety of styles and lifestyles to be featured

Sex sells – especially a sports car—but it can be done with style . . .

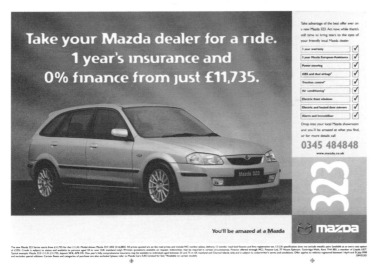

Plate 9 . . . but most press ads for cars are 'moving metal', and the brands are interchangeable

Plate 10 'Advertorial' style ads get read, especially in the right magazines. This is tailored to Saga readers (the over-50s)

Plate 11 Interactivity is supposed to belong to the Net and digital TV. Here's how to do it in the press

Plate 12 Simple, stylish, witty advertising has built a massive global brand—all it takes is bottle

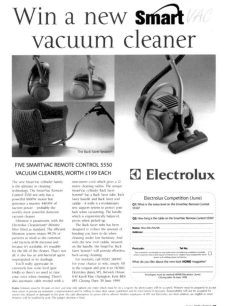

Plate 13   Magazines have editorial authority. So why not let the magazine do your advertising, and clean up

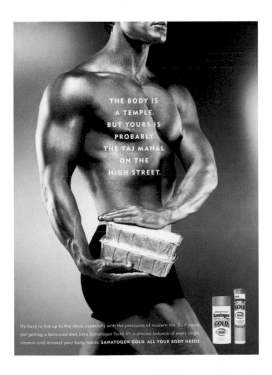

Plate 14   An ad that intrigues and invites questions (page 99)

Plate 15 The questionnaire is one of the oldest devices in advertising. This one combines with the visual to be a bit different

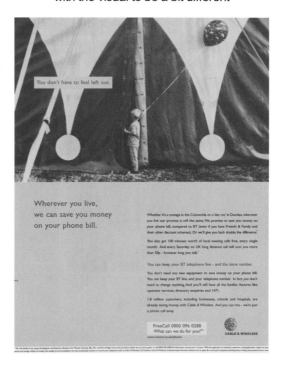

Plate 16 Consistent use of yellow gives C&W's campaigns coherence and consistent identity, across all media

15 Advertising and the law

It is well recognised that advertising is considered by the public as hyperbole. The use of such puffery does not in itself make advertising dishonest

Sallie Spilsbury, *Guide to Advertising and Sales Promotion Law*

Advertising as a business and the advertisements it produces are subject to many laws, statutes and regulations and to various Codes of Practice. In this chapter, I shall set out the main principles that should ensure that an ad is acceptable both under the law and under the relevant codes, and provide the necessary guidance for anyone who is in any doubt to get assistance. Too often, advertisers (in particular) and more junior people in agencies are remarkably ignorant of the existence of restraints on what can be done in advertisements, and distinctly cavalier about the legal status of intellectual property (copyrights, trademarks, etc).

The advertising industry has a long history of trying to steer clear of legal controls, because these are seen as being rigid and expensive. In its defence, the industry, nationally and internationally, has developed a system of 'self-regulation'. (The inverted commas are there because I suspect that this project has led to a situation where the self-regulatory apparatus is sometimes more legalistic than the law itself, at least in the UK).

Nonetheless, the primacy of the law means that we should start here. If you obey the Codes of Practice, there is no absolute guarantee that you will be legal—though the Codes insist, rightly, that you should try to be. If you fulfil the requirements of the law, you may still fail to conform to the Codes—in some areas, the law provides no specific guidance, but the Codes have clear rules.

Law in the UK is increasingly intended to harmonize with EU law, especially in areas affecting commerce. Nonetheless, there is a way to go, and the precise form in which EU Directives are turned into law by national parliaments can vary considerably—as can the interpretations of the courts. This chapter is specifically concerned with the UK, though the scope of the law and the character of self-regulatory institutions are increasingly similar across Europe. The UK's Advertising Association has recently published a summary of relevant EU legislation and policy development.[1] The situation in the US is rather different, while elsewhere in the

---

[1] *The Commercial Communications Compendium*, Advertising Association, London, 1998.

world laws and practices vary widely, though the International Chamber of Commerce (ICC) Codes of Practice have some general currency.

The law

The law affects advertisers and advertising in a number of areas (see Box 15.1). A full list of laws and regulations that may be relevant to at least some advertisers'

Box 15.1   Aspects of the law affecting advertising

- Contract.
- Trademarks.
- Copyright.
- Passing off.
- Defamation and libel.
- Trade descriptions.
- Price indications.
- Data protection.
- Misleading advertising.
- Comparative advertising.
- Obscenity, indecency and blasphemy.

In addition, advertisements may be affected by a wide variety of product-specific legislation, relating, for example, to health-related products, gambling, financial services, and so on.

---

situation is simply vast. The important thing is to be aware of the areas where legal problems can arise, so that you are able to check with a legal adviser. Apart from a growing number of law firms that have expertise either in advertising or in key areas such as intellectual property, the IPA has competent and helpful legal advisers who may provide valuable help either with the law or the Codes.

Contract

The law of contract is complex, though the principles are simple. A contract is a legally binding agreement between two parties. You sign and exchange contracts when you buy a house; an agency and client will draw up a contract to seal their working arrangements. When an advertiser is selling to a broad consumer market, there is—obviously—no formal contract of this kind, but if the consumer buys on the basis of claims made in ads, there is an implied contract. If the product then fails to deliver, the advertiser is in breach of contract. The classic case that established this is *Carlill* vs. *The Carbolic Smoke Ball Company* (1892).

A Mrs Carlill bought a 'smoke ball' which was claimed to prevent colds, flu, etc., and promptly caught flu. She asked for compensation offered in the ad, was refused, sued and won.

For the law of contract to apply, an actual purchase has to be made: a price in a shop window is 'merely an offer to treat', so if the shopkeeper has mistakenly under-priced a product, there is no obligation to sell.

Trade descriptions and price indications

The Trade Descriptions Act 1968, and the related Code of Practice for Traders on Price Indications 1988 (actually under the Consumer Protection Act 1987) are concerned with ensuring that products and their prices are correctly and fairly described. The scope of the Act covers not merely the physical make-up of the product but such areas as endorsements and claims to meet official or industry standards (both of which must be genuine). The Code of Practice, which is complicated, is a potential minefield for retail advertisers, in particular, and needs careful study.

Intellectual property

Trademarks and copyright are areas where it is easy to go wrong. To have legal force, trademarks need to be registered, and this can be done either on a country-by-country basis for those territories where the product or service is sold, or, now for the European Union through the CTM (Community Trade Mark) office in Alicante, Spain. The CTM has proved so popular that the office has been swamped by applications, and—at the same time—the CTM is so new that there is no case law to clarify how it will work in practice.

Trademarks confer on their owners monopoly protection for their brand names and related elements (such as the shape of distinctive packaging—the Coca-Cola bottle or the Jif lemon) against imitation or misuse by competitors. Because trademarks, company names, etc., are essentially national in character, there is an increasing range of problems arising from advertising on the Web, which is, of course, global.

The symbol ® can only refer to a registered trademark. TM, on the other hand, may apply to either a registered or non-registered mark. A non-registered mark does not confer any monopoly protection, though it may become protectable through usage.

This is important in the case of *passing off*—basically, trading on someone else's goodwill. This is usually done by getting up your product to look very like someone else's, or appropriating elements of their distinctive presentation for your product. Examples include the use of the name 'sherry' to describe fortified wines from Cyprus; Asda's Puffin biscuits, which were judged to be passing off as Penguin biscuits; Cadbury's Swiss Chalet chocolate, which the Swiss chocolate-makers successfully challenged as passing itself off as Swiss.

Copyright is in some respects similar to trademarking, but applies to original work in (broadly) the arts and literature. There is no copyright in a brand name or book title, nor in advertising slogans (though this is inadequately tested in the courts). The aim of copyright is to prevent copying or performing a work without acknowledgement and/or payment. It applies for a considerable period of time, which varies by type of material, but is typically 50–70 years after the death of the author or composer.

The copyright in a work is owned by its originator, or the employer of the originator. Thus, copyright in an advertisement initially belongs to the agency that creates it, though it is the normal practice for agency contracts to assign copyright to the client. If the ad is created for the agency by freelances, the copyright belongs to the freelances—again, unless it is assigned. Similarly, if a photographer or illustrator is commissioned to produce the pictures for a campaign, the copyright is theirs—and the agency has to be careful to stipulate in its contract with the photographer the range of uses to which the pictures may be put. If a picture for an ad is then used in a brochure or a point-of-sale piece, or the campaign is extended to new countries or the picture appears on a Website, the photographer will be quite entitled to ask for extra payment, unless the shots have been bought on this basis.

Similar thinking underlies the fact that performers in commercials have property rights in the use made of the ads: thus, they earn repeat fees whenever the ad is aired, and may demand extra payments if the commercial is used overseas. In the same way, elements in a commercial—the music, for example—will need to be cleared for use wherever the advertiser wishes to use it, ideally in advance.

Finally, while an ad itself may be copyright, there is no copyright in a general idea or concept. (This is relatively untested in the courts, and it could be considered analogous to the case Apple Computers brought against Microsoft for imitating the look and feel of the Apple graphical user interface.) It may be considered bad form or unoriginal to take an advertising idea from one market and apply it to a different brand in another, but it is rarely an infringement of copyright, unless it goes right down to quite significant detail.

Comparative advertising, trade libel, etc.

Under current UK law, it is possible to compare your product in advertising to th
of a competitor, so long as this is done fairly and without denigrating tl
competitor. The process involves some legal risks. You may infringe their trademark; you may commit a trade libel (which may, even, be a malicious falsehood);
you may produce a false price comparison; and you may simply be making a
misleading comparison.

A trade libel involves a false reference to a competitor's brand which is published
maliciously and leads to direct financial loss to the competitor. It will be costly.
Clearly, if you are going to make comparisons, you should have supporting
evidence that will stand up in court—and have it in place before the claim you
make is published. The more specific the claim, the better the evidence should be.
What's more, even if you do not actually name the competitor, it will still be a libel
if the reference could be reasonably interpreted as referring to them. If you have
deliberately falsified the evidence in some way, this is even worse.

Comparisons, then, need to be clear and fair, unbiased, comparing like with like
and substantiatable. An EU Directive, which should be embodied in UK
legislation by April 2000, is somewhat stricter than this, though milder than
existing German law. By contrast, in the US 'knocking copy' can be used much
more freely.

Endorsements and personalities

Misuse of individuals in ads can lead to a variety of problems. There is a blanket
prohibition in the UK on the use of royalty (and of claiming royal patronage
without an appropriate royal appointment). The obvious problem with using
people in ads (especially without their permission) is the risk of defamation.
Here, an old case shows what can happen. Fry's chocolate used a picture of a
leading amateur golfer, Cyril Tolley, in an ad, and were sued for defamation: Mr
Tolley considered that Fry's had compromised his amateur status, which was then
very important. He won.

More recently, stars have bought cases claiming spurious endorsements were
damaging their goodwill, with mixed success; and some have registered their
names as trademarks, something that may be made more difficult by new
regulations. In the UK, unlike some other countries, there is no automatic legal
right to privacy—though its adoption of the European Convention on Human
Rights should change this. The Codes of Practice (see below) are ahead of the law
here.

Data protection and direct marketing

The Data Protection Act 1998 embodies the latest EU Directive, and is more tightly drawn than previous UK legislation. If you collect, process or disseminate personal information of any kind (including personnel files) on computer, you have to register with the DP Registrar. You have, too, to make clear to the people from whom you are collecting the data what it will be used for, and give them the option of preventing its use for these purposes. They, in turn, have the right to ask to see what information is held about them, and to correct any errors. Because the EU rules are stricter than those prevailing in many other countries, it is forbidden to transmit the data to any country outside the EU, unless the local laws are at least as strict. This causes potential problems with the US, where practice is far freer: at the time of writing, the US Department of Commerce is negotiating a legal form that companies who wish to handle EU personal data will have to subscribe to in order to do so.

An EU Directive on distance selling is due to come into force by the year 2000, which will effectively ban unsolicited cold calling by telephone and cold faxes. This may also be extended to junk e-mails ('spam'), which can probably be prevented under existing UK laws on the misuse of computers.

The self-regulatory system

The British system for regulating ads revolves around the British Code of Advertising and Sales Promotion Practice (BCASP), which is drawn up and regularly revised by the CAP committee, a body containing representatives of all sides of the industry and consumer organizations. The BCASP applies to print advertising, and is paralleled by the closely similar codes drawn up by the Independent Television Commission and the Radio Authority, covering both commercials and broadcast sponsorship.

None of the codes has the force of law, but they intertwine with the law, and all support the aim that any advertising should be legal.

The BCASP is a set of guidelines that is 'policed' by the Advertising Standards Authority, and is done retrospectively: pre-vetting the vast number of print ads would be physically impossible. By contrast, the ITC and RA codes are enforced by pre-vetting of ads, by the Broadcast Advertising Clearance Centre (BACC) and the Radio Advertising Clearance Centre (RACC) respectively. Complaints about press, poster and print advertising are accepted by the ASA, from trade complainers (competitors, usually), Trading Standards Officers and the general public. The ASA also regularly reviews ads in controversial or difficult areas, and sometimes initiates its own complaints. Complaints about TV or radio ads should go to the ITC or RA, and are often passed on to them by the ASA.

The ASA advertises to consumers, to encourage complaints about unacceptable ads, carries out regular research—for example, into consumer responses to certain types of advertising or ads in particular fields—and publishes monthly reports of its findings on ads complained about. It has an extremely informative website at www.asa.org.uk.

The ASA is able to insist on an advertiser withdrawing an ad, or modifying it for subsequent use. Persistent or flagrant offenders may be instructed to seek advice from the CAP, which provides a free copy advice service; and if they offend further, the ASA may recommend to publishers that they do not accept the ads. For advertisers who offend with poster campaigns, the ASA may insist on pre-vetting by the CAP copy advice team (see Box 15.2). In extreme cases, the ASA may refer a misleading ad to the Office of Fair Trading under the Control of Misleading Advertisements Regulations 1988, which was introduced as a final sanction in case the self-regulatory system should fail to prevent abuses.

Box 15.2   Poster pre-vetting powers

The ASA's power to insist on pre-vetting of posters is relatively new. One of the first victims was the Commission for Racial Equality. The Commission wished to encourage consumers to draw attention to racist material in ads and other media. They ran a poster campaign which was intended to work in two stages: the first 'teaser' stage displayed gratuitously racist material, and the 'reveal' asked why people had not complained. The ASA decided that this idea, though doubtless well-intentioned, had been extremely ill-conceived, and was capable of not merely causing offence and distress, but of provoking racist attitudes. In fact, they took it so seriously that they ordered the CRE to have any future poster campaign pre-vetted.

The 'reveal' stage of the ad showed the original poster, and asked which was worse: the offensive ad (which showed, e.g., an ape playing basketball alongside a picture of a 'normal' basketball player), or people's failure to complain about it.

The CRE declined to allow an ad to be reproduced here, even though the one described has been on their website throughout 1999, and may still be there – try www.cre.gov.uk/about/worse.html. For full details of the ASA judgement, and their perspective on the campaign, look up Commission for Racial Equality in the advertiser index on www.asa.org.uk, Adjudications, November 1998.

Codes of Practice

All the codes start from the premise that advertising should:

- Be legal, decent, honest and truthful (the main message of the ASA's consumer advertising);
- Have a sense of responsibility to consumers and society;
- Respect the principles of fair competition;
- Not bring advertising into disrepute;
- Conform to the code.

The accepted principle is that all material claims should be capable of substantiation, before publication. The BACC and RACC are able to demand this, because they will not accept a script unless they are satisfied about the validity of such claims. The ASA are strict with the ads submitted to them, especially concerning the status of tests and testing in the area of health claims, where they insist on direct clinical evidence of tests on humans.

Other areas of particular concern to the ASA include: the use of 'small print', which should not be used to alter the import of the main copy and headline of the ad; testimonials and endorsements, which must be either genuine or clearly fictitious; and pricing, where prices have to be complete (e.g. including VAT) and refer to the product (e.g. a specific car model and variant) featured in the ad.

The most publicized areas of complaint, however, tend to cover areas of decency—especially anything to do with sex (for examples, see Box 15.3)—and emotional appeals, especially those playing on fears or superstitions.

Box 15.3   Sex and the single ASA

The ASA's monthly reports regularly include examples of ads that have offended (or been complained about) under the Code's clause 5—'Decency'. While the main offenders are small advertisers in specialized motor trade magazines (there's an obvious association between gunk and sex, isn't there?), better-known advertisers found to have offended during 1998 include, for example, Gucci, *The Times*, French Connection, JVC and Talk Radio. The best defence appears to be that the ad was recognizably humorous in intent, or that it was designed especially for the (broad-minded) readers of a specialized magazine. But even the alleged seriousness of intent failed to get Talk Radio's picture of a barcoded naked bottom, which was to advertise a programme about prostitution, past the ASA; and although French Connection have won out with some of their adaptations of their logo, the ASA drew the line at 'fcuk ... advertising'.

Source: *ASA Monthly Reports, 1998*—see www.asa.org.uk, 'Adjudications'

The Codes have a series of special provisions, which anyone involved in the markets concerned needs to be well aware of, in the following areas:

- Alcoholic drinks (>12 per cent by volume).
- Motoring.
- Environmental claims.
- Health and beauty products and therapies.
- Medicines.
- Vitamins, minerals and dietary supplements.
- Cosmetics.
- Hair and scalp products.
- Slimming products.
- Financial services and products.
- Distance selling.
- Employment and business opportunities.

In addition, there is a whole separate Code applying to cigarettes and tobacco (but not pipe tobacco) and related products, including products that carry the colours, livery, insignia or name of a cigarette brand (e.g. Marlboro Classics clothing).

The ASA , as Sallie Spilsbury's recent book[2] points out, 'has a tendency to adopt a restrictive and literal approach to the interpretation of claims ... the ASA makes little allowance for puffery', even though the Codes state that puffery is allowed, provided that it does not affect the accuracy of the advertisement in any material way.

The number of ads complained about by the public to the ASA has been historically quite small, running around 8 000; but 1998 saw a sharp increase to over 12 000. Most individual ads attract very few complaints, though the champion ad of 1998, for Irn Bru, collected nearly 600 complaints (which were turned down).

TV and radio

The BACC acts as a pre-clearer of commercials for all but a few cable TV companies; while the RACC covers virtually all radio ads, except for a few local ones in non-controversial fields.

The BACC normally vets commercials initially at script stage—it is not worth any agency making a commercial that may be unusable—and subsequently as a finished ad before transmission. Where factual claims are made, the BACC will insist on substantiation, and it helps to submit this with the ad. Technical and scientific

---

[2] S. Spilsbury, *Guide to Advertising and Sales Promotion Law*, Cavendish Publishing, London, 1998.

claims are passed by BACC to appointed experts for evaluation. BACC has a series of guidance notes for advertisers.

BACC can suggest any changes it sees fit, and may impose restrictions on scheduling of particular ads, for example that they should not be in breaks around children's programming.

BACC clearance is, of course, solely concerned with the Codes: they are not legal advisers. What's more, the ITC may sometimes overrule a BACC clearance, deciding that an ad does not conform to the Codes.

The RACC procedures are closely similar to BACC's, but allow for speedier clearance to fit with the faster pace of radio production.

The TV and radio codes

Both codes are, in essence, closely similar to the BCASP, but with provisions specific to the medium. For example, there are restrictions on the use of broadcasters in advertisements. On TV, news, current affairs and advice programme presenters are barred from appearing in ads, while ads using performers from other programmes must usually be scheduled well away from the programmes in which they appear. On radio, presenters may read ad scripts on air, but it must not be implied that they are in any way endorsing the product. Similarly, product placement is banned on TV.

On TV, there is ban on subliminal advertising (as in most of the world, in spite of the absence of any evidence that it works).On both media, testimonials are only acceptable with documentary evidence and the signed permission of the people concerned. Both media have a list of products that may not be advertised—cigarettes, most forms of gambling, dating agencies, and the like.

Sponsorship is an area where the rules are likely to change as channels proliferate, thanks to the new digital technology. In general, the rules are reasonably straightforward at present. Sponsorship has to be clearly identified as such, and the brands sponsoring the programmes effectively excluded from programme content. TV excludes sponsorship from news, business/finance programmes and current affairs, and restricts it on consumer advice or controversial issues. Radio's limits are narrower—only news is excluded.

Summary

□ Advertising can interact with the law in a wide variety of ways. You need to be aware of the possibilities and at least the basic principles.

- ☐ Then, if in any doubt at all, take advice.
- ☐ There are Codes of Practice that provide a great deal of guidance on how to produce acceptable advertising. Read them, and understand what they mean.
- ☐ For TV and radio, all ads have to be pre-vetted. This ensures that they should clear the Code—but is not a guarantee of legality.
- ☐ Be especially careful with: comparative advertising; copyright (throughout the process); factual claims of superiority (have objective supporting evidence available); the use of third parties (testimonials/endorsements, the use of celebrities and public figures without their permission).

As an exercise ...

Take any issue of the ASA's monthly report. Go through it, and study the decisions. Get hold of one or more of the ads successfully complained of, together with those for competing products. Why did the complaint succeed? What do direct competitors do that is different and so does not breach the code?

16   Advertising and economics

Advertising is the rattling of the stick in the swill-bucket of capitalism

George Orwell, *Keep the Aspidistra Flying*

In this chapter, I will look briefly at the role of advertising in the economy as a whole, and in the economics of companies and markets.

Advertising in the UK economy

Advertising is an activity with significance for many countries' economies: total ad spending runs around $+/-1$ per cent of GDP in most developed countries.

In the UK, while ad agencies, as such, employ only some 15 000 people, it has been estimated that advertising as a whole is responsible for nearly 100 000 jobs, or 0.4 per cent of total employment. This includes people working in businesses supplying the ad industry—studios, TV production houses, printers, etc.—and advertising staff in client organizations and the media.

Advertising expenditures, as shown in the statistics published by the Advertising Association, consist of two elements: display advertising and classified advertising, of which display is the dominant sector, though classified is very important for some media. Advertising is sensitive to the state of the economy as a whole—it is not merely vulnerable to both downturns and upswings, but it moves rather rapidly in response to either. Classified advertising, in fact, is a valuable 'lead indicator' of economic progress, because virtually half of it, at least in the UK, consists of recruitment advertising, which reflects companies' experience and expectations of their markets very precisely.

Advertising thus shows considerable 'mood swings' in line with the growth or stagnation of the economy. Through much of the 1970s, the industry in the UK was in decline: the 1980s saw a sustained boom after the 1981–82 recession, followed by hard times in the early 1990s, and by 1998, display advertising had still not recovered to its 1989 percentage share of GDP (see Figure 16.1).

The movement in advertising expenditures is closely related to that of companies' profits, which are, of course, heavily influenced by the performance of the economy. Given that companies, especially public companies with shareholders to keep

Year	Advertising expenditure (current prices £bn)	% of GDP
1985	5.05	1.64
1986	5.80	1.77
1987	6.57	1.82
1988	7.61	1.90
1989	8.64	1.96
1990	8.93	1.86
1991	8.53	1.72
1992	8.86	1.71
1993	9.14	1.67
1994	10.14	1.75
1995	10.98	1.82
1996	12.02	1.89
1997	13.14	1.94

Figure 16.1. UK advertising expenditure and GDP 1985–97 (Source: A.A, *Advertising Statistics Yearbook 1998*, NTC Publications)

happy, aim to grow their profits over time, an economic downturn puts heavy pressure on them to cut costs. Since advertising, though it is a form of investment, is an investment in intangibles, involving very limited resources within the company, it is very easy to save money by cutting the advertising budget. What's more, you can do it at almost any time, quickly, and transfer a substantial sum directly to profit.

At a time—early 1999—when the UK shows every sign of entering a period of recession, and there is a very real threat that the current euphoria of the US economy may collapse, it is educative to look back at research compiled during earlier recessions.[1] This shows, rather consistently, that firms that do not cut their advertising during a recession will usually increase their market share, to an extent that their return on investment will be significantly higher in subsequent years than that of firms that have cut their advertising. What is more, it also shows that firms that do cut advertising do not manage to save their profitability in the short term, any more than do those who carry on spending.

This, of course, depends on the inevitable fact that, in any market, at least some, and probably most, of the firms will, in fact, cut back: if they all carried on spending, they would merely all lose margin, with no significant changes in market share. Certainly, the instinct to cut the budget is totally understandable, but the logic of market behaviour favours the bolder course—not least because it is an observable fact that few marketing directors have the strength and standing in their

---

[1] For example, A. L. Biel, 'The cost of cutbacks', *Admap*, May 1991.

companies to win a battle over budget cuts. It is therefore actually easier to gain market share in a recession than it is in a period of growth—and there is ample evidence to show that higher market shares tend to lead to higher profitability. (Much of the evidence for this comes from the PIMS database, a very large bank of data on companies and markets assembled initially by General Electric in the US but now owned by the Strategic Planning Institute (SPI).

What this means, in practice, is that advertising is usually used to support what should be favourable circumstances for sales growth, but not, necessarily, for market share gains; while it is more likely to make a greater contribution to the company's business if it is used in unfavourable market conditions. What is more, because a weak market for advertising should lead to weaker prices for advertising time and space, the cost-effectiveness of the advertising should be higher in a recession than in times of economic growth.

One final point in this section. There is an underlying reason why ad expenditure as a whole has not returned to its 1989 peak share of GDP in the UK. Advertising is not the whole of the communications mix, and most advertising statistics do not include direct marketing, let alone PR, sales promotion, design and corporate identity, sponsorship and some minor media—nor do they yet include the Internet, which is undoubtedly the fastest-growing form of marketing communication, though still from a very small base everywhere outside the USA. All the available evidence shows that direct mail has been growing faster than media advertising in recent years, and PR expenditures have certainly grown very fast in the last three years. Data on sales promotion expenditure are extremely hard to come by, but US evidence, and broader estimates by WPP,[2] suggest that advertising accounts for only 42 per cent of total marketing communications expenditure world-wide (including market research), and less than 35 per cent in the UK. As long ago as 1986, the WPP annual report highlighted the rapid growth of sales promotion expenditures, and this remains a world-wide phenomenon.

Advertising and markets

There is little evidence that advertising is an important factor in the growth (or decline) of individual product markets, though there is more evidence for this happening in small segments of larger markets which are gaining competitive shares of the larger whole (see Box 16.1). Certainly, it is often possible to find rapidly growing markets where advertising expenditures are also growing substantially in aggregate, but there is little to suggest that it is the advertising that is driving the growth. What is happening in these markets is that individual competitors, having identified a growth market, are piling in to compete for

---

[2] WPP Group plc, *Annual Report*, 1997.

market share. Similarly, what seems mostly to happen if advertising in a market is cut is that this means that it has reached maturity, the competitive frenzy has gone out of the market and it can settle down to a more sober and steady competitive pattern.

Box 16.1   Does Advertising Affect Market Size?

A study by the economics committee of the Advertising Association concluded that there is no general answer to this question, and none should be expected. More specifically, they concluded that an increase was less likely when: a market is already large and has no obvious scope for expansion, in terms of unsatisfied consumer needs, or is at very high levels of aggregation (broad market sectors). Conversely, there is a greater chance of expansion: in small markets with many similar products; in new markets or markets with many new products; in markets where there are many new ('trialist') consumers; when a single brand dominates, and its growth can only come from expanding the market; when there are other factors favouring growth (population segment increase, for example); and when a group of producers combines to mount a generic campaign.

Source: S. Broadbent (ed.) *Does Advertising Affect Market Size?* Advertising Association, London 1997.

In grocery categories, where this happens, UK experience has been that the market is gradually taken over by the multiple chains' private label brands: 'me-too' products sold at prices 15–20 per cent (typically) cheaper than the leading brands. Detailed analysis of grocery markets by the A. C. Nielsen research company shows clearly that there is a correlation between low private label share of market and the combination of consistent advertising and product innovation by the manufacturers. High private label shares occur in markets where the manufacturers appear to have walked away from active competition, for whatever reason.

The one area where advertising could, theoretically, affect total market development is that of 'commodity' marketing, where the various interests in a market combine to promote—say—tea, meat or fish. There are relatively few examples of this, and the evidence for or against success is at best equivocal. Part of the reason for this lies in the fact that these programmes are usually introduced at a time when the commodity concerned is under threat, often because of fundamental changes in the marketplace, so that the generic advertising and promotion appear to coincide with declining market sales. (Of course, this simplistic view fails to take account of what might have happened *without* any promotion.)

For example, the International Tea Promotion Council, which has a variety of programmes around the world, came into being largely as a response to the joint threat of successful competition by coffee and by soft beverages. Trying to maintain the astronomically high per capita consumption of tea in countries such as the UK and Ireland was probably always doomed to failure, but the organization has had some modest success in building less developed markets.

Perhaps the most successful long-term piece of market building, using a combination of advertising (which has always been the spearhead) and a variety of other communications activities, has been the work of De Beers with diamonds. De Beers effectively *is* the diamond industry, at least in consumer terms, and has successfully developed new markets for diamond jewellery all over the world. This has involved, for example, literally inventing a diamond engagement ring custom in countries like Japan. Although diamond jewellery sales are very vulnerable to economic circumstances, the long-term trend in sales worldwide is consistently upwards, and some of this is certainly due to De Beers' advertising.[3]

In the UK, the Meat and Livestock Commission (MLC) has been faced with the task of sustaining sales of carcase meat (beef, lamb and pork) in the face of the rise of cheap broiler chickens on the one hand and vegetarianism (which reaches some 15 per cent of teenagers there) on the other. This task was made doubly difficult by the BSE crisis which effectively destroyed the UK (and European) beef market from the mid-1990s. Nonetheless, the MLC has been able at least to start rebuilding beef consumption, and has certainly helped to improve attitudes to the product.

> **Box 16.2   Building the market ...**
>
> It is claimed that BT's 'It's good to talk' campaign is a unique example among IPA Award prize-winners of a strong brand leader using advertising to expand an already bouyant market.
>
> BT's strategic insight was to recognise the role of the men in families as 'gatekeepers' to the extended use of the telephone. Men tend to talk less on the phone, and to object when other members of the family do so, at length. The campaign that resulted, used Bob Hoskins as a sort of invisible 'agent provocateur', who wandered around people's homes making encouraging remarks to get men (usually) to use the phone more. The aim was to help men loosen up their attitudes to long phone calls by other members of their families, and – even – to talk more themselves.

---

[3] For a detailed description of De Beers' activity, see G. Duckworth (ed.) *Advertising Works 9*, NTC Publications, Henley-on-Thames, 1997, Chapter 13.

While it was women who admitted to spending more time on the phone as a result of the campaign, there was a marked softening in men's attitudes, especially among the more resistant over-35 age group, and total call minutage rose as a result of the campaign (See *Advertising Works 9*, chapter 7).

... *or building brand equity*

The BT campaign is in sharp contrast to the activities of other phone companies, including the mobile phone operators. Here, the thrust of the advertising is almost exclusively about winning market share, and it is generally assumed that the combination of social pressures and the industry's collective advertising and marketing activity will suffice to grow the market.

The most recent IPA Award-winner in this sector was Orange, whose mainstream advertising could, conceivably, be viewed as intended to grow the market, and who had to introduce a radically new way of looking at their brand in order to succeed against already-entrenched competition, as shown in their 1996 award-winning case (*Advertising Works 9*, chapter 1).

Nonetheless, the case put forward to the awards judges two years later (*Advertising Works 10*, chapter 2) focused not so much on growing the market, or even on gaining market share, as such. The marketing objective was, clearly to grow the brand, and this was achieved, in terms of a substantial increase in subscribers to the service. However, the slant that the agency and the brand managers put on their success was primarily about their success in growing shareholder value for the company, and the contribution that advertising made towards this.

With the aid of independent evaluation by analysts from Lehman Brothers, it was possible to demonstrate that the advertising had been able to add something over £3 bn. to the company's value. At the operational level, in competitive terms, Orange had been able to maintain a price premium against the market, achieving higher revenue per customer than other networks, operate at a lower level of 'churn' (the industry's jargon for customers dropping out or switching to another network), and continue to increase numbers of subscribers in spite of intense competitive pressures.

Comparing the two Orange case studies in *Advertising Works*, it is interesting to see the ways in which the content of the advertising had to change, from initial brand awareness and positioning to very hard-nosed, content-based material designed to ensure the brand's continued competitiveness in an increasingly aggressive marketplace.

Overall, though, the relationship between advertising and market size is usually one in which the adspend is the effect, rather than the cause. The money goes where the sales are, rather than the reverse.

Advertising and the company

Advertising can be viewed either as an investment or as an operating expense, within a company's accounts. In practice, accounting conventions treat it as an operating expense, though modern theory about brands is more inclined to regard it as a form of investment. This makes the position of the advertising budget within a company both vulnerable and equivocal.

Whatever its technical status, how does it effect the economics of the company? Companies exist to use their resources of capital and personnel, and raw materials bought in, to produce goods and services which they sell at a profit. Their objective is to provide a return to their shareholders or owners, and to maintain a viable business over time. Advertising, clearly, is one of the tools of the process of selling. As such, as we have seen (Chapter 3), advertising accounts for a share of selling expenses, which tends to remain fairly constant over time. Advertising both helps to sell the company's products and to build the strength of the company's brands—and, perhaps, also the corporate reputation.

It is this latter role that takes it from being merely a sales expense to something more like an investment (see box 16.2).

It is important to recognize this role, because it is quite unusual for advertising to clearly pay for itself, in the short term, in terms of increased profit. A burst of advertising will usually lead to a short-term increase in sales, but this will very rarely generate enough profit, within the period of the advertising, to cover the cost of advertising.

There are two things to be said about this. First, advertising is part of the built-in cost of selling the product: it is unrealistic to expect it to produce enough 'extra' profit, in the short term, to 'pay for' itself. Second, if it is doing a good job, the advertising will have actual sales effects some way beyond the period in which it appears (these may be either increased sales, or sales sustained at a higher level than would otherwise have occurred); and it will have helped to strengthen the overall standing and reputation of the brand in the long-term. These days this is often called 'brand equity', even though no one can quite agree what this means or how best to measure it.

Obviously, for a company that has not previously advertised, it can be distinctly disheartening to find that advertising, for which such high hopes may have been held, is merely—or so it appears—an added cost, eating into profitability. It is important to recognize that advertising can *substitute* for other expenses, over the longer term, rather than simply being added to them, and that its benefits are also relatively long term. (Equally, if you cut an established advertising budget, you need to put some other form of communication or promotion in its place, to take up the slack, or you will lose sales and/or market share.)

As part of the company's business, advertising acts both as an aggressive competitive weapon and as a form of defence. It is a means of gaining sales from competitors—usually more by a process of attrition than by the instant conversion suggested by dated theories (see page 44)—and of defending a market share against competitive inroads.

Box 16.3   *Advertising and economic theories of the company*

Economic theorists classically take a very narrow view of the role of advertising within a company, leading to the conclusion that advertising is an expense, without which the cost of the company's products would be lower. The same would be true if they reduced the number of salesmen, or the amount of steel in the car body—but they would soon be out of business. The implicit assumption is that businesses are unable to keep their costs under control—in other words, that they are stupid. While this may indeed be true of some, it seems unlikely that it should be true of most of the world's major companies and their managements!

For a more detailed analysis, see H. Lind (ed.) *Making Sense of Advertising*, Advertising Association, London, 1998.

Advertising and price

Advertising can also act effectively to support a product's price. Very simply, if consumers become in some sense loyal to a brand, they are prepared to carry on buying it even if its competitors become quite significantly cheaper. There is, for most people, a point at which they will give up their brand and start buying a cheaper one, but quite a substantial gap can open up before this happens. Otherwise, we would all buy the private label brands, all the time, and no one would ever buy premium-priced brands. (Of course, the justification for many premium prices is a genuine difference in quality—of ingredients, manufacturing or design—but there is often little easily perceptible, objective difference between mainstream manufacturer brands and their own-label equivalents, or even their cheaper branded competitors.)

This ability to charge a higher price is a reflection of successful branding, in which the advertising is often an essential part. The fact that this phenomenon occurs has led economists and consumerists to complain that advertising pushes up the cost of goods and services, and to suggest a variety of mechanisms by which advertising should be restrained. In practice, research[4] shows that advertising has little or no effect on the overall level of prices, because it has the main effect of providing the manufacturer with economies of scale that reduce costs and allow the savings to be passed on to the consumer—which the supplier has to do, in order to remain competitive.

Monopolies

Monopoly is a dirty word to economists and politicians, and anything that tends to create monopolies is suspect. Economists often suggest that advertising can be used to develop monopoly power and, once this is achieved, to maintain it and, by inference, exploit customers. In practice, studies of heavily advertised markets by the UK's Monopolies Commission and others have shown that these markets tend to be highly competitive and that the prices charged are by no means inflated.

Similarly, there is no quantifiable evidence that advertising is the major force in establishing or even maintaining monopolies. Certainly, large companies with big market shares use advertising—as they use advanced distribution systems, economies of scale in production and buying and more efficient administrative systems, based on intensive use of information technology—to defend themselves against competition. The monopoly they have, however, if it is one, is usually based on the ownership of intellectual property—patents, copyrights, trademarks and the like. It is worth remembering, too, that very few companies have a *real* monopoly in any large market: UK legislation, for example, defines monopoly, arbitrarily, as a 25 per cent share.

There are, in fact, plenty of examples of apparent monopolies or dominant market shares being attacked and significantly eroded—regardless of any advertising efforts. The incipient erosion of Microsoft's (real) monopoly of PC operating systems by Linux has nothing to do with advertising, nor, indeed, has Microsoft's creation and maintenance of that monopoly. Usually, the loss of a monopoly comes about through technological innovation or, in these days of the privatization of state-owned monopolies, through changes in regulations and controls. Thus, in the UK, British Telecom (BT) has seen its share of the telecommunications market steadily eroded by a string of competitors, once they were allowed into the market: this is especially true of specialist subsegments of the market, but there has also been

---

[4] See, for example, S. Littlechild, *The Relationship Between Advertising and Price*, AA, London, 1982.

substantial switching by households to the cable TV companies. This is in spite of a regulatory regime that forces BT to reduce its prices, in real terms, by a significant amount annually.

A more technological form of share erosion is being suffered by Barclaycard, whose long-standing dominance of the UK credit card market is under heavy attack from mainly US card operators using sophisticated database analysis techniques to mount aggressive mailing campaigns behind card offerings with markedly lower interest rates and in some cases more open and valuable customer reward schemes than Barclaycard's.

Gillette's historical dominance of the wet shaving market has on several occasions, in a number of countries, been threatened, and sometimes severely damaged, through technical advances by competitors, ranging from the low-tech of the original throw-away BIC razors to far more sophisticated products from Wilkinson and Schick. In spite of this, Gillette's investment in R&D has enabled them to fight back, and their strategy now is evidently to pre-empt competition by moving the technical goalposts before the competitors can take aim. To be sure, advertising is a significant part of the marketing side of these contests, but without the technical developments there is no way that advertising could sustain Gillette's position.

The media

Most of the day-to-day media that inform and entertain us are at least partly financed by advertising revenues—and commercial TV and radio rely almost entirely on advertising, as do 'free' newspapers and magazines. As a result, your daily newspaper will usually have about half its pages consisting of advertising, and without this it would be a very sorry affair. What's more, it would cost, probably, nearly twice as much as it does today. This accounts for the relatively high cost of newspapers in some continental countries, where the advertising content of the papers is considerably less than the 40–60 per cent of pagination found in UK national papers.

This theoretically gives advertising—taken as a whole—a massive influence on the editorial policies of the media. Fortunately, perhaps, this is not how it works. Because, as I made clear at the very beginning of the book, 'advertising' is a very abstract way of looking at an extremely fragmented and diverse business, there is no consensus that could enable advertising to bring influence effectively to bear on the media. This is not to say that some large advertisers, especially in the US, do not try. To take a couple of examples, Coca-Cola have an extremely detailed specification for the kind of editorial material against which it is appropriate to run a Coke ad; and the *International Herald Tribune* (6th May 1997) reported an extensive set of examples of large US corporations attempting to influence the editorial content of various media.

Fortunately, while a single large advertiser may be able to make things a trifle uncomfortable for—in particular—a struggling publication or channel in the short term, there are enough other large advertisers to ensure that the problem should not be a long-term one. This is true, of course, where media are independent and economies diverse. A small country with most of the advertising in the control of the government might produce a different situation—but in that case the government would probably own the media anyway.

As it is, we should be at least moderately grateful for the fact that advertising enables the media to thrive—how grateful you are depends, of course, on how you regard the quality of the *Sun* or *Star TV* or *Bild*. What's more, it can legitimately be claimed that it is the availability of advertising money that enables you to enjoy the media you love at a price you can readily afford.

Benefits to the consumer

It is quite easy to go way over the top, once you have started, by claiming that advertising brings untold benefits to consumers. Quite apart from its role in making the media cheaper, its role in helping producers to achieve economically efficient volumes has the effect of keeping the prices of goods and services lower than they would otherwise have been. The information that ads—some ads, anyway—provide helps consumers to make informed and reasonably rational choices of what to buy, so reducing their search costs. Without advertising, many products would be more expensive, and buying them a much more difficult and hazardous process.[5]

Certainly, advertising is part of the cost of an advertised product: in a sense, you have to pay for the advertising. However, given the competitive nature of most markets, you have to recognize that if the advertising did not exist, some other aid to selling would have to take its place, and this would probably be more costly and less efficient—so the price would ultimately be higher.

It can be argued, too, that advertising is a cost to society in terms of aesthetic or moral values. Research among consumers consistently shows that this is certainly not a major concern.

---

[5] For an extended discussion of this and related topics, see W. Fletcher, *Advertising Advertising*, Profile Books, London, 1999.

Summary

- Advertising is a small factor in overall economic activity, and is very sensitive to economic cycles, because it is linked closely to company profits and can easily be reduced.
- There is at best limited evidence that advertising can affect market size, though there is a little to suggest that campaigns specifically designed to affect the total market—as opposed to competitive brand advertising within a market—can sometimes have an affect.
- Within the economics of the company, economists have traditionally seen advertising simply as a sales expense that can therefore be reduced at will. Advertising practitioners prefer to regard it as an investment, and as something that is necessary to maintain the health of the business.
- Advertising has, clearly, to be paid for. But the evidence is that advertising helps create economies of scale, or of selling efforts and expenditure, that more than offset the cost of the ads in the price.
- Monopoly: there is little convincing evidence that advertising either creates or sustains monopoly.
- Advertising finances the media, to a substantial extent. Without a thriving advertising market, media find it hard to survive and prices are liable to be higher.

Points to consider

- Comparative statistics show that—broadly—advertising expenditures are more significant as a proportion of GDP the higher the per capita income of the country. Does this mean that high per capita adspends are a sign of prosperity, or of consumerism gone mad?
- We saw in Chapter 3 that A/S ratios vary quite widely from one product market to the next. What does this tell us about the cost structures, or the competitive character, of the markets concerned?
- In Britain, the BBC does not carry advertising, either on TV or radio. Both types of broadcasting are paid for by an annual licence fee. What effects might allowing ads on the BBC have on (a) other media (b) the programmes and competitive success of the BBC?

17   Advertising and society

No one now can escape the influence of advertising

Pope John Paul VI, Message for World Communications Day, 1997

Advertising is blamed for many of the ills of society. Significantly, the word used when a politician—or a judge, a social worker, a clergyman, a pressure group or even the person next door—accuses advertising of some heinous crime against humanity is virtually always 'advertising'. Rarely 'advertisements', far less 'that advertisement'. 'Advertising' is a convenient shorthand for the great capitalist conspiracy that threatens us all. It clearly sets out to encourage that growing bogey 'consumerism' (a word that used to mean concern for consumers, but suddenly changed meaning, somewhere around 1990), and, as such, exploits the gullibility of people who cannot afford the goodies portrayed in the ads.

Box 17.1

Perhaps worst of all, the free market exploits children. Tobacco and alcohol marketers have not hesitated to capture the juvenile market so that 60 per cent of 12–15 year olds report taking alcohol, while more than a third of 14–15 year olds are regular smokers. At Christmas, skilful advertising induces children to pressurise low-incomed parents to purchase expensive presents. The market insistence that children are no more than consumers contrasts with the values of Jesus.

Bob Holman, community worker from Easterhouse, Glasgow, *The Guardian*, 12 December 1998).

While tobacco and alcohol are specific, (and controversial) cases, where it is not at all easy to prove the connection between advertising and the taking up of either smoking or alcohol by children, the *general* point in Box 17.1 is considerably more questionable, as we shall see below. To exaggerate a little, it is quite difficult to ascribe this sort of threat to—say—the Heinz commercials with music by Ladysmith Black Mambazo, or even an overt innuendo from fcuk, but quite easy to blame a nice, big abstraction.

Undoubtedly, there are real criticisms that can be levelled at advertisements, and possibly at the industry that produces them as well. Most of these criticisms, as illustrated by Box 17.1, which is, from an article entitled 'Morality and the market', are in fact more criticisms of the market economy and its workings than specifically of advertising, though they recognize advertising as its most obvious commercial face. There are, I believe, a number of areas where society can reasonably attack advertisements and advertising—and plenty more where someone may find cause to complain about an individual ad.

The main areas are:

- Influence and effects on children.
- Encouragement of antisocial or dangerous purchases or behaviour.
- Dishonesty, misleading or cheating the public.
- Bad taste, exploitation and devaluing of the arts, defacing the environment.
- The encouragement or acknowledgement of sexism, racism and other 'isms'.
- The creation of unattainable desires among people who cannot realize them— the encouragement of 'consumerism'.
- The insidious undermining of standards and values.

Advertising and children

As we have seen in Chapter 14, the Codes of Practice are especially stringent in the attempt to control and regulate the content of advertising to children. In the UK, it is recognized that advertisers can aim to influence children, but that this has to be done in a restrained manner. In some other European countries, especially in Scandinavia, advertising to children is banned, or subject to a variety of specific limitations.

There are four related issues involved here. First, are children capable of recognizing that ads are ads, and understanding that the aim is to sell them something? Second, should we, in any event, regard them as a legitimate target for advertising? Third, because the way in which most advertising to children has to work is through 'pester power', is it right that advertisers should be encouraging children to put pressure on their parents in this way? Fourth, specific to nutrition, is the argument that the concentration of food advertising on 'junk' food (of a variety of kinds, according to current theories, or who is doing the complaining) leads to the development of a whole range of ailments.

Children do, in fact, learn to recognize ads as ads from quite an early age. Research by both commercial and academic researchers shows that they are well aware, as young as four or five, of what an ad is, and what it is trying to do.[1] (This is younger

---

[1] See J. Hardman, 'Advertising to children', *Admap*, May 1998.

than classical child development theory, exemplified by Piaget,[2] would suggest, but the evidence seems clear). The Code of Practice aims to control the effects of advertising by (for example) ensuring that ads make clear to children the size and capabilities of, in particular, fantasy toys.

The broader issue is the one of involvement in the market, and how this affects parents. I do not see how children can avoid the market. It therefore makes sense that they should learn how to deal with it. This will (inevitably) mean that they meet with disappointments, when they have believed too much of the (inevitable) hype. You can argue that they should not have to cope with this until they reach a certain age—but what age makes sense? Eight? Ten? Fifteen? Some people already remain incurably naïve until they reach their dotage. It seems to me that—almost—the earlier you learn not to believe everything you hear in the ads (just as you should learn not to believe everything you read in the papers or see on TV) the better. If the education system can be persuaded to help in the process, so much the better: I am all in favour of schools teaching their pupils how to deconstruct ads, and to recognize what they are trying to do. (I am not at all in favour of the growing number of attempts to infiltrate schools with advertising material, because I think this is a quite inappropriate marketplace).

It is worth noting that children in the UK, at least, are from quite a young age articulate and perceptive critics of advertisements, with strong likes and dislikes, which do not necessarily seem to relate closely to brands they want or use, except that some brands are seen as incurably naff.

'Pester power' is a phrase the ad industry has saddled itself with, and which the media pick on enthusiastically every time someone from the commercial world uses it. Children have pestered their parents for things they want from time immemorial, and it does not require advertisements to create the effect. (To this day, I do not know how, as a five or six-year-old, I 'knew' that a toy manufacturer was about to launch a new range of die-cast model cars: I know I wanted one, and that I pestered my parents like crazy. I can be reasonably sure that I did not learn about the products from an ad.) Yes, parents get pestered, and often pestered to buy very expensive things—trainers, perhaps, above all. It is all too easy for the fat and affluent (and many people in advertising are one or the other) to say that all it takes is the word 'No'. The fact remains that it is a part of parenting to be able to deal with this, as with every other demand from children. This, too, is part of an education process. If we live in a capitalist, free market economy, learning the way it works is part of life. (It is worth remembering that the Code of Practice, reflecting EU Directives, expressly forbids any ad from inviting children to 'ask your parents' for a product).

---

[2] For example, J. Piaget, (trans. M. Gabain), *Language and Thought of the Child*, 3rd ed., Routledge & Kegan Paul, London, 1959.

The nutrition issue is more complex. The fact that the majority of food advertising is for packaged and processed foods is a more or less inevitable result of the workings of the market: the manufacturers who are most likely to advertise food products are in the business of adding value (in terms of convenience, packaging, recipe) to basic commodities. The problem raised by the nutritionally concerned is not really a problem with advertising: it is a problem of industrial structure and social behaviour (changes in meal patterns, etc.). This is a classic example of a situation where advertising happens to have its head over the parapet, and so gets the blame for a much more deeply rooted phenomenon.

Encouraging antisocial and dangerous products and behaviour

This is an area where the Code of Practice and the self-regulatory system, together with a growing body of law, has the effect of making it very difficult to use advertising to promote anything harmful. Except, of course, that smoking and alcohol are both addictive and at times antisocial; and driving fast cars, to take the other main area, is potentially antisocial and dangerous. (Illegal drugs, by contrast, are not advertised, but there is frequent—sometimes justified—criticism of individual ads for using the language of the drug culture. It is extremely difficult for those not in this culture to prevent this happening: most people over about 30, even in ad agencies, find themselves in much the same position as the much-criticized judges who have to be told who Robbie Williams is.)

So, of course, we shouldn't advertise alcohol and fast cars, let alone tobacco, should we? Well ... we allow people to sell these things, and governments earn massive revenues from taxing them. So what do people really want? Perhaps we should ban them—and recreate the beauties of Prohibition in the US in the 1920s, with criminal gangs bootlegging the banned commodities with the support of thugs with machine guns.

The EU is in the process of banning tobacco advertising, which has already been excluded from TV and cinemas. France has its *Loi Evin*, which severely restricts alcohol advertising (probably to protect local producers, as much as for public health reasons), and there are at least some restrictions on alcohol advertising in place all over the Continental Europe. In the UK, the Codes of Practice are extremely strict on ads that could be seen to encourage fast driving or even emphasize a car's speed.

Again, this is an area that is seen to affect children, as the quote in Box 17.1 shows. It is inevitable that children are exposed to at least some ads for cigarettes and alcohol, so long as these ads are permitted. It is quite difficult to attribute their use of these products to advertising, as such, especially for cigarettes, where the ads are not allowed to say anything meaningful about the products—except that they can kill you—or to build any meaningful brand imagery. There seems to me little doubt that smoking starts largely from either peer group example or adolescent defiance of parental bans, or both. It is not a sufficient argument by those who claim it is ad-induced to point out that the brands smoked are the most advertised (since the most-advertised brands are the most widely available, by and large, and are the brands the kids see their peers and parents smoking), or even that children recognize best the most advertised brand names. The recent case of the 'Reg' campaign for Royal cigarettes seems to show how a campaign can influence children, but it is by no means clear that their familiarity with it, or liking for the ads, led to smoking, let alone to smoking Royals.

More generally, the very extensive literature on the relationship between advertising and smoking is distinctly inconclusive as to whether ad bans lead to a reduction in smoking, or the presence of advertising creates extra volume demand. The manufacturers argue that the advertising is solely about brand competition; their critics vociferously disagree.

Alcohol is a more complex issue, because it is quite possible for children from quite a young age to see ads that sell the brands and the habit of drinking in a reasonably appealing way, even though the (UK) 'rules' aim to avoid any suggestion that young people should drink, or allow ads to demonstrate too much enjoyment. Again, however, it is by no means clear that it is advertising that *starts* people drinking: parental example—and, indeed, encouragement—seems the most potent factor, followed, again, by peer encouragement. Certainly, it is easy for a young person to use ads as a means of finding a repertoire of drinks to explore.

On the positive side, it should be pointed out that government-sponsored advertising to prevent many of the dangers and abuses discussed in this area has been quite successful in changing attitudes—to drink and driving, in certain areas of the drug culture (a highly successful and totally unadvertised vice, incidentally), and so on.

Dishonesty, misleading, cheating

'Legal, decent, honest and truthful' is the ASA's mantra (page 236). But doesn't most advertising set out to mislead people?

Ever since the first snake-oil salesman (or the snake in the Garden of Eden), selling has relied on persuasive argument, and on making the best of the product being sold. Buyers, from time immemorial, have learned to beware. It is even a principle of English common law (*Caveat emptor*). By now, very few ads in the UK, except from actual fraudsters, can get away with cheating and misleading—or even try to do so. What does, undoubtedly, happen is that ads put the best face of the product forward, and may well conveniently forget to point out the disadvantages. This is a recognized part of the way the game is played.

Interestingly, however, there is a growing trend towards greater frankness, which has arisen alongside the apparently growing interest among consumers in the companies they deal with. If there is pressure on companies to be, and to be seen to be, ethical, environmentally concerned, and so on, there is definite pressure on their brands and their advertising to conform to the same sorts of standards. There is probably a great future for campaigns that acknowledge (small) weaknesses, at the same time as boosting the brand's advantages. Shell, one of the largest companies in the world—and one of the most frequent targets for attack on ethical and environmental grounds—started such a campaign in early 1999.

In the long run, it is in no advertiser's interests to mislead the public. A dissatisfied customer is the worst sort of advertisement: people are up to ten times as likely to tell their friends about a bad experience with a purchase as about a good one.

Exploiting the arts, defacing the environment

The ad business has a quite incestuous relationship with the arts. Many people who work in the arts have worked—or even do work—in advertising, and advertising uses the arts all the time. Ads parody films, imitate paintings, borrow music (classical as well as pop), quote from literature (from *The Bible* down), and so on. Writers like Fay Weldon and Salman Rushdie have worked for ad agencies; cartoonists Gerald Scarfe and Ralph Steadman have produced distinguished series of advertisements; film directors like Adrian Lyne and Alan Parker cut their teeth on TV commercial production. The relationship is complex, and complicated by the fact that every now and then people in advertising act as if their latest ads actually are works of art. In fact, the only advertising form that seems to have got recognition as art is the poster, though there are those that claim some TV commercials to be works of art.

Of course, too, ads damage the environment. Think how much prettier our townscapes would be without all those posters, shop signs, street furniture. Think how much nicer it would be if we did not have to wade through pages of ads to get to the editorial material in *Vogue* or the *Daily Telegraph Magazine*. How tedious it is when our favourite TV programme is interrupted by those nasty, loud, pushy commercials. Think of all the paper wasted on printing all these ads that encourage us to consume, to deplete the earth's resources, to deposit rubbish (most of it packaging, which is also advertising) and further pollute the environment we live in.

Well, of course, if you feel like that, you probably should not be reading this book. On one point, the arguments seem to me to be plain daft: posters (and neon signs) are actually an integral part of a lively cityscape. Before the anti-communist revolution at the end of the 1980s, the drabness of most east European cities, where there were no posters, was infinitely depressing. Even where the whole process gets carried to excess, as in the neon-lit canyons of Hong Kong's central streets, the effect is exciting.

Much of the rest of this argument is built on a failure to recognize that without the ads, the media we live with would not exist—or not in the form that they do. You can argue that that might be a good thing, but then you might not have tried living with media where there is no advertising to help finance quality and variety. (Yes, the BBC used to set world-recognized standards, and still sometimes does, but be careful with the nostalgia: it was extraordinarily stuffy and slow to change). Advertising, in fact, pays for the whole of ITV, Channel 4 and Channel 5; for commercial radio; for rather over half the cost of your daily paper—and 68 per cent of it if you read a 'quality' title; and for nearly one-third of the cost of the average consumer magazine. If you read a local paper, over 80 per cent of its revenue will come from ads, many of them useful classifieds.

Sexism, racism . . .

Individual ads can be appallingly insensitive, in all sorts of ways. More than this, in the UK at least, a lot of advertising at present seems to be written by and for 20-something 'lads', who are sharp (yes), but also brash, rather vulgar (my age is showing, probably), and with a very limited cultural framework. This sort of advertising finds it easy to treat women as objects, not people, and ignores the growing black (in the broadest sense) proportion of the UK population. It is very rare to see a non-white face in a British ad, unless it is that of a celebrity (comedian Lenny Henry, say, or footballer Ian Wright, or supermodel Naomi Campbell). A notable recent exception to this is a poster campaign for Chanel's Allure, which included a black model; and other examples include the (imported) TV commercial for Maybelline and the stylish Gap TV campaign.

Part of the problem here is that advertising tends to talk in stereotypes, not with the aim of promoting the stereotype, but as an essential form of shorthand. In a 30-second commercial, you have to get to the point; and it is simpler to do this by using people who 'fit' into the majority of the audience's preconceptions. This works both with gender and race (and age, come to that). The result is that a lot of advertising starts from the premises that, for example: a woman is a housewife; a mother's sole interest is in feeding her family; all men are interested in football (and all women are not); black people are funny; old people have trouble coping with the pace of modern life; the disabled are invisible.

In so far as there is any evidence about this, it suggests that, contrary to common practice, ads that treat people as individuals, with their own character and quirkiness, work much better than the stereotypes. But you have to work much harder to create ads like this.

More importantly, too, there is at least the beginning of a recognition that the stereotypes are breaking down, or outdated, and that it is actually more interesting, and therefore appealing, to question the stereotypes. Mostly, this is done in pretty obvious ways, with fathers doing a very minimal parenting job, or being slightly inefficient at the housework (another stereotype, of course), while women are occasionally allowed to be seen to have jobs. By and large, the disadvantaged are still invisible.

Promoting 'consumerism'

Ads encourage wasteful and excessive consumption. They promote the idea that all that matters is to own things and consume things. They persuade people to buy things they cannot afford—or else rub the noses of the poor in the fact that these desirables are out of reach.

Well, yes, sort of. This is another of those areas where advertising is the tip of the iceberg, but gets the blame because it's visible. Unless you are a whole-hearted believer in the 'strong' theory of advertising (page 47), it is very hard to believe that advertising, on its own, can do much of this. Certainly, it is one part of a capitalist market system that is predicated, to a large extent, on consumption. But the willingness and ability to consume have little to do with advertising. And have you ever noticed how it is always other people who are 'compelled' by advertising to buy things they don't want? Advertising never *compelled* anyone to do anything. People are free agents.

The Marxist critics of advertising, who are strong exponents of this stream of thinking, have clearly identified advertising as a potent tool in the hands of the boss class. Capitalism is driven by its inner logic to produce ever more, and advertising is the tool that is used to ensure that the workers consume what is produced—thus ensuring the continued enslavement of the working class. The flaw in all this is the belief that people are somehow helpless in the face of advertisements, and that advertisements are the key factor in people's buying behaviour. It also ignores the evident resistance of consumers—in the mass—to buying things that they do not want. Modern thinking about marketing in general, and advertising within it, is that the only way to be successful is to provide consumers with what they want, and to talk *with* them, not *at* them, about satisfying their needs. This sits very uneasily with the Marxist analysis, to put it mildly.

Undermining standards and values

Advertising is, of course, all about cheap-jack commercialism. It panders to the lowest common denominator. It helps to drive out what is good, in favour of what is popular—and, of course, that's simply awful. If there was less advertising, or even if it was more responsible, standards and values would be higher. (I almost said 'like in the good old days', because I think this is a classic case of 'golden age' thinking: everyone believes in a mythical time, usually their grandparents' day, when nearly everything, from the weather to social mores, was better. The idea goes back at least as far as the Roman poet Horace, in the first century BC. It is not true, but gives a nice excuse for grousing about today.)

In practice, because advertising is trying to connect with people's feelings, ambitions, lifestyles, and so on, it is most unlikely that it *creates* any of these. It acts, in fact, as a mirror of society as it is, rather than acting to change society—simply because society is too strong for advertising to have a hope of changing it (but see Box 17.2). The problem is that the mirror is a distorting one. It's a mirror made by people who are atypical (advertising agencies, and their clients, are inhabited by ABs and C1s, mostly under 35). These atypical people then try to produce material that their target market, who are mostly fairly unlike themselves, will aspire to, or, at least relate to. This doubles the distortion.

Box 17.2   Changing the World

It is difficult, through advertising, to change people's behaviour. But this is what much government advertising seeks to do—and what Fascist and Communist governments used propaganda posters for, quite successfully, at least so long as they were supported by the boys with the armbands and large boots. The pages of *Advertising Works* include a number of examples of more or less successful government campaigns that are worth examining. Recent examples include the following:

From *Advertising Works 8*:

- □ HIV/AIDS prevention.
- □ Smoke alarms.
- □ Smoking—Scotland.

From *Advertising Works 9*:

- □ Promotion of adult education.

From *Advertising Works 10*:

- □ Promoting healthy exercise—Scotland.
- □ Drugs education.

Most of these and similar cases to be found in the IPA database or on WARC (see page 300) show clear changes in attitudes, and at least some changes in behaviour, though the latter mostly seem to affect the more marginal members of the target group: it is very difficult to shift deeply engrained habits and attitudes.

Nonetheless, the distorted picture usually has something in common with observable reality, even if the people in the ad are too good, or too nasty, to be true.

Understandably, though, critics react in a jaundiced way if they see a world in which women worry endlessly about whether they are using the right washing powder, or kids rush around saying 'Gimme this' or 'Gimme that', and asking if you've been Tango'd yet. This surely is what advertising has done to society—and the ads merely reflect what advertising has achieved?

It seems quite difficult for many people to accept that advertisements are, individually, merely attempts by individual companies to sell their goods; that they do this in ways that, they hope, will connect with their target audiences (not always the same as the critics); and that there is no ulterior motive in their minds beyond the bottom-line profit. If the only way they can get a response from their audience is by some gross form of crassness, this says a lot about society, and rather little about advertising. But it is probably fair to say that ads do not just reflect society, they exaggerate it, and they may well *contribute* to accelerating some of the developments within it. The Pontifical Council of the Catholic Church's *Handbook on the Ethics of Advertising* (1996) is a balanced discussion of some of these potential effects.

Servant or Seducer?

Advertisements are, of course, one way of separating people from their money. Judging from the relative cost per thousand of a 30-second national commercial and a good in-store demonstrator, I have to conclude that the public has gained from the substitution of Anthony Valentine's voice on the telly for the blandishments of the snake-oil salesman. The vast majority of ads are at a substantial distance from the point of sale, both physically and in time. What's more, they are clearly, recognizably, trying to sell something. And they have to obey the rules as discussed in Chapter 15.

Of course, what the ads display can be very enticing: that is what selling is, and always has been , about. There are, however, plenty of defences against enticement: there is always the word 'no'; and there is the simple expedient of running out of money, though the prevalence of plastic means that that can take longer these days.

And then you can postpone a purchase—in spite of Barclaycard's rather naff appeal 'Don't put it off—put it on'.

It is true, however, that people want to buy things. They have needs to be met—however far up Maslow's scale (see Box 17.3) they may be—and they may have to work quite hard to find ways to meet them (very hard, if they try on the Internet!). An important source of information in their search is advertising. As soon as you talk about ads as information, you hit the philosophical question of whether, and how far, it is an ad's job to persuade or to inform. The argument misses the point that one person's persuasion is another's information.

Box 17.3 Motivation

Understanding the way in which consumers behave requires an understanding of psychological motivation. There are a number of different theories of motivation, but the one that has become most widely known and referred to in marketing and advertising circles is Maslow's theory of the way in which human needs are structured.

Maslow proposed that there is a hierarchy of human needs, and that those at the base of the hierarchy need to be satisfied before the higher levels come into play. Until we have satisfied the basic requirements of food and shelter, other needs are essentially irrelevant. The implications of this for advertisers are that there is no need to persuade people of the value of—say—potatoes or rice or flour: people will buy those anyway. It is only once we have food and a roof over our heads that we start making choices, and it is here that advertising has a role to play. This becomes especially important once we reach the higher levels of Maslow's triangle (Figure 17.1), and we are able to pursue our more selfish interests. And, as Maslow points out, ' . . . the human being rarely reaches a state of complete satisfaction except for a short time. As one desire is satisfied, another pops up to take its place'.

And it is here that the critics of advertising can, in fact, have a field day. Much of what advertising turns out to be about is, at least arguably, so much candyfloss—the trivia that float to the surface of life once the realities have been sorted out. There is, certainly, a degree of truth in this. However, it is quite possible to look at things rather differently. If we believe that human beings have the capability of higher thoughts, and higher ideals, our aspirations are worth catering for and stimulating. The market economy offers a variety of possibilities that compete for our attention, many of them—theatres, concert programmes, exhibitions, as well as exotic holidays and (possibly) improving books—that are not simply consumer articles, but a source of potential spiritual good.

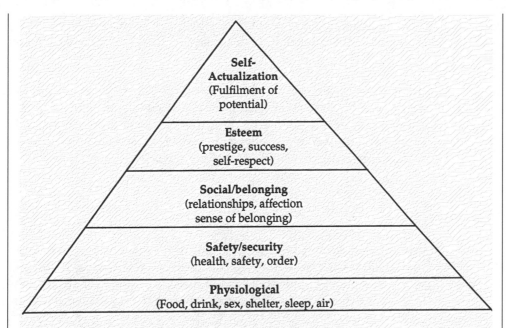

Figure 17.1.   Maslow's hierarchy of needs (Source: Adapted from A. Maslow, *Motivation and Personality*, Harper, New York, 1954)

Even at a lower level on Maslow's triangle, the opportunity to choose, while it may be anathema to rationalists who believe that either there is no need for choice or that choice is wasteful, is, in fact, one of the freedoms that has been earned by economic progress. And because it is almost impossible to make fully informed choices, advertising exists to make choice easier. You want a pink shell suit? Here's just what you need.

It is, in fact, quite difficult to assess the value of ads as information, not least because if you ask people how they heard about a product, almost the last thing they'll volunteer is 'advertising'. But if you ask people how they go about buying a washing machine or an insurance policy, a substantial proportion will mention ads as one source of information. And if you ask people more obliquely, about which media they use to get information about products, it is clear that they are in fact talking about ads, much of the time.

Conclusion

No one is perfect, and it would be mad to suggest that all ads are socially responsible and dedicated to the furtherance of humanity. It is considerably less easy to accept any of the blanket condemnations of advertising, at least without agreeing that the capitalist market economy in which we mostly live and work is fundamentally immoral and damaging. (Which may be true, but raises a different agenda.)

What is unhelpful and misleading is to blame advertising for all the faults both of the market and of society, without recognizing that it is merely an element in that system, and not necessarily the source of the problems under consideration. In particular, it is very easy to attribute to advertising powers that it does not possess. If it did, everyone in the business would be mightily richer!

Summary

- It is very easy to criticize 'advertising' as an abstract symbol of capitalist society, but considerably less easy to do this when individual ads or campaigns are at issue. It is difficult to believe that the 6000-odd advertisers in the UK are held together by a conspiracy to subvert society and mould it to some over-arching end.
- Where advertising is most vulnerable is in its relationship with children. Here, we need to recognize just what children do and do not understand about advertising, at what ages, and recognize that they are in fact remarkably perceptive critics of ads from quite an early age.
- Advertising campaigns, on the whole, reflect society, rather than changing it— and this is primarily because it is remarkably difficult to change society by active intervention: societies evolve, in response to a very complex range of stimuli, of which advertising is a small part.
- Advertising is, however, a very visible part of capitalist marketing—and can easily be used by critics as a proxy for the system as a whole.

Points to consider

- You have been asked to give a talk to your old school about advertising and its effects on society. What specific topics would you want to bring up with a teenage audience? What would your key arguments be?
- You work for a snack food manufacturer. A food lobby has accused your company of promoting bad diet by advertising, intensively, products that are full of empty calories and excessive fat. Draft a reply.
- A Sunday paper has published a 'heavy' article analysing advertising's deleterious effects on the visual arts. Write a letter to the editor defending the role of advertising.

18 Global, glocal, local? How international should advertising be?

Thus may we see, quoth he, how the world wags

Shakespeare, *As You Like It*

Globalization

The formalized concept of globalization of markets and commerce has been around for over 25 years, and the idea of global advertising is nearly as old. If firms can produce products to a uniform specification for the world's markets, why should they not have global brands under which to sell them, and back these with global advertising? Production facilities have begun to migrate around the world, seeking suitable low-cost locations, and companies have grown ever larger, through internal expansion and through mergers and acquisitions. At the same time, as we have seen, media companies have begun to develop worldwide coverage, and even to sell space and time on an international basis.

In response, ad agencies have become more multinational in character, continuing a process which started in the 1920s, when, for example, J. Walter Thompson had an agreement to open an office wherever their then largest client, General Motors, asked them to. Agencies, again, are the subject of frequent mergers and acquisitions, as well as the forming and reforming of international alliances. There is an interesting contrast between the acquisitiveness of major US agency groups such as Omnicom and Interpublic, and the alliance-based strategy of the Japanese giant Dentsu.

The WPP Group's 1997 Annual Report carries an interesting brief analysis of the parallel processes of agency mergers and the consolidation of very large multi-national advertising accounts into a small number of agencies on a worldwide basis. While 23 of the top 30 US agencies are now owned by just nine multinational groups, major multinational client companies such as Colgate, IBM, S. C. Johnson, Reckitt & Colman and Citibank have reduced their roster of agencies from as many as 40 or more to just one or two. This means that the big global networks have an overwhelming advantage—for now—over even the best local agencies in trying to win business from most major multinational clients. I say 'for now' because there seems to me to be an element of fashion in all of this; and, as we shall see in the final chapter, there seems to be absolutely nothing sacred about agency arrangements or

265

structures. The fact that a major world brand such as Coca-Cola could suddenly start to buy advertisement ideas from a creative 'boutique' organization that was not even really in the business of producing advertising shows how potentially fluid the situation is.

The rationale for consolidating international business into just one or two agencies is largely one of management efficiencies: shorter chains of command and simpler co-ordination of activities, leading—hopefully—to reduced costs. These latter can certainly accrue from a reduction in the amount of management time that needs to be devoted to dealing with the agency, and may include a reduction in the amount that the agency or agencies is or are paid. At the same time, too, centralized negotiation, whether through the creative agency operating as a full-service agency, or through a multinational media specialist agency, could lead to reduced total media costs. In practice, it is worth noting that at least some financial arrangements reported (by agencies) appear to give the agency *more* than the traditional 15 per cent commission (or its equivalent in fees), rather than any reduction.

What about the ads?

Part of the economy of effort to be looked for from international agency consolidation lies in the cost of creating and producing the ads. If you can produce one campaign, centrally, and use this all over the world, there should be savings to be gained: with a good major TV commercial costing perhaps £300 000 or more to produce, a 30-country campaign could spend nearly £10 million before ever putting an ad on air. In theory, you can instantly save about 90 per cent of that total, by developing and producing just one commercial.

Of course, this is naïve. The ad will have to be translated and the verbal part of the soundtrack rerecorded, at the very least—but this need not be very costly, except where the commercial's dialogue has been produced in lip-sync, where dubbing may be unacceptable in some key markets, such as the UK. We are still going to be well ahead—just so long as the ad works as well in every other country as in the one for which it was originally produced.

What's more, the process will be making the maximum use of the most difficult bit of advertising development: having a great creative idea—always assuming that we have one. Great ideas, the argument goes, are too valuable to be wasted on a single market or group of markets: it would be sheer dereliction of duty on the part of the advertiser's management if they failed to use the idea in as many markets as possible. At least one major global marketer, Unilever, has a policy of taking excellent, successful advertising concepts, wherever they have been developed, and applying them elsewhere to *whichever* of their many brands seems appropriate. Because of the company's history, its brands tend not to be global, but their ad concepts sometimes are. By contrast, another multinational, Mars, has spent the last few years globalizing long-established brands, so that the UK has seen Marathon become Snickers, and Treets become M&Ms, for example, as part of this harmonization.

The big question, assuming we have a great idea—and the ability to recognize it as such—is whether it is realistic to expect it to work equally well all over the world; or, failing that, what we will have to do to adapt the idea to enable it to do so.

Again, there is a naïve assumption, most frequently, but by no means exclusively, found among senior managers of US multinationals, that what works there will work anywhere else. After all, the US is a very large and quite diverse set of markets, so a successful ad there has to have a degree of acceptability among people of widely differing backgrounds and, even, languages. And, as is well known, if it works in Peoria, it will work in the US as a whole.

There are a number of reasons why this assumption is naïve—even though it is not necessarily wrong. These can be divided into two broad categories: country-specific and market-specific.

Market-specific reasons for questioning the assumption derive primarily from the standing of the brand in different countries. Very few brands are equally strong, or equally well developed in terms of their product life cycles, in more than a few of the countries in which they are sold. A brand may be a long-established market leader in the US; a well-known second or third brand in some other English-speaking countries such as the UK and Australia; a struggling newcomer in (say) France and Germany; and a luxury brand for the very rich in most of the South. In each of these markets or groups of markets, it may be faced by a different group of competitors (which will, to be sure, consistently include some well-known multinationals), and these, again, will occupy different positions within the market. A well-known example of the sort of differences that arise in this way is Levi's: in the US, Levi's jeans are mass-market and price-competitive; but in much of Europe, Levi's is a premium-priced, high-quality brand.

A further complication may be the way in which the product or product category is used or consumed in the various countries: Kelloggs have had a long uphill struggle to develop a market for breakfast cereals in Continental Europe, where some of their products have found a completely unexpected (to an American or Briton) niche in the snack market. As we have seen in Chapter 16, De Beers have had to create a diamond engagement ring market in some countries where the practice simply did not exist. The long-established British fragrance, Yardley's Lavender, is in Britain something you give your grandmother for Christmas; in France it is a fairly upmarket unisex brand; and in parts of Latin America it is an extremely macho male fragrance.

Clearly, where a brand's position can be so radically different from country to country, and if the optimum advertising strategy should be derived from a detailed analysis of the brand's specific position in its market, it is logically improbable that the same advertising could fit every country equally well, simply on the grounds of the brand's competitive situation.

Then there are *country-specific* factors. These interact with the market factors, but are primarily concerned with the nature of the society in the individual country, the values of that society, and characteristics of the culture that may involve body language, frames of reference, sense of humour, taboos, religion, and so on. It is quite easy to construct a case that makes it very difficult to believe that an ad that works excellently in one country could ever work as well in another. A most convincingly argued example of this is a recent book by the Dutch writer Marieke de Mooij,[1] who starts from academic analyses of the differences between cultures and uses these to argue that any 'global' advertising campaign must be quite radically adapted to local needs if it is to stand a chance of success.

A particular aspect of de Mooij's argument depends on understanding the different ways in which different cultures carry on the business of argument and persuasion: at the one extreme (e.g. the US or Germany), these can be highly rational; at the other (Spain, the Middle East), they may be extremely emotional and metaphorical in character. It is unlikely that successful advertising from one type of country would work very well in the other. The emphasis of US copy-testing methods on 'persuasion' and a suggestion by a German agency account man that the rest of Europe should adopt the highly rational style of advertising common in Germany are examples of the way in which culture can influence our overall approach to advertising.

That there *are* national styles of advertising is undoubtedly true, as anyone who goes to any of the growing number of international advertising awards festivals would readily acknowledge. What is more, these styles seem to emerge most strongly in the best work from each country, which suggests that they are reflecting the reality of the national cultural character.

Tribes and tribulations

It is often suggested that particular groups of consumers have common characteristics and interests that transcend national boundaries and that, therefore, it is right to target them with international advertising campaigns. The two groups that have traditionally been cited in this way are businesspeople and

[1] Marieke de Mooij, *Global Marketing & Advertising: Understanding Cultural Paradoxes*, Sage, London, 1998.

teenagers. Businesspeople, it is claimed, are now so used to travelling across national boundaries and interacting with other nationalities that they may be regarded in a way as international hybrids; while teenagers, as is well known, listen to the same music, wear the same (grungy) uniform, eat the same fast food and are, therefore, simply a global tribe. To these two groups can be added the growing 'Internet Community', which is assumed to have completely globalized instincts and interests—in the apparently total absence of any evidence.

As far as I know, all three 'tribes' are linked merely by a few superficialities, while remaining pretty consistently American, German, Japanese, Thai or whatever their country of origin may be. There are very few people, even in the boardrooms of multinational companies, who are genuinely at home in an alien culture, unless they have lived there for many years. And these homogeneous dark-suited business folk have a habit of acting out national stereotypes with startling faithfulness in the heat of a long international meeting.

One final argument that is sometimes used to support the concept of the global campaign is that with tourism rapidly becoming the world's number one industry, it would be immensely confusing to people if they travelled to another country and saw their familiar brands advertised in a totally different way. Quite apart from the fact that the numbers of people involved are still small when viewed against the total populations of either the hosts' or visitors' countries, there are two highly questionable assumptions built into this argument. First, that the tourist will be remotely in a frame of mind in which ads are relevant; and, second, that he or she can understand an ad in a foreign language.

So, we should forget about global advertising, then, should we?

Actually, no.

Glocal advertising

De Mooij's argument about the cultural differences between countries looks extremely powerful. Indeed, it is, as it applies to the ends of the various scales of culture, attitudes and beliefs that she quotes. The only problem is that most countries are not at the extremes: they tend to cluster towards the middle, where the differences are far from clear-cut. The result of this is that it is frequently feasible to group broadly similar countries together, and to run the same—or virtually the same—advertising within the group. For example, you might treat northern and southern Europe as two rather different areas, or run a common campaign in most of the Middle East, or Latin America, without striking major problems.

What you do have to take account of, however, is a phenomenon identified by Mary Goodyear, an extremely widely travelled qualitative researcher. She argues that there is a sort of scale of advertising literacy, linked primarily to the experience of a country's consumers of sophisticated advertising (see Figure 4.4, page 49). You have to be prepared to tailor the way in which your ads work to take account of the sort of ads that people in the target country are used to. When the countries of eastern Europe and the former Soviet Union dropped communism and became—in various degrees—free market economies, it rapidly became clear that it was not possible to run ad campaigns lifted directly from western Europe or the USA. However, consumers in these countries, who had been watching western TV surreptitiously for some time, expected the production values of the commercials run by western advertisers to be as high as in western Europe, even if they treated the messages contained in them in a different way.

Overall, then, the message from research seems to be that it is difficult, if not impossible, to run an absolutely homogeneous campaign across national borders, unless the countries concerned have a lot in common. You have to adapt: you have to take account of local idioms, metaphors, body language, sense of humour. You have to recognize national styles. In a word, the ideal multinational campaign is not 'global', but 'glocal': it embodies the widely quoted view that you should think global, but act local—or even, as De Mooij puts it, market global, but advertise local.

The fact remains that there are successful multinational—or even global—campaigns. Marlboro and Coca-Cola, to take two prime examples, have successfully sold what is, in effect, an American dream to the world for years. Esso's (Exxon's) tiger is pretty much global. Even, slightly surprisingly, British Airways' arrogant and improbable repositioning of itself as the World's Favourite Airline worked, with remarkably little variation, more or less all over the world: the one country where the campaign simply failed to communicate was Japan (see Box 18.1).

Box 18.1 *The World's Favourite Advertising?*

It was in 1982 that BA started to turn itself from a rather ordinary airline into something special. The advertising campaign that started with the 'Manhattan' commercial represented a complete sea-change in the airline's view of itself and its ambitions, and a management attitude that aimed to make BA the leader in its market. Originally greeted with incredulity by outsiders, the campaign reflected a marketing policy that permeated the whole company, and led to the realization of the objective: it gradually both converted customers and enthused and motivated personnel. What is more, not only did the campaign—and the enhanced experience of travelling with BA—raise the airline's prestige and reputation, but it enabled BA to sell seats at a higher average price than its competitors. They did more business and they earned more per passenger. Research from all over the world showed clear improvements in BA's reputation and imagery over time, even though there remained substantial differences between countries.

Source: *Advertising Works 8*, Chapter 2.[2]

'They're all out of step but our Tom'

What happens in practice, in the real world, illustrates the difficulty of pontificating and generalizing about the global transfer of campaigns. Take one of the largest advertising markets—cars—with a quite small number of brands (40-odd) on any international scale. Car manufacturers have been more or less global for years, though national 'champions' remain in most major producing countries. If you look at car advertising around Europe, you will find that in this tightly competitive and pretty homogeneous marketplace, car companies' advertising ranges from the completely local and unco-ordinated to the almost completely uniform: the whole length of the spectrum. On the whole, Japanese manufacturers are the least likely to have co-ordinated international campaigns, while the most tightly co-ordinated are those of the Italian Fiat group—Fiat, Alfa Romeo and Lancia. Most other manufacturers use at least some campaigns across national boundaries, but very rarely for every European market. Even the manufacturers who might be expected to regard their marques and models as pan-European in character—Volkswagen, Ford, General Motors (Opel/Vauxhall)—seem quite chary of using pan-European campaigns. In most cases, even where an idea is used across national boundaries, it tends to be quite heavily 'tweaked' to take account of the local situation.

To take a more up-to-date example, in the mobile telephone market all the big manufacturers—Ericsson, Nokia, Motorola, Alcatel, Philips—are running substantial multinational campaigns; but the different circumstances of the individual markets mean that targeting and model choice vary quite significantly within each brand. The campaign concepts remain broadly constant, but the executions are tailormade to the country concerned.

Conclusion

This careful tailoring and adaptation of core campaign concepts seems to me to be the inevitable way forward for most global brands' advertising, if they are to reap the full benefits of their creative ideas. In some cases, it may be impossible even to do this type of adaptation in an individual market, and a specific campaign will be

---

[2] Chris Baker (ed.), *Advertising Works 8*, NTC Publications, Henley-on-Thames, 1995.

required. The sort of example I have in mind is one reported by researchers Millward Brown, where a claim made in a multinational campaign they were pre-testing was new and attractive in several countries, but had already been used in another country, where it was, therefore, of limited value.

The ideal remains, I believe, the purely local campaign, because this will be created and fine-tuned to its direct market, with all the style, humour, panache or whatever that is relevant to the local market situation. The one problem this inevitably raises is that it is unlikely that an advertiser can call on comparable levels of creativity and production excellence in all markets, and that the costs of production will be disproportionately high. If the results can be good enough, this would not be a problem: the best ads can be shown to outsell even average ads by so wide a margin that they can justify the expense.

So, the final message has to be one of compromise. Get a really good campaign—from somewhere—and adapt it as carefully and imaginatively as possible to local market conditions. And be prepared to reject it in one or two markets if all the evidence is that it really will not do the business.

Summary

□ A number of factors encourage the concept of global advertising campaigns: the spread of global brands: the increased reach and centralization of TNCs; the apparent economies of scale of creation, production and management of advertising; the increased convergence of lifestyles and attitudes around the globe; the specific development of identifiable international 'tribes' (teenagers, the jet set).

□ Experience shows, however, that these factors can be illusory. In particular, there are substantial and fundamental cultural differences between countries (or even between regions within countries) that demand consideration, and suggest caution.

□ Increasingly, sophisticated managements are treating their advertising on a 'glocal' basis: using, as far as possible, global or regional strategies, but executing the ads locally, or adapting them heavily. There *are* genuinely global campaigns, but they are likely to remain few in number.

Points to consider

□ Think of commercials you see on your national TV stations that are recognizably produced in some other country. How do you know? What is wrong with them?

□   What distinguishes them from commercials for multinational brands that do *not* appear to be recognizably 'imported'? (Of course, these may be locally produced, but a lot of them will not be: examples are most Coca-Cola ads, P&G's Pantene, many fragrance ads.)

□   What categories of product would you most expect to be able to advertise with multinational ads? Why?

□   And which would be most difficult? Why?

19   The future

Prophecy is the most gratuitous form of error

George Eliot, *Middlemarch*

It is a resounding cliché that we live in a time of rapid and omni-present change, and that this is not merely a source of stress for anyone in business but an opportunity for management. As I pointed out in the first chapter the advertising agency business has been remarkably slow to change in recent years, and there are by now plenty of doom-sayers to suggest that this has sown the seeds of its downfall. This chapter looks at some of the key themes for the future that will affect advertising and the context in which it is created and managed.

There are six of these:

- Globalization—of clients, agencies and media.
- The 'unbundling' of the traditional functions of the full-service agency, and their erosion by specialist and non-specialist consultancies.
- The increased focus on integrated communications or 'total communications'.
- The development of consumer-centred marketing, based on interactive and one-to-one responsive communication, sales and delivery systems.
- The growing importance to management of (rapid) evaluation of all of a firm's commercial activities.
- The continuing development of technologies that affect the creation, production and distribution of advertising messages.

I should probably add a seventh: the growing resistance of consumers to consumerism, their growing sophistication at decoding the messages advertisers put before them, and the developing complexity of their responses to the commercial world about them.

Globalization

The last chapter took a hard look at the way in which advertising can be effectively global, and outlined the pressures behind globalization. It has been estimated that the top 1000 advertisers account for 90 per cent of the world's ad expenditures. Assuming that this is remotely true, one possible implication is that there is room for no more than 40-odd global agencies, each handling, on average, 25 of these advertising giants. The vision in Pohl and Kornbluth's sci-fi classic *The Space Merchants*, of just two vast advertising mega-agencies effectively controlling the world, appears to be almost conceivable—especially since it seems reasonably certain that at least 10 per cent of the top 1000 advertisers will merge with, or acquire, one of the others in the next couple of years.

The question is then what good does this sort of giantism do? For whom? And, for an advertising text, does it help produce good, or excellent, advertising? It seems to me that this process of corporate aggrandisement runs counter to most other trends within the advertising business and—more significantly—within society as a whole. Huge organizations progressively lose contact with their customers, and become entirely reliant on bureaucratic system-building and system maintenance. This removes the possibility of any creative response to changing circumstances, and encourages a paralysis of the *status quo*.

In other words, the corporate behemoths, and the vast agency networks that are coming into being to serve them, carry the in-built seeds of their own destruction. Nonetheless, it seems to me inevitable that the processes of globalization will continue, at least for the foreseeable future, to affect both advertisers and their agencies. The pace of agency mergers on a grand scale showed no sign of slowing as the millennium neared its end, with the last two months of 1998 seeing Japanese giant Dentsu taking a major stake in Leo Burnett, and Omnicom consolidating its UK market position by acquiring the rest of AMV-BBDO to add to their earlier purchase of GGT-BDDP.

This progressive giantism offers numerous opportunities for the smaller, swifter, more agile operator to start to pick off the juicy bits around the edges. Large businesses neglect their smaller, outlying operations, and this applies both to advertisers and their agencies. For many years now, the leading Italian ad agency has been the local Armando Testa—the only non-multinational in the top 20 agencies in Italy. They have attained and held this position by being good at being Italian : something that none of their competitors is any longer able to do so well. As their founder says, this process has been helped by the agency's refusal to go public, which has relieved it of the need to damage the structure of the business in the search for ways to boost profits for the shareholders.

The problem for the smaller operator remains that it is difficult to penetrate the businesses of the large multinationals. Multinational executives find it a source of comfort that their agency has offices in outlying parts of the world—there is almost a process of ticking off the flags on the map, and no one got fired for buying IBM (or McCann or Ogilvy). The fact remains that it is perfectly possible for any agency to place advertising in a country where it has no office of its own, and perfectly possible for an advertiser to buy advertising from a creative source that has no agency network and to use this all over the world.

Agency commentators—mostly from the large groups—have for long observed that it is very difficult to be a medium-sized agency in most developed markets. In practice, most such agencies get taken over by larger groups, and this leaves a fertile source of material for smaller agencies to feed on. Meanwhile, there is an observable ebb and flow in large corporations' relationships with agencies: consolidation and concentration tend to be followed by a period in which local (especially) reins are loosened, and smaller firms are allowed to get a bite at the peripheral and minor brands where the pressures for conformity and the safe solution are fewer, and the opportunity to do something spectacular greatly enhanced.

If to this is added the current fashion in corporate management for 'focus', which means, in effect discarding brands, divisions and whole markets that no longer fit the vision of the company's expertise and future, and there are lots of quite rich pickings for the less gigantic agency to feed off. This will continue, in one form or another.

Unbundling

Creative and media started to separate as long ago as the end of the 1960s in the UK, and the process is far advanced in most major advertising markets. It has proved less easy to hive off the creative function from the main agency that remained, and most of the creative boutiques seem to have transformed themselves into something else, while it is now more common to find freelance creative teams operating on a small scale. Yet Coca-Cola was able to reinvent the concept by going to CAA, which was, in effect, a talent agency. Ogilvy and Mather in the US has recently announced an arrangement whereby its clients may, if they wish, use the resources of any of seven small regional 'hot shop' creative agencies: if you can't beat them, join them!

More recently, the UK's planning initiative has begun to develop 'splittist' tendencies, with a variety of planning consultancies and individual consultants providing services that compete with, or complement, those of the agencies. These strategists do not have the monopoly of thinking about brand strategy, however: there is a new breed of brand strategy consultants, and the marketing divisions of the big management consultancy companies are also starting to intrude in this area—to the disquiet of some agency managements, who recognize that the consultants have access to higher levels of clients' management, and therefore pose a threat to the agency's assumed leadership in brand thinking.

By now, in fact, you can buy almost any advertising agency function from a specialist organization or consultant—there are even account managers who will run an account for a period if an agency is for some reason short of people to handle it.

However, the fact that it is possible to do this does not necessarily make it the right thing to do. While it is tempting to think that, as an advertiser, you should buy the best expertise available to perform every process involved, there is no guarantee that the experts you assemble will be able to work together as a team, especially as a creative team and creativity is, above all, what advertisers seek from their agencies, and the point where the agencies' advantage over management consultants identifiably lies. Certainly, what this 'cherry-picking' will achieve—unless you buy the services of an account manager to organize the whole process—is an enormous increase in the detailed workload that you have to undertake.

There is, however, a more fundamental problem with unbundling, and this lies in the way in which advertisers are, increasingly, looking at their communications.

Total communications

If a brand is the sum of its physical characteristics, plus whatever intangible values may be derived from the various brand communications, and if it is becoming more difficult to differentiate brands physically so that their emotional values become more important, then it becomes vital that every message the customer or consumer receives about the brand works to build a coherent story. This means that the brand's communications have to be, in the jargon, integrated.

Further, as the media available become more fragmented and complex, and the possible ways of using them move from straightforward ads to a variety of forms of sponsorship, product placement, editorial and advertorial messages, and so on, the need to approach all of these options with both understanding and imagination begins to demand new ways of thinking about both the media and the creative material that should go into them.

If all these elements are being assembled from a range of different and specialist agencies and organizations, the task of co-ordinating and orchestrating the diverse contributions rapidly becomes awesomely complicated, and extremely difficult—both because of the technical requirements of the different activities and because of the politics of the various parties involved.

It can be argued, too, that because the ways in which media can be used are proliferating, the primary communications planning decisions should now be about the media, and that media thinking should *precede* any creative planning: this would turn traditional practice on its head, though the more enlightened agencies have long tried to keep media thinking at least in parallel with creative.

The logic of this, of course, is that unbundling media from the creative agency is a strategic mistake, however enticing it may be in terms of apparent economics. Either you have to create a new breed of media planner, separate from the media buying agency, and closely linked to the creative agency; or you have to reintegrate media with creative into a new type of full-service agency. Media agencies have already recognized part of this, by force of financial pressures: by the time they had turned buying successfully into a commodity business, they desperately needed to find ways of adding value to their operations, by developing more sophisticated planning systems and approaches. Indeed, the specialist media magazines in the UK are already suggesting that the next move by media shops will be the acquisition or establishment of creative subsidiaries or units.

What is very clear is that any large and forward-thinking advertiser will be looking to manage its use of media (of all kinds) and of the types of communication it puts through each medium in a much more sophisticated, coherent and synergistic way than in the past. For large users of media advertising, in particular, this requires something of a sea-change in thinking, and a reappraisal of their whole marketing communications function. Past surveys in the UK have shown little enthusiasm among either consumer advertising agencies or consumer advertisers for the whole concept of integrated communications, together with very equivocal views about who should manage the integration. Advertisers have tended to claim that it is their responsibility, and agencies have been fairly happy to leave it to them.

A key problem is that there are very few people available who have the expertise to conceive and control large-scale communications programmes that genuinely make the best possible use of a combination of media advertising in a variety of media (which may all have rather different jobs to do), PR, sales promotion, sponsorship, direct marketing and the deployment of new forms of interactive media. A few very large clients have people like this, and very few large agencies have them though there is probably a wider range of potential candidates for this sort of task in the agencies: the fact remains that large agencies have grown fat on a diet of TV commercials for too long, and done too little to develop the integrating skills that could be extremely marketable. Indeed, in the UK, Dominic Owens, a former agency man who has marketing management experience with BT and other large advertisers, recently set up a new type of media consultancy, BridgeWorks, to act as consultants in 'communications architecture', to fill the co-ordinating role that seems to be missing.

The One-to-One Revolution

'Post-modern' marketing (see Box 19.1) sees a situation where marketing no longer seeks to sell to the mass audiences that characterized the heyday of consumer branding in the 1950s and 1960s. Refinements in market research and analysis, and fragmentation of markets and consumer desires, combine to make it both necessary and possible for the company to target, quite precisely, those customers that are currently or potentially most valuable to it, and to engage them in an interactive, one-to-one communication process. This is at the heart of the dynamic growth of direct marketing in the past decade, and will be massively aided by the development of interactive digital TV and the spread of access to the Internet. We are all direct marketers now—or we should be.

Box 19.1 *Post-modern Marketing*

Marketing in the past 100 years or so has progressed through a number of stages. The heyday of the advertising business, which started in the 1920s, and has continued through to the 1980s, saw first the development of brands as a means of identifying a maker's products and offering a guarantee of consistency; then, with increasing competition, the development—aided by advertising—of brand image and personality; with market saturation, marketing had—at last—to become more genuinely customer-focused. By this stage, advertising was beginning to be questioned and direct marketing was gaining ground; and this process is continuing as the post-modern period takes over, with segmented and fragmented consumers increasingly sceptical and advertising-literate (see Figure 19.1). The figure, taken from an excellent account of qualitative market research and its role in marketing, shows from a researcher's point of view how this process has developed. Not all markets, nor all consumers, have reached the 'super consumer' level suggested by the chart. But that's the way things are going.

Well, perhaps.

The underlying dynamics of the technology and the marketplace certainly point this way. There is (limited) evidence that consumers actually *want* to engage in dialogue with at least some of the suppliers of goods and services with whom they deal. There are plenty of data to enable firms to identify their best customers, and to target reasonably accurately their most desirable prospects. Whether the economics of direct marketing are sufficiently enticing to offer a viable alternative to more broadscale advertising for every advertiser is a good deal more questionable: media advertising is a highly cost-efficient way of contacting numbers of people, even if there is substantial wastage involved—because there is substantial wastage involved in direct marketing, too, though you rarely hear a spokesperson for the industry acknowledge this.

There is, however, a much broader problem with the 'universal one-to-one' agenda. One of the basic premises is that—over time—the marketer comes to know a great deal about each individual customer, and then is able to make specific, tailored offers or propositions to them. This will usually reveal to the customer that this knowledge exists: and some—perhaps many—will resent it and react badly. It is certainly true that people tell researchers that they prefer to be contacted by mail by

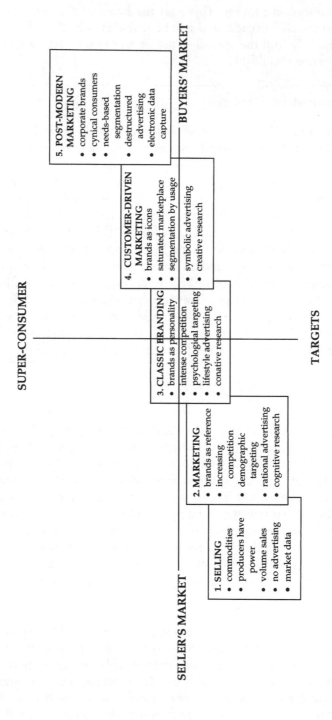

Figure 19.1. Steps to post-modern marketing (Source: Goodyear M. in *ESOMAR Handbook*, 1998. Copyright © ESOMAR® 1999)

firms they already know and do business with. I have not seen the research that says that they welcome with open arms a mailing that shows the firm knows their most intimate secrets. I believe, too, that people will become even more suspicious about digital interactive media, where the implication of much of the technology is already that Big Brother is watching. It may merely be the 'elite' innovator/early adopter group who resist 'spamming' (the sending of unsolicited e-mails), but I rather doubt it.

In a world where the post-modern consumer is defined as being cynical and suspicious about corporations and about marketing activity generally, the possibilities for screwing up customer relationships through insensitive use of interactive, one-to-one communications will grow exponentially with the accumulation of customer information by large corporations.

What is certain, however, is that the next 5–10 years will see an enormous growth in this kind of communication, and in the development of the technological and analytical infrastructures to support it. This means, inevitably, that moneys will migrate out of traditional media advertising into these 'new' areas; and this, in turn, will lead to changes in the ways in which communications agencies operate and combine. Traditional ad agencies will have to become more involved with direct marketing—and integrate it with their other operations, if it is to be effective. While the big advertising agency groups all have substantial direct marketing subsidiaries, there are only limited signs of this integration being fully implemented: mostly the direct operations are separate, specialist companies, even if links with the conventional agencies are encouraged, and this seems to me to be a fundamental obstacle to true integration.

One final point about the rush towards direct, one-to-one communications. While these are fine for maintaining the business of well-established brands, they do little or nothing to build the brand's future: without publicity, a brand is confined within the circle of the people who know about it. Yet, people like to buy brands that are well-known—famous, even. Something—it may be brand advertising, or PR, or sponsorship—has to be available to keep the brand famous for the long term, because in the long run, as Keynes said, we are all dead, and this applies to the leaky bucket of a brand's consumer franchise, just as much as to people.

Evaluation and assessment

One of the forces that favours the developing acceptance and use of direct marketing techniques is the perception that they are readily measurable, in a way that media advertising is not: not only are results apparently directly attributable to specific actions, but the results are available comparatively quickly—thus fitting with the corporate desire to measure marketing effects within financial reporting periods, which means quarterly for US corporations.

Certainly, there is no possibility that marketing as a discipline can escape corporate management's demands for more precise accountability; and since most of marketing's spending is on communications, this means measuring the effects of advertising, PR, promotions, direct marketing, and so on.

There are two ways in which this can be done: either by treating each element individually, and trying to isolate its effects; or by recognizing that a brand's communications must be an integrated total, and measuring the combined effect. The former is what has been done in the past in the IPA Advertising Effectiveness Awards and their imitators: great effort has been made to demonstrate the effect of *advertising*, and to eliminate other elements from the calculation of these effects. The latter is the concept that underlies the measurement of brand equity, though relatively few commentators have yet identified exactly what this implies.

It seems to me that senior management should be primarily interested in the progress of the *brand*, and hence in the effects of the total of the communications investment behind them. It is therefore a valid objective to demonstrate to management that the brand has profited from the investment, *in the ways planned*. However, this should not be enough for *marketing* management: they should be concerned to identify which elements within the overall communications mix are contributing how much to the achievement of the brand objectives. What is needed, therefore, is not simply *advertising* effectiveness measures, but, ideally, measurement of the effectiveness of each element in the mix: the concentration on advertising merely reflects the historical fact that advertising has usually been the most significant single part of the communications budget.

This, too, however, risks over-simplification. If the communications mix depends for its success on synergies between the various elements, it is likely that—even if we can precisely isolate the contribution of each and achieve some kind of cost-effectiveness ranking—any change in the balance of the elements could lead to a different result. The implication is that we are still a long way from the Holy Grail of assessing communications effectiveness. But the pressures from top management dictate that the attempt will have to go on.

Technology

Technology has permeated the advertising world since the invention of the printing press. It affects the availability and nature of media; the ways in which we can create and produce ads; the ways in which we communicate our plans and strategies to colleagues and clients or agencies; the ways in which we conduct research into the media, into our ads, into our customers. Most recently, it has created a whole new range of media opportunities, through the Internet, digital TV, interactive point-of-sale material of all kinds, the new plasma video screens appearing in shopping centres, and so on. Even printing is going digital, so that in theory one could, for example, tailor a customer magazine to a single customer.

The technological revolution has had its most obvious impact on advertising in three areas: in media research, where modern computers make it possible to analyse vast tracts of data almost in real time; in production, especially for TV, where post-production wizardry has almost no bounds; and in the understanding of consumer information that underpins modern direct marketing. Next year, it will be safe to add the development of interactive digital media—the Internet and digital TV—to this list, because both will have attained, or be on the verge of attaining, critical mass.

Agencies have so far tended to be erratic and cautious in their acceptance of most forms of new technology. Few have gone far in investing on their own behalf, and they have preferred to use specialized suppliers to provide the specific services that they have wished to adopt. There are exceptions to this, and I think that the next few years will see the larger agencies embarking on a quite massive move into owning, as opposed to merely renting, a variety of technologies. In particular, it seems very clear that the life of so-called 'new media' agencies as a specialist group is going to be relatively short-lived: the good ones will be bought by established ad agencies, and the poor ones will die. Similarly, as production facilities become more computerized, the existing tendency for large agencies to acquire their own will gather momentum.

Quite simply, if the agencies do not become wired, to a high degree of sophistication, they will find themselves losing business. This will come to apply, too, to more mundane facilities such as video-conferencing: for international business, this is becoming an essential tool in most large client organizations and, although agencies tend to hate it, they will have to learn to live with it.

What this means is that agencies are going to have to invest, and continue to invest, in machines as well as people. Recently, they have not been as good as they should have been at investing even in people, and adding technology is going to put pressure on costs and profitability. A recent review of the agency business in *M&M International* (January 1999) several times refers to the embarrassing statistic that margins on sales for ad agencies average only 12–14 per cent, while those for consultancies and other forms of specialist communications are in the range 20–30%. Agencies will have to find new and better ways of charging their clients if they are to fund their necessary investment.

Consumer attitudes

Advertising depends on understanding the target customer. I have already referred above to post-modern marketing and the post-modern cynicism of many consumers. It is clear that advanced industrial societies have reached a stage where much consumption is purely discretionary for large numbers of people, and this means that widely different products or services may compete for consumers' attention. The malaise in the UK's conventional retail sectors at the end of 1998 could be contrasted with the euphoric spending of consumers on mobile phones.

There is, too, the wider possibility that consumers are becoming satiated with consumption *per se*, and beginning, too, to respond, in at least a tentative way, to the doom-saying of environmental lobbies. At present, these seeds of resistance to the market are relatively thinly spread, and it is unclear whether enough will germinate to lead to a real revolution in behaviour: a cynical observer would say that however sceptical consumers may be, they will not go this far.

What does seem to be happening, however, is that consumers are far readier to question commercial messages, and to want to know more about the companies from which they are buying. This has been effectively fuelled by the media—as a senior marketer from DIY retailer B & Q pointed out recently, if an investigative TV programme finds a B & Q supplier who does not conform to B & Q's environmental standards, the TV programme will blame B & Q, not the supplier.

Box 19.2   The GM Food Controversy

An example of consumer scepticism and resistance to manufacturers' agenda comes from the rapidly developing field of genetic modification (GM) of foodstuffs. Encouraged by consumer groups, environmentalists and the media, many people in the UK are highly suspicious of the safety of GM foods, and of the motives of the huge multinational companies that now dominate the global agricultural seed business. In summer 1998, Monsanto, the most overtly aggressive marketer among this group, decided to run an advertising campaign to put its side of the case and to invite readers to comment. The net result of this was a flood of adverse comment, both in the media and to the company's web site, and subsequent consumer surveys (winter 1998) show that resistance to GM foods in the UK is still growing. The issues are complex, and the scientific community are quite divided about the way in which the development should procede, although the Reay Committee of the House of Lords came out in favour of the developments in January 1999. The argument continues, at a variety of levels. (And Britain is not alone: a similar ad campaign ran in France, with the same sorts of response, and resistance to GM foods is reported from, for example, Germany and Australia.)

The lessons of this seem to be:

- That consumers are increasingly suspicious of 'scientific' developments, especially where these affect their food (this appears to be a UK and European response, more than a US one).
- That advertising—on its own—cannot defuse suspicions.
- That the way in which this suspicious consumer must be approached needs to be very carefully thought through.

That you may make more trouble for yourself by attempting to appear open than by keeping your head down.

The fact is that still, more than 50 years after Dr Dichter started using the new science of motivational research to inform advertising development, we are far short of understanding as much as we should about our target customers. This goes all the way from the psychology of how their brains process commercial stimuli to our ability to recognize and respond to the fact that people buy different products in different states of mind or need.

The consumer, in all his or her rich variety, remains the great challenge, and the great fascination of the advertising business. In the second century BC, a Roman comedian said '*Homo sum: humani nil a me alienum puto*'—'I am human: I reckon nothing to do with humans is foreign to me.'

If you wish to succeed in advertising, this should be engraved close to your heart—or, more probably, these days, tattooed on your left buttock.

Summary

- Globalization will continue to affect the advertising business, the clients it serves, and the media it uses. This appears to run counter to the growing expectation of sophisticated consumers that they will get individual attention from companies.
- The traditional full-service agency has been progressively 'unbundled' as functions have been spun off: this runs counter to the growing pressures for integrated marketing communications, and raises the question of who is going to do all this integration.
- Customer-centred, one-to-one marketing is a strong trend, which threatens media advertising budgets, but also calls in question most of the effects of globalization. A role for media advertising will remain, but it may be substantially smaller, within overall marketing budgets, than today.
- Firms are increasingly expecting to measure the value of marketing inputs. This puts heavy pressure on advertising, as opposed to some other marketing communications disciplines, to improve measurement techniques.

□ The entire advertising industry is being changed and moulded by technology, to a greater extent than ever before. This is affecting, and will continue to affect, the production of ads, and is changing the balance of the media used for advertising. It also has a significant impact on the way in which agency businesses can be organized and managed, especially on an international scale.

One final exercise

You have been asked by the management of large international agency to design an agency for the future. List the key features of your recommendations. Assume that you have total freedom to exploit new technology and new thinking about people in organizations.

Glossary

A Guide to jargon and acronyms used in this book—and, in some cases, elsewhere[1]

AA Advertising Association (joint body of IPA and ISBA).

AAAA American Association of Advertising Agencies.

AAR Advertising Agency Register.

ABC Audit Bureau of Circulation.

A/B split Press test of direct response copy. Alternative ads are printed on alternative copies, to randomize distribution.

Above-the-line Media advertising, as opposed to other forms of marketing communication.

ACORN A Classification of Residential Neighbourhoods. The original geodemographic analysis.

Added value Perceived value added to a brand through communications.

Adstock The accumulated carryover pressure from advertising investment.

AIDA Attention, Interest, Desire, Action.

AI Awareness Index (Millward Brown tracking studies).

AIR Average Issue Readership. Standard measure on NRS.

Ambient media Non-mainstream, often ephemeral media used to get 'under the radar'. Frequently found close to the point of sale, and used promotionally.

ANA Association of National Advertisers (US).

ARF Advertising Research Foundation (US).

ASA Advertising Standards Authority.

ATR&N Awareness, Trial, Reinforcement and Nudging. Ehrenberg's reinterpretation of AIDA.

BACC Broadcast Advertising Clearance Centre.

Banner ad Standard small ad used on the Internet.

BARB Broadcasters' Advertising Research Board—responsible for TV audience research.

BCASP British Code of Advertising and Sales Promotion Practice.

Below-the-line Communications other than media advertising, especially sales promotion. See above-the-line.

Bleed Illustration carried out to the edges of a page—'bled off' the edges.

---

[1] Much of this material has appeared during 1999 in *Admap*, and is reproduced here by permission. A more extensive list appears on the public pages of WARC (see p. 300)

BRAD   *British Rate and Data*. Standard guide to UK media.

Brand equity   1. Financial value attached to a brand. 2. Estimate or measure of the marketplace strength of a brand.

Brand essence   Core characteristic(s) of a brand that differentiate it from competitors.

Brand identity   Outward features of a brand's make-up: shape, logo, name, colours, textures, pack design, etc.

Brand image   The cluster of qualities and attributes that enable consumers to identify a brand and distinguish it from its competitors.

Brand loyalty   Degree to which a consumer is committed to a brand: considered to be a very weak connection by Ehrenberg and his followers.

Brand personality   The character of a brand, expressed as if it were a person—either by consumers in (qualitative) research, or as a creative objective.

Brand stretch   The ability of a brand to be 'stretched' to include products or categories other than the brand's original product. Virgin is a widely stretched brand.

Brand values   Positive attributes associated by consumers with a brand. Could be based on performance ('cleans really well') or psychological/emotional ('ultra-modern, trustworthy', etc.).

Broadsheet   Large size newspaper (e.g. *The Times*).

b/w   Black and white—monochrome, as opposed to colour.

Call report   Contact report of client-agency meeting.

CAP   Committee on Advertising Practice.

CAVIAR   Cinema and Video Audience Research.

Classified advertising   Small, individual ads, often used by private individuals, and organized by the media into categories to aid buyers' searches.

Clickthrough   A measure of the effectiveness of web ads, arrived at by counting the number of surfers who click on the ad and visit the next linked page.

Cluster analysis   Statistical technique of survey research analysis, which segments a population into clusters with similar characteristics (these may be behavioural or attitudinal or a blend of the two).

ccm   Column centimetre.

Commission system   Traditional method of remunerating ad agencies. Media pay 15% of gross cost to agency.

Conversion   Index of penetration, used in media analysis. If readership among all adults is 10 per cent (= 100), readership of 14 per cent among AB men =140: a conversion of 140 to AB men.

Conversion theory   Proprietary system for measuring consumers' commitment to brands. In the UK, licensed to TN-AGB.

Copy test   Pre-test of advertising (mostly US, where it is usually quantitative, and designed to provide a go–no go decision, based on established brand or market norms).

Cost ranking   Analysis of candidate publications (or programmes) for an ad campaign, listing them in reverse order of CPT.

Cover, coverage Measure of the proportion of a target audience reached by a medium or a campaign. (= US reach).

CPT Cost per thousand—also cost/000. Measure of how much a medium, or a campaign has cost per thousand OTS (*qv*). (In US, often CPM.)

Cut-through The claimed ability of an ad to attract attention among the mass of competing 'noise' in the marketplace.

DAGMAR Defining Advertising Goals for Measured Advertising Results. 1960s system for planning advertising.

Database Organized and detailed computerized listing of customers and contacts.

Database marketing Sophisticated marketing system relying on a database.

Data Protection Act Legal framework for controlling the commercial use of personal data. Administered in UK by the Data Protection Registrar, with whom virtually any commercial database should be registered.

Data warehouse Computerized assembly of a range of company information on its operations, markets and customers.

Day-after recall Technique for researching the effect of TV commercials, fashionable in the US in the 1970s. Now generally discarded because of lack of evidence of relationship with sales effects.

Daypart Division of the day used in planning TV schedules, and in TV company ratecards.

Direct response Any form of advertising that invites consumers to respond directly to the advertiser (as opposed to visiting a dealer or shop).

Dirichlet Mathematical model underlying Ehrenberg's analysis of consumer purchasing behaviour. Uses penetration and weight of purchase to predict brand shares.

Display advertising As opposed to classified (*qv*), advertising designed to appeal to a wide public, and appearing in more or less solus (*qv*) positions.

DM 1. Direct mail. 2. Direct marketing.

DMA Direct Marketing Association.

DPS Double-page spread.

Drip Media scheduling , especially TV, using near-continuous light weight. Natural output of recency planning (*qv*).

DRTV Direct response TV.

Econometrics Mathematical analysis of marketing factors, used to evaluate performance of ad campaigns, to set budgets, and to evaluate media schedule alternatives.

Effective frequency Number of ad exposures judged to be necessary, within a given period, to have an effect on consumers. Now widely believed to be no more than 1.

Endline Line that rounds off or signs off an ad. More execution-specific than a slogan or strapline (*qv*).

EPG Electronic Programme Guide (digital TV).

ESOMAR European Society for Opinion and Marketing Research.

Exposure Opportunity to see an ad—OTS (*qv*).

Factor analysis Statistical technique used to extract 'factors' that appear to explain a market's structure. Frequently used in conjunction with cluster analysis (*qv*).

Fast marketing Proprietary technique that combines TV advertising with intensive product sampling.

Fmcg Fast-moving consumer goods—e.g. groceries.

FCB grid Way of classifying markets or brands in terms of involvement and consumer approach.

Flame Computer system for producing special effects in post-production of TV commercials (cf. Harry).

Focus group Group discussion that is structured to focus on a particular issues or question. See Group discussion.

Folder test Research test of print ads which are presented to subjects in a folder or file.

Frameworks A view of the different ways in which advertising is expected to work, derived from the research of Hall and Maclay.

Freesheet A free newspaper or magazine.

Frequency Number of times a given member of a target audience is exposed to advertising in the course of a campaign.

Full-service agency Ad agency that provides the complete range of advertising functions, under one roof. Relatively few large clients now buy advertising under full-service agreements.

Geodemographics Analysis of research data using postcodes, to identify geographical clusters of similar categories of consumers.

GHI Guaranteed Home Impressions. Advertising 'package' offered by TV and radio contractors.

Group discussion Qualitative research group that is essentially open-ended, as opposed to a focus group (*qv*). Frequently used interchangeably with focus group.

GRP Gross Rating Point (see also TRP, TVR, TARP) Measure of weight of an ad campaign. 1 GRP means that the equivalent of 1 per cent of the target audience have had 1 opportunity to see (OTS) the ad.

Harry Computerized system used in TV post-production to produce special effects (cf Flame).

IDM Institute of Direct Marketing.

Infomercial Long commercial used in DRTV and on TV shopping channels.

Impact 1. Strong effect (of an ad). 2. Another word for OTS. 3. 'Equal impacts': in UK TV planning, allocating funds between TV stations so that each produces the same level of TVRs.

Implicit memory The ability of people to 'remember' ads that they are unaware of having seen.

Impulse purchase Unplanned purchase, decided on at the point of sale.

IMC Integrated marketing communications.

Inter-media choice Selection between media.

Intra-media choice   Selection within a medium.

IPA   Institute of Practitioners in Advertising. UK agency association.

ISBA   Incorporated Society of British Advertisers. UK advertisers' association.

ISP   Institute of Sales Promotion. Sales promotion agencies' trade association.

ITC   Independent Television Commission. Responsible for overseeing UK independent TV.

ITV   Independent television. Frequently used as shorthand for ITV-1 (Channel 3 in the UK), but sometimes for all three terrestrial commercial channels.

JIC   Joint Industry Committee. One of a group of research bodies set up to administer and co-ordinate media research. Most of the original JICs have now changed their names (JICREG—regional newspapers—is the main exception).

JICREG   Joint Industry Committee for Regional Newspaper Research.

Line-and-price   Typical retail press ad, which lists a range of products sold and features prices as a guide to customers (also price-and-line).

M&A   Mergers and acquisitions.

Marketing mix   The organization of all forms of marketing activity for a brand.

Maslow's hierarchy   Structured view of human needs and motivations, from basic subsistence to spirituality.

MNC   Multinational corporation.

Modelling   Construction of mathematical models of markets to facilitate understanding.

MOSAIC   A geodemographic (*qv*) system.

MPX   Multiple page exposure.

MRG   Media Research Group.

MRS   Market Research Society.

NRS   National Readership Survey. The JIC (*qv*) for national press media, and the survey it publishes.

NSV   Net sales value. Ex-factory sales value—usually after discounts to stockists have been deducted.

Omnibus survey   Research survey covering several product fields, usually for different clients, simultaneously, to save costs.

OSCAR   Outdoor Site Classification and Audience Research. Predecessor of POSTAR (*qv*).

OTH   Opportunity to hear (see OTS).

OTS   Opportunity to see. Standard industry measure of coverage. Definition varies between media: for TV, it means presence in the room with the set switched to the right channel; for press, it means (usually) having 'read' the publication, which can mean no more than spending 2 minutes with it.

QRS   Quality of Readership Survey.

Page dominance   Used to describe an ad that takes up the major part of a page—usually a half page or larger.

Page traffic   In press reading research, the percentage of readers who say they looked at a particular page.

PBR   Payment by results.

People meters   TV audience research devices that are set up to measure the presence of individuals when the TV is on—as opposed to household or set meters. Peoplemeter is a registered trademark of the A.C. Nielsen Company.

Persuasion   Generic for a school of ad pre-testing which aims to measure shifts in attitudes and/or buying intentions as a result of ad exposure.

PEX   Page exposure.

Positioning   Definition of how a brand is intended to fit into the market so as to gain the best advantage.

POSTAR   Poster Audience Research. Sophisticated system of poster site rating and audience measurement, which could lead to a poster OTS being better value than most other media.

Post-testing   Generic term for research once an ad has run. May include tracking studies (*qv*).

PPA   Periodical Publisher's Association.

Pre-testing   Research into ads before they run. In the UK used more as quality control and to check communications; in the US—see Copy test—used as a hurdle that an ad must cross.

Proposition   Short, focused statement of what a brand offers its consumers, used as the core of creative briefs.

RAB   Radio Advertising Bureau.

RACC   Radio Advertising Clearance Centre.

RAJAR   Radio Joint Audience Research. The JIC (*qv*) for radio, and the research it publishes.

Readership   Measure of the number of people who read, as opposed to buy, a publication. For what this may mean in terms of ad exposure, see OTS and page traffic. Magazines, in particular, may reach up to a dozen readers per copy but over an extended period.

Recency planning   Media planning based on the theory that an ad is most effective if it is seen, once, as close to the moment of purchase as possible. Logically, this leads to 'drip' (*qv*) schedules.

Response function   Shape of response to an ad or campaign. Usually talked about in the abstract: the 'response' could be measured in terms of sales, awareness, etc., to taste.

Response rate   Percentage of target audience or mailed group who respond to a direct response ad.

RISC   Research Institute on Social Change. Leading survey organization providing value and lifestyle segmentation.

ROI   Return on investment.

ROP   Run of paper. An ad that the publisher may place anywhere.

ROW   Run of week. An ad may run any time during the week, at the media owner's discretion.

RSP   Retail sale price.

Salience   Approximately, 'relevance', 'significance' or 'importance'. Term used rather differently by Ehrenberg and Hall (see Index).

SAP Station average price. The basis on which UK TV is negotiated. Total station revenue is divided by achieved ratings for the major audience breaks to arrive at the SAP, retrospectively.

Semi-display Half-way between display and classified: either a display-style ad in a classified section, or a relatively small display ad inserted among a group of ads for related products—e.g. the travel sections of colour supplements, or the financial pages of some papers.

Slogan Advertising line that is closely associated with a brand, to the extent that it may become almost part of the brand identity. Used as an endline or strapline (*qv*).

Solus An ad appearing as the only ad on a page, or in a commercial break.

South, the Generic term for the developing countries.

Spot A single TV or radio ad.

Spot colour A single colour added to a b/w ad, to help it stand out.

Strapline Regularly used endline in a brand's advertising. May carry over from campaign to campaign, but usually longer and more meaningful than a slogan.

Subliminal Literally, 'below the threshold'. Advertising, usually audio-visual, that is alleged to work even though its appearance is too fleeting for the audience to be aware of it. The only reported case has been shown to be a hoax, but the practice is legally banned in numerous countries.

SuperProfiles Geodemographic (*qv*) system.

SWOT analysis Analysis of a business's Strengths, Weaknesses, Opportunities, Threats.

Tabloid Small size of newspaper—e.g. *The Sun*.

TARP Target audience rating point. Like a GRP, but more specific.

TGI Target Group Index.

TNC Transnational corporation.

Tracking study Continuous survey designed to monitor effects of advertising.

TRP See GRP.

TVR Television rating (= GRP).

U&A Usage and attitude survey.

Umbrella brand A brand that covers a variety of products, probably, but not necessarily, in disparate fields. Cadburys is a good example.

VALS Values and Lifestyles. Survey research designed to identify consumer segments by attitudes and behaviour.

Visual transfer Recall of TV ad images derived from exposure to radio ads.

Wastage The proportion of a media schedule's or medium's coverage that falls outside the defined target group.

Wear-out Measure of the loss of effectiveness of an ad or campaign, over time.

Further sources of information

Bibliography

The following books, most of which are referred to in the text, have been useful to me in writing this book, and may reward study. They are only a small selection of the stacks of books that look at advertising from all angles, so if you find something else that looks interesting, don't be put off by not finding it here!

Aaker, David A., 1991. *Managing Brand Equity,* Free Press, New York. Arguably the best American account of brand equity and the techniques of branding and brand management.

Advertising Association,1998, with 6-monthly updates. *The Commercial Communications Compendium,* AA, London. Detailed directory of EU legislation and policy relating to advertising and marketing communications. Summaries of the debate and legislative development, together with the AA's position on each issue. Not a light read, but well worth knowing about.

Bird, Drayton, 1982 (4th edn, 1998). *Commonsense Direct Marketing,* Kogan Page, London. Excellent guide that justifies its title, and written with charm and humour.

Broadbent, Simon, 1989. *The Advertising Budget,* NTC Publications, Henley-on-Thames. Still the definitive book on budgeting for advertising. By now, it needs a companion piece covering the whole marketing mix, but it is a mine of sanity.

Broadbent, Simon,1997. *Accountable Advertising,* Admap Publications, Henley-on-Thames. A lucid, but eventually quite technical, account of using market data and modelling to measure advertising effects. Part 1 is an excellent introduction to thinking quantitatively, in detail, about brand marketing and advertising effects.

Bullmore, Jeremy, 1999. *Behind the Scenes in Advertising,* NTC Publications, Henley-on-Thames. Light but amusing canter through adland by JWT London's creative chief from the 1970s. Many unexpected insights and cautionary tales.

Butterfield, Leslie (ed.), 1997. *Excellence in Advertising,* Butterworth Heinemann, Oxford. 11 contributed chapters, by leading UK practitioners, clients and academics, covering most of the advertising process. Slightly variable, but especially good pieces by Mike Sommers on the client, Roddy Glen on qualitative research, and Steve Henry on creative briefing.

Cooper, Alan (ed.), 1997. *How to Plan Advertising,* Account Planning Group, London. Completely new edition of original edited by Don Cowley. Range of different views of the account planner's role and contribution, and how it relates to the rest of the agency, the client and to competing strategists. Lots of good insights.

De Mooij, Marieke,1997. *Global Advertising and Marketing: Cultural Paradoxes,* Sage, London. Excellent overview of the cultural minefields that lie in wait for global ad campaigns, based on academic and practical research. Worth remembering that there's a lot of similarity lying between the extremes of most measurement scales.

Dru, Jean-Marie, 1997. *Disruption,* Wiley, Chichester. Lucid description of the founding father of BDDP's philosophy. Very French formal analysis that aims at breaking—disrupting—the established rules of a market. But what happens if disruption itself becomes a rule ... ? Lots of interesting, international examples, not all of which seem to fulfil the philosophy.

Ehrenberg, ASCE, *et al.,* 1997. *Justifying Our Advertising Budgets,* South Bank University, London. (For journal references, see Ehrenberg and Scriven, *Admap,* September 1997, p.37.) Series of papers setting out the advertising implications of Ehrenberg's Dirichlet model and the 'weak' theory of advertising. Coherent and frequently compelling view which runs counter to most ad people's idea of what they are, or hope to be, achieving. Read carefully, and recognize the underlying truth that most brand ads are about preserving the *status quo.*

Fletcher, Winston, 1999. *Advertising Advertising,* Profile Books, London. Highly readable statement of the benefits of advertising, from former AA chairman. Lengthy and detailed up-to-date bibliography.

Franzen, Giep, 1994. *Advertising Effectiveness,* NTC Publications, Henley on Thames. A complex and rather unorganized review of a very wide range of advertising research material, much of it—unusually, in English—from Continental Europe. Rewards careful mining, but it *can* be used to 'prove' almost anything!

Jones, John Philip, 1995. *When Ads Work: New Proof that Advertising Triggers Sales,* Lexington Books, New York. Ground-breaking analysis of single-source data, which provides the main underpinning for the 'recency' theory of ad scheduling. Over-simplistic for the technical purist, but the main message seems unarguable. Weak in its account of longer-term effects, which is theoretically naïve.

Halsey, Bryan (ed.). *The Direct Marketing Guide,* Institute of Direct Marketing, Teddington, 1998. Everything you ever wanted to know.

Hedges, Alan, 1998. *Testing to Destruction: A Critical Look at the Uses of Research in Advertising,* IPA, London. New edition of classic 1970s booklet, which packs its 100-odd pages with wisdom, together with up-dating comments from two leading 1990s ad planners. Good short bibliography of key, mainly UK, ad research articles.

McDonald, Colin. 1992. *How Advertising Works: A Review of Current Thinking,* AA/NTC Publications, Henley-on-Thames. Quite short, very practical review of the state of our knowledge. Only marginally dated, by Jones (1995), who is building on McDonald's own work in the 1960s, and perhaps by Ehrenberg's (1997) JOAB papers, though these add little to Ehrenberg's earlier thinking which is covered by McDonald. The Brand Dynamics and Brand Commitment theories are also post-McDonald.

McDonald, Colin, 1997. *Monitoring Advertising Performance,* Admap Publications, Henley-on-Thames. Brief but authoritative overview of ad campaign measurement techniques. Updates and extends McDonald 1992.

McDonald, Colin and Vangelder, Phyllis (eds), 1998. *ESOMAR Handbook of Market and Opinion Research,* ESOMAR, Amsterdam. Blockbuster compendium that covers all aspects of research, but includes(at least) three chapters well worth reading: Paul Freeman on market models, Mary Goodyear on qualitative research and Paul Feldwick on brand research. All three add depth and breadth of understanding to complex subjects.

Peppers, Don and Rogers, Martha,1993. *The One-to-One Future,* Piatkus, London. They 'wrote the book' on what they now call 'mass customization'. A bit evangelical, but lots of good examples and insights.

Pontifical Council of the Catholic Church, 1996. *Handbook on the Ethics of Advertising,* (can be downloaded from http://advertising.utexas.edu). Almost excessively balanced discussion of the main ethical issues that affect advertising and society.

Ries, Al and Trout, Jack, 1990. *Positioning: The Battle for Your Mind*, Warner Books. Detailed analysis of how and why brand positioning matters, by the people who claim to have invented the concept.

Spilsbury, Sallie, 1998. *A Guide to Advertising and Sales Promotion Law*, Cavendish Publishing, London. A lawyer's guide to the subject, the only up-to-date book on UK legislation and regulation. Covers most obvious pitfalls, but—surprisingly—ignores contract, which is where it all starts.

Sullivan, Luke, 1998. *Hey Whipple, Squeeze This*, Wiley, Chichester. One of very few readable recent books by a creative adman about creating ads. Worth reading for the insights.

Various Editors, 1981–99. *Advertising Works, 1–10. Papers from the IPA Effectiveness Awards*, NTC Publications, Henley-on-Thames, for IPA, London. Each volume contains approximately 20 award-winning papers, and typically covers a wide range of markets and market types. All the papers, and most of the non-winners, too, can be found on the Internet on WARC (see below).

Reference material

Directories

Advertisers' Annual. Hollis Directories, Teddington, Middlesex. Annual guide to the industry. Lists agencies, advertisers, service companies and at least some agency-client affiliations, though these tend to be dated.

ALF, incorporating BRAD A&A. BRAD Group, London. Monthly. Regularly updated listing of agencies and client companies.

BRAD (British Rate & Data). EMAP, London. Monthly guide to advertising ratecards, in all media. A companion volume covers mailing lists.

Statistics and specialist publications

NTC Publications, Henley-on-Thames publish a range of annual 'Pocketbooks' that provide a wealth of statistical data on aspects of the UK market. Especially relevant for advertising are:

The Marketing Pocketbook
The Media Pocketbook
The Lifestyle Pocketbook
The Geodemographic Pocketbook
European Marketing Pocketbook
UK Marketing Source Book

Useful annual statistical sources for advertising, also published by NTC, include:

The Advertising Association Advertising Statistics Yearbook
The AA/AIG European Advertising & Media Yearbook
World Advertising Trends
TV Europe. The European Television Databook

Some media-specific materials include:

Newspapers (regional):

The Regional Press Fact Book, 1998. The Newspaper Society, London.

Magazines:

Consterdine, Guy, 1997. *How Magazine Advertising Works II*, Periodical Publishers' Association, London.

Smith, Alan and Taylor Nelson AGB, 1998. *Proof of Performance II*, Periodical Publishers'Association, London.

Radio:

The *Radio Advertising Handbook* (annual). Radio Advertising Bureau, London.

Macmillan, Malcolm and Fletcher, David (undated). *How Radio Advertising Works*, Radio Advertising Bureau, London.

Wilson, Chris (undated). *The Grammar of Radio Advertising*, Radio Advertising Bureau, London.

Posters

Maiden Outdoor, 1996. *Posters in Perspective*. Maiden Outdoor, London.
Maiden, 1998. *Maiden Research Booklet*, Maiden, London.

Direct marketing

The DMA Census (annual). Direct Marketing Association, London.
The Letterbox Factfile (annual). Direct Mail Information Service, London.
Royal Mail,1995. *The Direct Mail Guide*, The Post Office, London.

The trade press

Although advertising is quite a small business, it is served by a wide range of magazines and periodicals, of varying quality and interest, internationally. Those listed are likely to be of most interest to readers of this book.

UK magazines

Weekly
Campaign.   The UK 'ad village's' gossip magazine.Unavoidable.
Marketing.   Official publication of the Chartered Institute of Marketing. Livelier than that makes it sound.
Marketing Week.   Stablemate of *Campaign*, competes with *Marketing*.
Media Week.   *Campaign* for media people (buyers and sellers).
PR Week.   Ditto for PR.

Monthly
Admap.   The thinking adman's monthly – practical, rather than academic.
Direct Response.   To my eye the more superficial of the two main DR monthlies.
Precision Marketing.   DR magazine with a more in-depth approach than *Direct Response*.
Research.   The Market Research Society's lighter publication (compared with the JMRS). Carries informative brief accounts of research projects and techniques.
Revolution.   Arguably the best of the new media magazines.

Quarterly
International Journal of Advertising.   The Advertising Association's heavyweight quarterly. A mix of academic and practitioner material, with a strong international flavour.
Journal of the Market Research Society.   The 'heavy' journal from the MRS. Frequently disappears into technical minutiae, but some good general material.

US magazines

Weekly

Advertising Age. Superior US equivalent of *Campaign*. All the news that's fit to print.

Monthly

Journal of Advertising Research. The only accessible US ad periodical—others are far too biased to academia.

Others

Media and Marketing Europe. Very similar to the following title. News and views of mostly European advertising scene, with a media bias. Occasional material on other regions.

Media International. Slightly more specifically about media, but similar to above. Wider geographical spread.

Stratégies. French cross between *Campaign* and *Marketing*.

Adformatie. Dutch equivalent of *Strategies*.

Advertising Age International. Quarterly supplement with often valuable material.

Web sites

With the constantly-changing nature of the Internet and its denizens, any attempt to provide a guide to worthwhile sites is inevitably doomed. That said, there are some possibly fairly permanent and useful sites available, one of two of which have been referred to in the text.

Account Planning Group—UK. www.easynet.co.uk/apg. UK planners' society, with a selection of quite useful links.

Account Planning Group—US. www.apgus.org. US Account planners' society, with links to University of Texas (*qv*).

Advertising Age. www.adage.com. Substantial range of data on US advertising scene, plus some international material.

Advertising law (US). www.lawpublish.com. Very extensive US site covering all aspects of relationship between law and marketing communications.

Advertising Research Foundation (US). www.amic.com/arf. Provides some research information, book search facilities, details of recent ARF conferences, etc.

Advertising Standards Authority. www.asa.org. Information on Code of Practice, ASA adjudications, etc.

CRM Forum. www.crm-forum.com. Range of data on one-to-one and relationship marketing.

IPA, London. www.ipa.co.uk. Provides access to IPA information services and database.

Radio Advertising Bureau. www.rab.co.uk. Informative site with research, advice, commercials, etc.

University of Texas. advertising.utexas.edu. Extensive site, well worth mining. Linked to APG-US.

World Advertising Research Centre (WARC). www.warc.com. Extensive database of advertising literature, including archives of Admap, IJOA, IPA Effectiveness entries and winners, JAR, etc.

It can always be illuminating to look up the sites of individual ad agencies, to see what they are saying about themselves. Yahoo (www.yahoo.co.uk) has an exhaustive list which you can link to from the UK APG site.

Index